Decentering Fashion on the Silk Roads

Decentering Fashion on the Silk Roads focuses on the dynamism of fashion, textile craft, heritage, and sustainability in Central Asia and beyond. The compelling series of accounts provides a comprehensive set of insights and impressions collected from both fashion academics, designers and practitioners from around the globe who journeyed through Uzbekistan and Kazakhstan and from those who live and work in this region. It showcases ways in which local textile craft practices can inform the modern fashion industry into becoming more sustainable.

The book opens by exploring the importance of the old 'Silk Roads' crossing through the heart of the world in Central Asia, serving not only as trade routes but also allowing knowledge, art, and practices to be transmitted between the Orient and the Occident – enabling ideas to flourish and cultural dispositions to develop from Antiquity until Modernity. The unique set of chapters that follow examine and highlight the growing opportunities and lessons this region has to offer to Western fashion through local artistry and craft, and points toward the urgent need to slow down and adopt responsible principles and practices. The book constitutes a warm appreciation of the experiences and grateful thanks to the many communities from all different backgrounds and ages who contributed.

This rich travelogue is a refreshing resource for international scholars and postgraduate students studying and researching fashion theory and management in particular. It will also be of interest to anthropologists, cultural studies, and textiles scholars.

Stefanie Mallon is a cultural anthropologist and textile scientist at the University of Göttingen, Germany, with a research focus on Materiality and Sustainability in Fashion and Textiles. Recent publications include an article on 'Digital fashion and the future of fashion' which analyses users' garment experience, a paper on 'Performative aging in swim wear', and an empirical study on fungus as an alternative for leather. Further works are the co-edited anthology 'Death and the thing' with studies about the meaning and functionality of textiles in the context of 'death', and an article titled 'Thinking through fashion – Thinking fashion through', which reflects on students' perspectives on the future of fashion.

Galina Mihaleva is an artist, fashion and wearable technology designer. Mihaleva's artistic practice and academic research deals primarily with the dialogue between body and dress, driven by the idea of having both a physical and a psychological relationship with a garment as responsive clothing.

Responsible Fashion

Editor: Ian King

The fashion industry has in recent years come under increased global scrutiny regarding its practices. The response by the fashion industry reveals a desire to change. But how and what do we record to demonstrate this change? This is our challenge. A reinvention of fashion – away from the frivolous and ephemeral toward one as an enabler of sustainable growth and innovation.

This book series records this change. Working in conjunction with a series of regular live/hybrid international events the series maintains academic standards, books in the series include authors from different backgrounds to purposefully encourage readers to re-think the potential of fashion and how it needs to evolve in a responsible way henceforth.

Sustainability and the Fashion Industry
Can Fashion Save the World?
Edited by Annick Schramme and Nathalie Verboven

Technology, Sustainability and the Fashion Industry
Can Fashion Save the World?
Edited by Annick Schramme and Nathalie Verboven

The Future of Fashion Education
Speculation, Experience and Collaboration
Edited by Kirsten Scott, Barry Curtis and Claire Pajaczkowska

Decentering Fashion on the Silk Roads
Craft and Responsible Fashion Dynamics in Central Asia
Edited by Stefanie Mallon and Galina Mihaleva

For more information about this series, please visit: www.routledge.com/Responsible-Fashion/book-series/RFASH

Decentering Fashion on the Silk Roads

Craft and Responsible Fashion Dynamics in Central Asia

Edited by Stefanie Mallon and
Galina Mihaleva

Routledge
Taylor & Francis Group
LONDON AND NEW YORK

First published 2025
by Routledge
4 Park Square, Milton Park, Abingdon, Oxon OX14 4RN

and by Routledge
605 Third Avenue, New York, NY 10158

Routledge is an imprint of the Taylor & Francis Group, an informa business

British Library Cataloguing-in-Publication Data
A catalogue record for this book is available from the British Library

ISBN: 978-1-03283-160-2 (hbk)
ISBN: 978-1-03283-161-9 (pbk)
ISBN: 978-1-00350-807-6 (ebk)

DOI: 10.4324/9781003508076

Typeset in Sabon
by KnowledgeWorks Global Ltd.

Contents

Figures and tables

Figures

Tables

Contributors

Sabine Albert holds a professorship for vocational pedagogy with a focus on diversity at the Institute for Secondary Vocational Education at the Vienna University of Teacher Education. There, she teaches and researches in the fields of vocational education, diversity, inclusion, and didactics. She is also an adjunct lecturer at the University of Vienna's Center for Teacher Education. After her teaching degree in Information and Communication, Applied Computer Science, she studied Pedagogy and a combination of Psychology and Political Science at the University of Vienna. The theoretical knowledge is complemented by 20 years of professional experience at an integrative vocational middle and high school in Vienna. In 2021, she received her PhD from the University of Graz, at the Institute of Education and Educational Sciences. In her dissertation, she dealt with the importance of concepts of human beings and respect in teaching at vocational schools.

Aika Alemi is an artist, business coach, mentor, speaker and contributor to Elle Kazakhstan and Forbes Kazakhstan. Through *Business of Creation,* she supports creative entrepreneurs and artists in various fields. She was nominated a womenswear finalist of International Woolmark Prize 2017 for the region of Europe and awarded Best Mentor of EBRD Women Entrepreneurs Program 2018 and Elle Style Awards Kazakhstan 2016. Amongst others Aika Alemi has organized and directed events like *Born Nomad*, Central Asia Creative Incubator and DMUK HUB, Responsible Fashion Series Silk Road. Aika holds a Higher Education Diploma in Political Economy from Moscow State University and MBA from Duke University's Fuqua School of Business.

Gulnar Dzhambulovna Bekibayeva is associate professor of the Department of Fashion and Costume Design of the *Kazakh National Academy of Arts (named after Temirbek Zhurgenev)* in Almaty, Kazakhstan. Her main research activities include researching the modern costume system, Turkic culture, and design education. Her research topics include semiosis of Turkic culture, digital methods in scientific research and education.

Ioana Corduneanu, driven by passion, tempered by method, decided to act as the most compact form of an advertising agency. She advocates for the art of embroidery and the idea of 'do it yourself, your own traditional Romanian shirt'. Ioana was born on 31 May 1975 in Bucharest, Romania, into a family of IT specialists and mathematicians. Summer holidays spent in areas known for their rich tradition of folk crafts, such as Bucovina and Gorj, introduced her to these practices and to the most beautiful face of mathematics: wearable geometry/traditional patterns. Inspired by the Romanian sculptor Constantin Brancusi, she tried to find ways to enhance the rural art of embroidery. After graduating from the National College of Computer Science and the University of Architecture, working in the competitive field of retail design, she turned her skills and experience into a lifelong mission. Using the latest technologies, she became a spokesperson for the design masterpieces created by communities. In 2012, she founded 'Semne Cusute' (Sewn Signs), proving that folk art could remain as relevant and inspiring as ever in a rapidly changing world.

Agnes Evangelista is a Junior Researcher at the Circular Business research group at The Hague University of Applied Sciences in the Netherlands, she holds a bachelor's degree in International Public Management from the same institute. She has published papers on sustainable fashion and sustainable business modeling/tools.

Sharifa Jamaldin is the editor and founder of GreyishGreen.com (a sustainable fashion magazine) aimed at inspiring creatives, writers, and educators to make everything ecological and ethical. After her studies in Human Ecology, she pursued a fashion journalism career following her interest in history, design, creativity, media, and publishing. For the last two decades, she has been occupied with sustainable fashion practices and concepts such as circular economy, transparency, organic materials, zero-waste design, sharing economy, upcycling and recycling, regenerative permaculture, people/planet/profit, craft, and social business, cultural appreciation and diversity. Concerned about the adverse effects of fast fashion, poor working conditions, and pollution, she joined Fashion Revolution Belgian to do advocacy work and to highlight solutions to build a fair, zero-waste, regenerative fashion system.

Sara Kaufman is an Italian Milan-based freelance fashion writer. She is a contributor to major international magazines for which she writes about fashion, contemporary art and culture. Her research topics range from more sociological aspects of fashion culture to sustainable and innovative practices within the industry. She is a feminist and the mother of a 6-year-old boy. Recent publications include: 'Fashion's problem with Motherhood' (Fashion +, ASP) and the curation of *Fashion Studies Journal Special Issue Fashion and Politics*.

Karan Khurana is an educator in the field of fashion business and management in Uzbekistan with experience of ten years in India, Ethiopia, and Belgium. He did his PhD in Management (consumer behavior regarding brand failures in India). Karan does research in Teaching Methods, Educational Management, sustainability in textile and apparel value, business development strategies for SME's and cultural governance. Along with experience in education, he also contributes to the industry with training on design development and good practices in the fashion and textile sector.

Assiya Ruslanovna Nurdubayeva is a doctoral candidate in architecture focusing on 'theory, history and restoration of architectural monuments' at the *Kazakh National Academy of Arts (named after Temirbek Zhurgenev)* in Almaty, Kazakhstan. Her main research areas are theoretical, structural-semiotic spatial systems, ethnological aspects of the spatial culture of the Turks and semiosis of the traditional culture of the Kazakhs. Her research topics include semiosis of Turkic culture, digital methods in scientific research and education. She regularly teaches seminars on semiotics.

Saumya Pande, design educator and textile revivalist for 25 years, has led and set up fashion departments across several design schools in India. She positions her creative work at the intersection of textile, space and form. Currently on a sabbatical, Saumya is writing a book on undocumented embroidered quilts from eastern India and researching weaving practices of the village of Kuthampully in southern India.

Elisabeth Lloyd Pfahl is an artist, anthropologist, and founder of Artisans Venture, who has been privileged to work with Central and South East Asian artisans since 2005. Her projects push traditional boundaries of repoussé, casting, textiles, and remanent materials. Her 30 years of photographic, graphite and sculptural works explore body identity, cultural norms, totems, and taboos.

Kim Poldner is a Professor for Regional and Circular Economic Development at the University of Groningen. She holds a PhD from the University of St. Gallen, Switzerland. She has published extensively on entrepreneurship, aesthetics and sustainability and specifically on sustainable fashion.

Jure Purgaj is a design researcher and holds a professorship for subject didactics in fashion and design. He is affiliated with the University College of Teacher Education Vienna, where he works in the Department of Fashion and Design at the Institute of Secondary Vocational Education (I:SBB). Additionally, he is part of the Center for Didactics for Art and Interdisciplinary Education at the University of Applied Arts Vienna. In 2005, he completed his fashion design studies at the University of Applied Arts in Vienna. In 2011, he received a PhD scholarship from the University in Ljubljana, Slovenia. Subsequently, in 2012, he received a research fellowship for a research stay at the Design Research Lab of the Berlin University of the Arts from the German Academic Exchange Service (DAAD). In 2013, he received his PhD in Design Research from the University of Ljubljana, Slovenia. Since 2008, he has taught at the Academy of Design in Ljubljana, Slovenia, and Raffles

University Iskandar, Malaysia, among others. His research interests are in the areas of subject didactics of fashion and design, inclusive vocational education, design practice, design theory, and AI in education.

Carlos Gago Rodriguez is an art director and fashion buyer focused on the synergies between retail reality and e-commerce. He has worked in different major Italian fashion luxury brands like La Perla and a long-time experience in Max Mara as a Retail Event Coordinator. Currently, Carlos as a fashion consultant develops 360° bespoke strategies such as trend forecasting, creative direction and digital development for brands like Bogner or Bulgari, The Row or Puma among many others. Recent publications include 'An intergenerational analysis of streetwear' (co-written with Anna Zinola and Sara Kaufman); 'Fashion and Disability: From Diversity to Equality? Analyzing practices in the fashion Industry (co-written with Anna Zinola and Sara Kaufman).

Annick Schramme is the academic director of the knowledge community Creative Industries at Antwerp Management School. She is also the academic coordinator of the Master Cultural Management and the Competence Center Management, Culture & Policy (Faculty of Applied Economics) at the University of Antwerp. Over the last years, she has published about the arts policy of Flanders, the creative industries, local cultural policy and the creative city, heritage policy from an international perspective, cultural entrepreneurship, etc. Finally, she is member/chair of several boards and/or advisory committees in the cultural sector in Flanders and the Netherlands, such as the Royal Ballet of Flanders/the Royal Opera, the Flemish Fund for Literature, The Flemish Children Theatre HetPaleis and the Strategic Advisory Board for Culture, Youth, Media and Sports of the Flemish Government and the Dutch Council for Culture.

Chiara Sebastiani is Alma Mater Professor of Bologna University where she has held courses in the fields of Public Communication, Local Government and Urban Studies. She is currently an independent researcher contributing as freelance to a newspaper and several web magazines. She has a special focus on Tunisia – where she has done intensive fieldwork before and after the Jasmine Revolution – and on gender issues. She is also a Jungian psychoanalyst with a focus on the relationship between Islam and psychoanalysis. She lives and works in Milan.

Ira Solomatina is a writer and researcher. Ira is currently finishing her PhD thesis at the University of Amsterdam on 'Politics and the political in contemporary fashion magazines' drawing on research data from India, Russia, and the United States. With her background in Southeast Asian studies and Cultural Studies, Ira has taught on culture and globalization at Humboldt and Potsdam Universities. Her research interests span fashion media and politics, gender and social media, and affect and intimacy online; she is a regular contributor to the fashion-critical publication Vestoj.

Richa Sood is a designer, consultant, conceptualizer, and educator at the Indian Institute of Art and Design in New Delhi. She is a specialist in graphic design for textiles and engineered (digital) prints for garments. With over 20 years of work experience in the Indian fashion industry, she has worked with most known Indian couture brands. Richa aims to blend her industry experience in design practice with design pedagogy and classroom learning.

Anna Zinola got her PhD in Research Methodology at the Università Cattolica del Sacro Cuore di Milano in 1997. She is focused on research methodology and consumer behavior. From 2004 to 2019, she has been Professor of Marketing Psychology at the University of Pavia. Currently, she is Professor of Sociology of Fashion at Master Courses Istituto Marangoni, Milano, and Professor of Research Methods at Università Cattolica, Milano. In 2023, she co-authored 'Aesthetic Renaissance against Western conformity: The Role of Indigenous Culture' and co-curated of a special issue of 'The Fashion Studies Journal' themed 'Fashion and Politics'. Zinola is a regular columnist for Corriere della sera and Micro & Macro Marketing.

Introduction

Stefanie Mallon

In March 2023, a three-week event took the Responsible Fashion Series (RFS) to Kazakhstan and Uzbekistan in Central Asia to explore some of the dynamics of the region's fashion and craft scene. The series regularly brings fashion scholars and practitioners from varied backgrounds together in locations all around the globe and on invitation from local stakeholders. The aim is to brainstorm on strategies for making the global fashion industry more sustainable from within local fashion contexts. This event was organised by fashion designer Aika Alemi, Kazakhstan, and fashion business scholar Karan Khurana, Uzbekistan. Their motivation was connecting local and international participants to exchange ideas, skills and experiences and advancing the sustainability of local fashion sectors in the global markets. With this, they are creating networks of awareness for the potentials and the subtleties of this region. This event constitutes part of a wider endeavour to 'decentre fashion' (Parsons Paris, 2022), which is at the heart of the RFS, by directing the focus on regions globally less conspicuous in the dominant fashion discourse and disrupting the reproduction of unequal power relations along the chains of value creation.

For Alemi, this also builds on her work as art director of *Born Nomad*, a project promoting cultural heritage and supporting female entrepreneurs (US Mission Kazakhstan, 2021). Her 'nomad' theme was picked up on for this event: the participants travelled between the cities of Samarkand, Bukhara and Tashkent, Uzbekistan, and Shymkent, Taraz, Turkestan and Almaty, Kazakhstan, by train, bus or car to engage with local designers and artisans, visit cultural heritage sights, craft fairs and fashion outlets and see the representative cities, the extremely expansive steppes and also the under-developed rural areas. Workshops, exhibitions and presentations were held in Tashkent, Turkestan and Almaty. This volume takes stock of some of the contributions, ideas, concepts and inspirations that were brought to or sprang from the trip and the first encounters of the various parties. But first, the interplay of fashion, textile and craft in the region is explored and contextualised.

DOI: 10.4324/9781003508076-1

Textiles as driving forces

Central Asian countries are positioning themselves to increase international cooperation and trade (Cohen, 2008; Kim & Park, 2019; Daryo, 2023). It is often stressed that Central Asia used to be – in the first one and a half millennia AD – the literal centre of the World, home to what is colloquially called the 'Silk Roads', the very symbol for global exchange. Trading between China, European and African empires such as Rome, Greece and Egypt went on to such an extent that cultural historian Rashmi Doraiswamy calls the traffic along the trade routes "pre-modern globalization" (Doraiswamy, 2023, p. 8). Eurasian textile researcher Emma Dick criticises the widespread and easy use of the concept 'Silk Roads', which is technically imprecise and is also being instrumentalised for political ends. In spite of its lack of precision, she writes, "the concept stuck and has become an evocative and effective myth" (Dick, 2018, p. 2; also, Wang, 2013, p. 165). Historians who write about this period – and don't shy away from its evocative effect – are fascinated by the words' signification of a phase of exchange that was formative for much of the world as we know it today – running counter to a widespread Eurocentric take on history (i.e. Bentley, 1993; Frankopan, 2015). Trade fuelled dynamic relations between people, peoples and innovation: As historian Jerry H. Bentley writes, that it "soon became apparent that beliefs, values, and cultural traditions could travel the silk roads alongside the merchants and ambassadors who opened them" (Bentley, p. 33). It is easy to be drawn into the enthusiasm for the dynamism of this period as a vibrant hub of productive competition and formation, even while the dark sides of humans dealing with each other and conflict are not at the centre of the narratives. They are, rather, included as another driving force for progress – in aid of overcoming challenges.

At the centre of these authors' attention is the occurrence of social and cultural changes when humans are engaged in close interaction. Here, trade and economic interest feature large as the motivating factor for the dynamics, and silks – while, of course, not the only trading articles – played an important part in this in the early centuries of the so-called Silk Roads (Trombert, 2013; Wang, 2013; Høisæter, 2017). Until the exclusivity of the skill and knowledge of sericulture was lost to Chinese producers, no other product, "with the exception of gold [...] has ever mobilized such tremendous energies and feelings of greed spanning such large distances, has ever promised traders such huge profits, has ever exposed them to such great risks, as the scarce historical sources of the first millennium A. D. plainly tell" (Klimberg, 1993, p. 35). In fact, even more generally, textiles and fashion – while often marginalised in research – have a long and vibrant history of being the aim of and even as a driving force for global exchange with ties around the globe for production and trade and its geopolitical potentiality (Kurkdjian, 2021). This had progressive as well as repressive effects: For example, while the textile industry has served as one of the motors of economic and technological progress leading to the industrial revolution (i.e. Landes, 1969), this development was also underscored by vast colonial and human exploitation (i.e. Beckert, 2014). In late modernity, the fashion system holds the globe in a dynamic, but deftly structured and powerful grip with an intricate system. We witness an enormous and complex entanglement with myriad facets of maximised efficiency: The established structures follow well-established patterns of economic value creation and exhaustive extraction, which impacts culturally, socially, economically and environmentally everywhere around the world (i.e. Dittmer, 2014). However, when working on changing the system towards becoming more responsible, there are local factors at play, too, and sensitivities of companies in the markets may be preventing pro-active sustainable positionings (Wolff, 2021). The fact that the industry provides the basis of reciprocal employment and business opportunities has to be taken into account (Tranberg Hansen, 2005). These are a consideration that countries take on board when taking concrete steps to develop their national textile industries.

Responsible fashion in Kazakhstan and Uzbekistan

Central Asia – though now in the wind-shadow of global economic activity – has long established and economically important textile production industries. In both Kazakhstan and Uzbekistan, the textile sectors are significant driving factors of the respective economies (Anderson, 1992; Madjidov & Khakimov, 2012; Yepanchintseva et al., 2023). Cotton and silk productions provide a substantial part of work and employment opportunities for Uzbek citizens (Khurana & Ataniyazova, 2020, p. 391). Khurana and Ataniyazova see potential for investment from the Chinese One Belt One Road project – informally called The New Silk Road Initiative – in a denser infrastructure leading through Central Asia to Africa and Europe. For a major producer of cotton and silk as Uzbekistan with a low-wage labour market, this "opens doors for trade and commerce in the fashion and textile export sector" (p. 390) and develops on Uzbekistan's potential as a business partner on the global stage.

Kazakhstan is poised to increase its textile production by innovating domestic textile enterprises, too (Pazilov et al., 2020). Its ready-made garments available for sale are mainly imported from South-East Asia and China though. After small businesses had thrived in Kazakhstan following a liberalisation of the market in the wake of the dissolution of the Soviet Union, stricter government regulation is increasingly impeding entrepreneurs (Petrick et al., 2017). There is a trend of difference for the two countries in the garment import and export volumes (WITS, 2021). In Uzbekistan, domestic consumption is met by inland production. This is facilitated by "government-provided incentives for manufacturers, extensive development of small business and private entrepreneurship, and a favourable marketing environment" (Turapovna, 2019, p. 50). A government decree from 2016 strives to ensure all value-adding is carried out within the country to increase the volume of textile, clothing and knitting industries (Khurana & Ataniyazova, p. 392). "While Uzbekistan is still the world's eighth largest cotton producer and its eleventh largest exporter, according to the State Committee of Uzbekistan on Statistics, the government wants to eliminate all raw cotton exports" (JustStyle, 2020).

A divergence from cash crops and the creation of more diverse employment opportunities can be seen as veering towards a more sustainable industry (meaning the prudent management of resources, i.e. combining environmental protection with economic interests and also with social responsibility; Tremmel, 2003, p. 117). The need for sustainability is pertinently felt in Central Asia and is important to fashion designers who we have talked to. They stressed that in line with economic development, it is important to mind social concerns and environmental protection, too. Central Asia also bears one of the most poignant symbols of the environmental failings of the global fashion and textile industry: the drying-up of the Aral Sea. This is mainly due to irrigation of agricultural fields in this arid region – of which cotton fields make up the largest part (Micklin, 2014, p. 21). As part of the Soviet empire, and even before, the region had been the source of cotton for Russian demand sustained by intensified monoculture cultivation, the systematising of irrigation systems and the implementation of chemical fertilisers (Nurzhanovna, 2011, p. 4036). While the climatic conditions are ideal (Khurana and Ataniyazova), the land doesn't naturally meet the water demands of the water-intensive cotton plant. Therefore, water is diverted from the rivers which would otherwise flush the Aral Sea (Micklin, p. 214). This is also detrimental to biodiversity. While the destruction of habitats had been particularly aggravated in the process from the early 20th century onwards, the "continued textile and agricultural developments" continue to be a threat to biodiversity (Nazarov et al., 2023, p. 22).

Between 1990 and 2011, Uzbekistan reduced cotton production by 27%, but due to the significance of cotton as an economic force, it is unlikely to be reduced further (Micklin, p. 367). So, the outlook of re-establishing the Aral Sea's biological and sustaining life force in the region isn't optimistic. But in another Decree of the President No. 5853 of the Republic of Uzbekistan (2019), the government shows commitment to "ensuring the rational use of natural resources and environmental protection" (Yusupov et al., 2021). Kazakhstan, too, has implemented a Concept on Transition to Green Economy (Green Economy Concept, nd.) by decree (Government of Kazakhstan, 2013). One of the most important measures taken is regarding energy use (which is double that of the average OECD economy), water and waste management (p. 23). Water use is to be reduced by replacing cotton "with less water-intensive vegetables, oil cultures and feedstock by 2030" (p. 16). A 2009 Law About Support the Use of Renewable Energy Sources benefits the textile industry. By Order of the Minister of Investment and Development of the Republic of Kazakhstan (2015), "financial, legal and technical assistance for the introduction of renewable energy in the textile industry of Kazakhstan" (Durru et al., 2021, pp. 51–52) is provided. In the face of climate change, pollution and financial strain, measures like the adoption of renewable energy sources have been implemented even by entrepreneurs in the industry, too (Huang et al., 2017, p. 72). Textile and fashion producers are themselves taking "active steps to improve their environmental performance and competitiveness" (Desore & Narula, 2018, p. 1453). Combined with state-subsidised renewable energy projects, recently, "there was a noticeable decline in [conventional] energy consumption by textile companies from 30% to 25%" (Durru et al., p. 53).

So, even though the cases of Kazakhstan's and Uzbekistan's textile industries are dissimilar, they share some of the same challenges and opportunities. Change towards responsibility/sustainability, so far, is brought about by rigorous interventions by the autocratic[1] governments, but also by independent adoption of measures by the textile industry.

Fashion's national and international reach

National importance is also given to fashion as a soft-power in 'fashion diplomacy' with which governments engage in international relations (Rabimov, 2023). Fashion events around the globe are shaping the geopolitical representation of Central Asia and are furthered with political support (Mentges, 2017a). In Uzbekistan, where fashion design is burgeoning and supported by the state, Dick marks this as being instrumentalised as a "geopolitical project" (Dick, p. 4). Clothes are, generally, an essential part of portraying geopolitical positionings and are implemented performatively to signify local and/or national interests (Behnke, 2017). They have always played an important role in forming concepts like the 'nation'; fashion historian Djurda Bartlett even credits fashion with a subversive power "capable of rearticulating hegemonies" (Bartlett, 2019, p. 22).

Sophie Kurkdjian, another fashion historian, states that fashion has become a powerful entity for international relations in the first half of the 20th century when French fashion became an export good for 'rich British people, US-Americans and Brazilians' and imbued with a cultural and economic power (Kurkdjian, 2021, p. 9). But it is also the fashion industry, which heeds the various national and international priorities and sensitivities. Russians, Qataris and Chinese count as among the most important fashion consumers for high fashion today (p. 11). Economist Don N. Thompson sees these important new markets for luxury fashion still looking to iconic European labels when choosing luxury fashion, because through a finely tarried-out web of strategies of value creation including a coherent narrative of tradition, they succeed in representing 'authenticity' (Thompson, 2021, pp. 177–187). But there are noticeable decentring dynamics: These markets – China in particular – have the attention of labels, designers, marketers, etc.

and, as they carry on gaining importance, the fashion industry is compelled to continuously adapt to their tastes and diffuse fashion's focus on Europe.

Central Asia has not, yet, arrived at being a player in the global fashion system even outside of the luxury sector, Aika Alemi points out in an interview (interview with Alemi, 2024). As the Uzbekistan (ufw.official) and Kazakhstan Fashion Weeks (kfz.kz) show, designers produce garments that follow some of the paths paved by design practices in the Western tradition (Rabimov, 2023, 2024). But they don't strive to simply emulate these, rather creating idiosyncratic effects with materials, producing distinct silhouettes and embracing ornament in a broad variety of ways. Acute discretion is articulated in two features: a) the many designs of 'modest' fashion, which is quite absent on Western runways, but also impacting the fashion scene in other parts of the globe (Sebastiani, this volume); b) often elements of national cultural heritage are being quoted in the designs – in the range between folkloristic dress styles to the subtle inclusion of intricately abstracted references to 'traditional' patterns.

In both Uzbekistan and Kazakhstan, cultural heritage becomes materialised in fashion as part of the construction of national identity. A broad array of textile crafts are even an integral part of that cultural heritage and the emblematic articulation of national identity (Nurdubaeva & Bekibaeva this volume). Alemi attributes this ardent focus to contour a national identity on the region's experience of the Soviet past (Alemi). While the 19th-century Russian colonialisation had already had an impact on undermining ethnic diversity, the "Soviet period saw intervention in the cultural sphere in Central Asia on a larger scale and in a more systematic Manner" (Doraiswamy, 2023, p. 11). Nomadism, too, is almost completely discontinued as a lifestyle today (Britannica, 2024). However, as textile anthropologist Gabriele Mentges writes in her study on Uzbek textile practices, the Soviet rule oversaw the 'invention of tradition' of 'typical' styles for each of the individual soviet republics. The "Soviet power supported an ethnic 'folklorism' that forms the basis of today's ethnic essentialism. Soviet rule tried to turn ethnicities into nations and thus invented and pushed forward the concept of the nation for the purpose of better differentiation between the various cultural groups" (Mentges, 2017a, p. 11). This affected textile crafts, too; however, some found their niches in museums or tourist/collector's markets. This provided the positive effect that unique techniques, beyond those, which have continued to be passed on through families (Mentges, 2017b, p. 42), survived and were ready to be explored after independence in 1991 (Chisti, 2023, p. 230).

The Silk Roads concept serves as a trademark and is instrumental in creating a market with tourists – products are, in return, adapted to the consumers' particular tastes (Dick, p. 7). There is an economic incentive to produce for tourist markets, "in which crafts and artisans are located within the matrix of an evanescent picturesque, reminiscent of times, traditions and persons considered anachronistic in the 'modern' world"

(UNESCO, 2005, p. 5). But a product "can only be marketable if it is attractive to the consumer, that is, if traditional skill is adapted and designed to suit contemporary consumer tastes and needs" (UNESCO, p. 5). This became evident to us visiting the stalls near landmarks that we saw in the region: even the hand-produced items were often stylised and typified products adjusted to what occurred to be contemporary tourists' tastes. But the creativity goes beyond this and in other locations independent artisans and designers offered their original products. As Dick writes "successful designers, artisans and entrepreneurs in Central Asia have become very good at navigating this complicated landscape between different stakeholders in the g/local contexts, understanding, embodying, fulfilling and fashioning multiple identities" (Dick, p. 8). Designers, too, have to design in a fraught place between expectations of national identity and developing new ideas and designs (Dick, pp. 10–11). Dick suggests that it might be time for the ethnic elements to be eliminated from fashion and that there is 'local dissatisfaction' with them. However, most of the fashion designs we saw in the specific places to which we were introduced or which we sought out ourselves would have involved some references to the respective region. Recognisable products position designers and also serve as advertisements in the global fashion scene.

Fashion and cultural heritage

Garments with traditional craft elements are worn for specific occasions and by specific groups. Gabriele Mentges has conducted two two-year-long research projects on the cultural and economic meaning of textile culture in Uzbekistan. Part of the study are interviews with – educated – Uzbek participants. They detail how they eclectically pick and choose according to the occasion whether to wear Western garments (i.e. when working) or garments with traditional elements (i.e. at home or for special events like the widely celebrated spring festival *navruz*) (Mentges, 2017b: 39f.). *In the streets* of the areas that we were traveling in, we hardly saw any clothes featuring 'traditional' craft, even for the special occasions of visiting landmarks. The main, quite uniform, look with dark colours dominating varied between a sober elegant style (worn by young urbanites) and 'modest fashion', which is often more decorated with ornaments. Modest fashion was seen everywhere but was particularly prevalent in groups of more mature people who seemed to be visiting the landmarks in the cities: Women wearing head-scarfs tied at the back and men scull-caps. In general, skin would only be visible on the head and hands, rarely around the ankles, too. But men occasionally sported short or pushed-up sleeves. Black and dark colours dominated everywhere, for urbanites often combined with white elements. Garments mostly seemed to be made from chemical fibres. But some denim (which is mainly made from cotton) was evident, too. The festively clad women at a meal for the *navruz* festival in the Farab Library in Turkestan, Kazakhstan, we were invited to, were wearing colourful head-scarfs tied at the back, white blouses and colourful skirts.

This picture changed, in the workshops and wherever we were meeting designers, their customers, design students and other people who are interested in fashion. Most of the labels were integrating materials or other references to 'traditional' crafts. A lady in one of the workshops was dressed in a coat with ikat material and chain-stitch embroidered items. When asked about her dress, she told me that she had dressed up specifically for the occasion of the event. Numerous students and other audience members at the workshops in Almaty had put on 'traditional jewellery'. Again, when I inquired, they said, this was done for the occasion of the event. Designers themselves and their customers were wearing these garments or jewellery. Some of us started wearing clothes which were locally made and sported recognisable patterns.

The divergence of consumption of fashion with traditional items according to consumer groups and events can be attributed to differences in fashion choices and distinctive tastes. Affordability of the produce could be considered, too. In this volume, Khurana and Annick Schramme lay out that there is a potential there for the domestic market (and beyond) which isn't used due to an underdeveloped production, but due to the industry's lack of necessary infrastructures. If the strengthening of crafting practices outside the luxury and premium section is a starting point to make the fashion system more responsible by, amongst other features, generating small enterprises with business and supporting local skills, wider accessibility should be taken into account – while at the same time ensuring that this labour-intensive production mode is enumerated to afford for the responsible work conditions and societal participation that are widely associated with this practice.

Crafting is labour-intensive and, therefore, expensive. But "craftspeople often have to resort to selling their unique works at mass production prices" (Tung, 2012). Tourist markets allow setting of more adequate price tags for solvent customers, but, also, collaborations between designers and local artisans can provide the stability needed for the artisans to weather challenges. Designers can play an important role here, if they join forces with artisans due to the 'problem-solving' ductus at the heart of their practice (UNESCO, pp. 5–11; Jure & Albert this volume). Some authors suggest a fluid line between hand-made and mass produced should be explored to open up new opportunities for artisans in the post-industrial era – implementing innovative technologies and entrepreneurial strategies (Cusumano, 1992). "Acting as catalysts of change, designers have the ability to help local craft industries by applying their knowledge to create new innovative business scenarios" (Tung, 2012).

The textile industry is one of the major employment sectors for women, too. Supporting female entrepreneurs is seen as one of the reliable ways to arrive at socially responsible industry. Many NGOs and smaller initiatives pursue a transformation of practices and discourse to re-adjust balances of empowerment and agency (Alemi, Jamaldin this volume). They educate consumers to effect consumption change and aim at exerting pressure on international businesses to adjust and act in a responsible way (Balsinger, 2020).

Today, 'the Silk Roads' don't constitute a geographical place of exchange; global trade does not compulsorily pass through Central Asia anymore and make it a definitive region of exchange and progressing ideas. They are, instead, part of the wider discourse of cultural heritage, which provides coherence and stability, giving meaning to and shaping contemporary fashion and crafting practices. It is a symbolic realm in which fashion designers and crafters can – or are compelled to (Dick) – position themselves nationally and internationally. Cultural history provides a rich source of techniques, skills and styles with the authenticity of its roots reaching into ancient history and any practices in the realm of this narrative of nomadism and tradition are often understood as inherently sustainable practices. While strong, this discourse is itself not impervious to change, because it is actively shaped by all the agents working with it: The government, financers of fashion shows, fashion designers, crafters and even customers/tourists who are on the lookout for 'authentic' products which will also adhere to their specific tastes.

Mentges' interviewees prize 'traditional' clothes, materials and techniques for qualities like being 'natural' and 'unchanging'. Crafts are often idealised in this way (i.e. British Council and Fashion Revolution India, 2023) and can, of course, utilise natural materials and natural dyes, but don't necessarily have to. In this context of responsible fashion, it is interesting to note that tradition and cultural heritage can carry this meaning though. Because of the connotations of the crafts' roots in ancient history and nomadic life in a finely tarried out relationship with nature, its potential for signifying sustainability and responsibility can be explored (Nurdubaeva & Bekibaeva this volume). As mentioned above, they can be drivers of change and fashion stands symbolically for change and renewal. Addressing any challenges in the vast industry should be implemented in the very dynamics of fashion, harnessing its potential for change. There is also a perceivable and idiosyncratic dynamic among designers and crafters themselves. They are the stakeholders vibrantly engaged locally, regionally, but just as much embracing global outlooks. Decentring, here, means to open up new channels of exchange for activism for responsible fashion.

Articles in this volume

As outlined above, combined efforts and diverse impulses are required to decentre the fashion system and effect change culturally, socially and politically. So, in this volume practitioners, economists, educators, entrepreneurs and academics share their heterogeneous insights, experiences and inspirations. It assembles scholarly articles next to personal perspectives, which provide into practitioners' understanding and view of responsible fashion the region. All contributions take up points that are inspired by questions concerning the fashion dynamics and responsible fashion development in the region and connect it in semantic networks to other regions.

Section *Decentring fashion in a responsible way* focuses readers' attention on the compelling dynamism of fashion and textile industries in Eastern regions. Sociologist and political scientist, Chiara Sebastiani, is inspired by Frankopan's prediction that, regarding trade in general, the globe's centre of gravity is about to shift Eastwards. She uses this as an impulse to explore the detachment of countries between Europe and Asia from Western fashion dominance. She builds on observations and on-site exchanges with locals to relate to us these distinct fashion practices. Three cases serve to illuminate facets of the various ways they are emancipating themselves and are, each in their own way, setting their own vestimentary priorities and developing distinct tastes, which are even catching on.

Asking how fashion can be made more responsible, Aika Alemi first guides the readers through a short history of the Kazakh fashion industry and then right into the heart of contemporary fashion design in Kazakhstan. Central Asian designers are situated in economies in the wake of centuries of foreign rule and now placed at the centre of a mighty field of forces emanating from the economic powers of the world. However, in this, Alemi observes a buoying craft and fashion scene that is not only re-discovering traditional crafts but utilising new technologies, networks and alternative sources for materials to create innovative business opportunities in a sustainable way. These small to medium-sized initiatives, writes Alemi, are one of the great potentials for responsible fashion providing infrastructures for sustainable fashion practices.

Another live-wire into Kazakh fashion design is provided by Asiya Ruslanovna Nurdubaeva and Gulnar Dzhambulovna Bekibaeva who take us into the *Kazah Academy of Arts* in Almaty for an introduction to costume and fashion design and their vestimentary methodology to a contemporary take on national identity in Kazakhstan. Using design examples, they relay vividly how cultural heritage provides the source of inspiration in the wake of austere style Soviet design. This design is exploring the aesthetic scope of expression and vestimentary styles for contemporary Kazakhs, aiming at creating lasting, sustainable fashion. This national identity at the core of the designers' work is always considering national as well as international gazes, not simply settling for a national consolidation, but tarrying out Kazakh fashion's positioning in the global fashion system.

Fashion management scholar Annick Schramme and fashion business scholar Karan Khurana examine the Uzbek fashion sector. They start on the premise that Uzbekistan can build on a suitable infrastructure, sufficient labour resources and raw material production. What interests them is how to go about situating it more effectively as a player on the global scene – with all the advantages of providing gainful employment and spin-off benefits for other sectors – while making this development wholly sustainable. The authors lay out how the industry should fine-tune networks and production to address the needs of the domestic and foreign markets. For this, the authors view the strengthening of the role that artisans play, as vital. The necessary structures to implement this have to be guiding the movement in a responsible way.

Craft is often thought of as grounding fashion, providing it with wholesome and natural attributes. On our journey, we were also exploring, whether crafting practices could be used as an inspiration to slow the fashion system down. In the section *Crafting decentred and responsible fashion* authors address specific cases of crafts featuring large in fashion. Circular fashion scholar Kim Poldner, fashion designer Galina Mihaleva and international public management scholar Agnes Evangelista emphatically embrace the practice of felting in Kazakhstan. They understand themselves to be building on the traditions of one of the most prevalent and recognisable of Kazakhstan's traditional crafts. The authors trace its history, its uses, symbolisms and the community-based production practices and above all the sustainable track record of felt to make sense of their own use of this method and drive towards a more sustainable fashion industry. They then illustrate the technique's potential in a circular fashion economy in two case examples, making the connection to contemporary technology and sustainable features in fashion design.

While crafting techniques can be implemented to achieve sustainable fashion production, they can also serve as a vehicle for social movement as the next article shows. In a suppressed society like Afghanistan's (another region on the former Silk Roads), where illiberal dress codes for women in particular are enforced, current embroidery practices constitute a tool of subversion of a totalitarian regime. Fashion journalist Sharifa Jamaldin immerses herself in the history of traditional Afghan dress and embroidery, exploring their aesthetic and social significance. Women who practice the craft use it to undermine the authority over their lifestyles and as a way to empower themselves. The author presents Western-Afghan craft cooperations, which support women in their endeavour and establish infrastructures and supply advice. This chapter shows how craft can be the crystallisation point for social change through empowering women while establishing sustainable practices.

Sometimes the specific role crafts play in fashion is highlighted in a collection. Ira Solomatina is reviewing how this is finding entry into selected fashion magazines in front of a backdrop of the pertinent issue of fashion's effect of unsustainability. She is struck by the discourse of social responsibility that is developed in fashion media on prominent roles of artisans: They are often used to develop on very specific narratives, essentialised in a variety of ways to serve as tropes in neoliberal narratives. Craft in this realm is an earthy counterpart against which to pit the narrative of a glamourous and productive fashion industry. It is imbued with positive attributes, which feed into the fashion industry, but also framed as confronted with challenges, which the industry is instrumental in overcoming.

In her *Embroidery diary*, Ioana Corduneanu characterises her relationship to crafts and outlines the transcultural significance of embroidery. For her as a crafter, embroidery constitutes a language beyond the verbal one. Only for this diary she, cautiously, translates her embroidery thinking into writing. The interpersonal exchanges with other crafters at a workshop she conducted in Tashkent reveal the communicative potential of craft without the barriers of a spoken language. In the second part of the article, Corduneanu's transcultural readings of Uzbeki *suzani* pieces (traditional embroidered wall-hangings) are an evocative immersion into a decoding of iconographies and symbolisms as global. This article is a reminder to fashion activists that knowledges in fashion and textiles are not just manifest in theory, but also very much so in practice and materials. Part of the work on decentring the fashion and textile industry is to integrate these knowledges into the processes.

This section is completed by a compelling argument for taking craft into a dynamic future, building on traditional skills and knowledge, but progressing them in innovative ways. In the face of societal phenomena like cultural homogenisation and the progressive transfer of social interactions into digital space, Elisabeth Pfahl argues for a radical creativity that will combine the powers of digital development like generative artificial intelligence with the idiosyncrasy and immanence of crafts. Re-conceptualising and advancing crafts by introducing new tools, methods and skills, the author details, will provide means to tap crafts' potential to expand its reach and open up new opportunities for artisans.

In the third section, *Collaborating and diversifying to decentre fashion*, design researcher Jure Purgaj and vocational pedagogist Sabine Albert draw attention to the need for diversity in design processes to achieve sustainable fashion. They focus on collaborations of designers and crafters (thereby the merging and diversifying their knowledges) to achieve diversity and, thereby, more sustainable fashion design practices by more fully addressing the needs of a very divers consumer-base. Their argument is backed by a survey conducted with participants of a workshop on the journey through Central Asia. Starting this early on in the production process of garments (at their very conception by designers and production by crafters) more items of clothing could be designed with specific needs of addressees in mind to avoid misconceived and quickly disposed of clothes.

India has a vibrant ecosystem of crafts which continues to thrive in the niches of an industrialised economy. Design educators Saumya Pande and Richa Sood provide another example of bringing designers and crafters together, here, with the aim of supporting crafters in wider outreach and extending their societal participation. The craft concerned, Kheta, is based on a unique construction technique with which distinct double-sided fabrics are created upcycling disused saris. The authors also describe how design students are presented with on-site experience of the crafting practice in a teaching project in the crafting region. Here, they become immersed in the specificities of the local environment and gather first-hand experience with the crafters as their teachers.

Carlos Gago Rodrigez, fashion journalist Sara Kaufman and fashion sociologist Anna Zinola are shining a bright light onto what is still a blind spot of the fashion industry. The occasional appearance of disabled models on the runway notwithstanding, it is still scantly considering persons with disabilities. Those that do are nevertheless treating disability and the garments created for them as 'other'. The authors outline a proposal for best practice – also touching upon the possible potential for Central Asian fashion production. Inclusivity in fashion design means investigating disparate garment-wearing experiences as well as exploring new routes in aesthetics, as the label Anna Bonny did with their breast patch for mastectomy scars. This would mean an additional real dynamic in the fashion system with a break on streamlining and hard-to-surmount structures.

The articles in this volume are all removed from central fashion narratives. Each picks up their own specific aspects that coin the scene in Central Asia and the wider region and develops poignant perspectives, thereby adding to and shaping a 'decentred' discourse. Together they build on a vibrant network of impulses to create new avenues of exchange. Decentring fashion, as fashion historian Marco Pecorari is quoted as saying, "actually means to displace and re-orient our focus. Constantly" (Parsons Paris, 2022).

Note

1 Both the government of Uzbekistan and of Kazakhstan are rated 'not free' in 2024 by the US-American non-profit organisation Freedom House (2024a, 2024b).

Literature and Sources

Anderson, K. (Ed.) (1992). *Trade and Development. New Silk Roads.* Cambridge University Press: Cambridge, UK.

Balsinger, P. (2020). *The Fight for Ethical Fashion. The Origins and Interactions of the Clean Clothes Campaign.* Routledge: London and New York.

Bartlett, D. (2019). Can Fashion Be Defended? In D. Bartlett (Ed.), *Fashion and Politics.* Yale University Press: New Haven, Connecticut, USA and London, pp. 17–57.

Beckert, S. (2014). *King Cotton. Eine Geschichte des globalen Kapitalismus.* Verlag C.H. Beck: München.

Behnke, A. (Ed.) (2017). *The International Politics of Fashion.* Routledge: London and New York.

Bentley, J. H. (1993). *Old World Encounters: Cross-Cultural Contacts and Exchanges in Pre-Modern Times.* Oxford University Press: Oxford.

Britannica Encyclopaedia (2024, April 9). Kazakh. In *Encyclopaedia Britannica*, Retrieved April 14, 2024, from https://www.britannica.com/topic/Kazakh

British Council and Fashion Revolution India. (2023). *Craft in the Age of Climate Crisis. Climate Resilience through Craft in India.* https://www.britishcouncil.in/sites/default/files/craft_x_climate_report_-_final_version_compressed.pdf

Cohen, A. (2008). *Kazakhstan: The Road to Independence. Energy Policy and the Birth of a Nation.* Central Asia-Caucasus Institute & Silk Road Studies Program: Washington, DC and Stockholm.

Chisti, R. K. (2023). The Silk Road Re-Visited. In R. Doraiswamy (Ed.), *Cultural Histories of Central Asia.* Routledge: London and New York, pp. 227–237.

Cusumano, M. A. (1992). Shifting economies: From craft production to flexible systems and software factories. *Research Policy*, *21*(5), 453–480.
Daryo (2023, November 22): Uzbekistan's Trade Triumph. *Daryo.uz*. https://daryo.uz/en/2023/11/22/uzbekistans-global-trade-landscape-charting-economic-frontiers-in-2023
Decree of the President No. 5853 of the Republic of Uzbekistan. (2019, October 23). On approval of the strategy for the development of agriculture of the Republic of Uzbekistan for 2020-2030. https://leap.unep.org/en/countries/uz/national-legislation/presidential-decree-no-5853-validating-agriculture-development
Desore, A., & Narula, S. A. (2018). An overview on corporate response towards sustainability issues in the textile industry. *Environment, Development and Sustainability*, *20*(4), 1439–1459.
Dick, E. (2018). Performing Eurasia in the textiles and clothing businesses along the Silk Road. *The Cambridge Journal of Eurasian Studies*, (2), Article #5N9400. https://doi.org/10.22261/CJES.5N9400
Dittmer, J. (2014). Geopolitical assemblages and complexity. *Progress in Human Geography*, *38*(3), 385–401.
Doraiswamy, R. (2023). Introduction. In R. Doraiswamy (Ed.), *Cultural Histories of Central Asia*. Routledge: London and New York, pp. 7–13.
Durru, O., Yessengeldina, A., Kosherbayeva, A., Shakeyev, S., & Shaikin, D. (2021). State policy of Kazakhstan on implementing of renewable energy sources in textile industry companies. *EconJournals International Journal of Energy Economics and Policy*, *11*(3), pp. 51–56.
Frankopan, P. (2015). *The Silk Roads: A New History of the World*. Bloomsbury: London.
Freedom House. (2024a). Uzbekistan. *Freedom in the World*. https://freedomhouse.org/country/uzbekistan/freedom-world/2024
Freedom House (2024b). Kazakhstan. *Freedom in the World*. https://freedomhouse.org/country/kazakhstan/freedom-world/2024
Government of Kazakhstan (2013, May 20). *Concept for transition of the Republic of Kazakhstan to Green Economy Astana 2013 2 Contents*. Approved by Decree of the President of the Republic of Kazakhstan on 20 May 2013 #557. https://www.oneplanetnetwork.org/sites/default/files/kazakhstan_concept_for_transition_of_the_republic_of_kazakhstan_to_green_economy.pdf.
Høisæter, T. L. (2017). Polities and nomads: The emergence of the Silk Road exchange in the Tarim Basin region during late prehistory (2000–400 BCE). *Bulletin of SOAS*, *80*(2), 339–363. https://doi.org/10.1017/S0041977X17000507
Huang, B., Zhao, J., Geng, Y., Tian, Y., & Jian, P. (2017). Energy-related GHG emissions of the textile industry in China. *Resources, Conservation and Recycling*, (119), April, 69–77. https://doi.org/10.1016/j.resconrec.2016.06.013
JustStyle (2020, January 2). Uzbekistan clothing sector eyes major hike in exports. *justsyle.com*. https://www.just-style.com/features/uzbekistan-clothing-sector-eyes-major-hike-in-exports/?cf-view
Khurana, K., & Ataniyazova, Z. (2020). Insights and future forward for fashion and textile value chain in Uzbekistan. *Research Journal of Textile and Apparel*, *24*(4), 389–408. https://doi.org/10.1108/RJTA-03-2020-0020
Kim, Y.-J., & Park, J. (2019). A sustainable development strategy for the Uzbekistan Textile Industry: The results of a SWOT-AHP analysis. *Sustainability*, *11*, 4613; https://doi.org/10.3390/su11174613
Klimberg, M. (1993). *Ikat. Textile Art from the Silk Road*. Kirdök: Wien.
Kurkdjian, S. (2021). *Géopolitique de la mode. Vers de nouveaux modèles?* Le CavalierBleu Edition: Paris.

Landes, D. S. (1969). *The Unbound Prometheus*. Press Syndicate of the University of Cambridge: Cambridge.
Madjidov, S., & Khakimov, B. (2012). Viewpoints about potential stimulation and possibilities of investments on textile industry Uzbekistan. *European Journal of Business and Economics*, 6, 22–24.
Mentges, G. (2017a). Introductory Remarks. In G. Mentges & L. Shamkhitdinova (Eds.), *Textiles as National Heritage: Identities, Politics and Material Culture. Case Studies from Uzbekistan, Kazakhstan, Algeria and Peru*. Waxmann: Münster, pp. 9–28.
Mentges, G. (2017b). Between Design, 'National Dress' and Nation Building. In G. Mentges & L. Shamkhitdinova (Eds.), *Textiles as National Heritage: Identities, Politics and Material Culture. Case Studies from Uzbekistan, Kazakhstan, Algeria and Peru*. Waxmann: Münster, pp. 31–56.
Micklin, P. (2014). *The Aral Sea*. Springer: Heidelberg, New York, Dordrecht, London.
Nazarov, R. A., Abduraupov, T. V., Shepelya, E. Y., Gritsina, M. A., Melnikov, D. A., Buehler, M. D., Lapin, J. D., Poyarkov, N. A., & Grismer, J. L. (2023). The Fergana Valley is an isolate of biodiversity: A discussion of the endemic herpetofauna and description of two new species of Alsophylax (Sauria: Gekkonidae) from Eastern Uzbekistan. *Animals*, *13*(15), 2516. https://doi.org/10.3390/ani13152516
Nurzhanovna, A. G. (2011). Cotton and textile branch of Kazakhstan State: Problems and prospects for the development. *African Journal of Agricultural Research*, *6*(17), 4035–4045.
Parsons Paris. (2022, November 22). *"Decentralizing fashion", ILFR x MAFS*. Parsons Paris Blog. The New School. https://blogs.newschool.edu/parsons-paris/2022/11/22/decentralizing-fashion-ilfr-x-mafs/
Pazilov, G. A., Ivashchenko, N. P., Bimendiyeva, L. A., & Aitymbetova, A. N. (2020). Textile industry. Issues of managing the growth of innovative activity in enterprises. *Polish Journal of Management Studies*, *21*(1). https://doi.org/10.17512/pjms.2020.21.1.
Petrick, M., Oshakbayev, D., Taitukova, R., & Djanibekov, N. (2017). The return of the regulator: Kazakhstan's cotton sector reforms since independence. *Central Asian Survey*, *36*(4), 430–452. https://doi.org/10.1080/02634937.2017.1392928
Rabimov, S. (2023, November 15). Kazakhstan strengthens its fashion diplomacy with Visa Fashion Week Almaty. *Forbes*. https://www.forbes.com/sites/stephanrabimov/2023/11/15/kazakhstan-strengthens-its-fashion-diplomacy-with-visa-fashion-week-almaty/
Rabimov, S. (2024, January 3). Visa Fashion Week Tashkent follows the Silk Road into the 21st century. *Forbes*. https://www.forbes.com/sites/stephanrabimov/2024/01/03/visa-fashion-week-tashkent-follows-the-silk-road-into-the-21st-century/
RFS (Responsible Fashion Series). (nd.). *About*. University of Antwerp. Accessed May 23, 2024 from https://www.uantwerpen.be/en/conferences/responsible-fashion/about/
Thompson, D. N. (2021). *The Curious Economics of Luxury Fashion. Millennials, Influencers and a Pandemic* (3rd digital ed.). Electronic book. DNT: USA.
Tranberg Hansen, K. (2005). From Thrift to Fashion: Materiality and Aesthetics in Dress Practices in Zambia. In D. Miller & S. Küchler (Eds.), *Clothing as Material Culture*. Berg: Oxford & New York, pp. 107–119.
Tremmel, J. (2003). *Nachhaltigkeit als politische und analytische Kategorie. der deutsche Diskurs um nachhaltige Entwicklung im Spiegel der Interessen der Akteure*. Ökom-Verlag: München.
Trombert, E. (2013). The Demise of Silk on the Silk Road: Textiles as money at Dunhuang from the late eighth century to the thirteenth century. *Journal of the Royal Asiatic Society, Third Series*, *23*(2), Special Issue: Textiles as Money on the Silk Road, 327–347.

Tung, Fang-Wu (2012). Weaving with rush: Exploring craft-design collaborations in revitalizing a local craft. *International Journal of Design*, 6(3), 71–84. http://www.ijdesign.org/index.php/IJDesign/article/view/1077/536

Turapovna, A. M. (2019). Clothes market in Uzbekistan: Competitive environment, development. *International Journal on Orange Technologies*, *1*(2), pp. 47–54.

UNESCO. (2005). *Designers Meet Artisans*. New Delhi. Craft Revival Trust. https://unesdoc.unesco.org/ark:/48223/pf0000147132

US Mission Kazakhstan. (2021). *Artisan empowerment project*. US Embassy and Consulate Kazakhstan. Nur Sultan. https://kz.usembassy.gov/artisans-empowerment-project/

Wang, H. (2013). Textiles as money on the silk road? *Journal of the Royal Asiatic Society, Third Series*, *23*(2), Special Issue, 165–174.

WITS (World Integrated Trade Solution). (2021). *Kazakhstan textiles and clothing exports, imports, tariffs*. https://wits.worldbank.org/CountryProfile/en/Country/KAZ/Year/2021/TradeFlow/EXPIMP/Partner/all/Product/50-63_TextCloth

Wolff, E. A. (2021). The global politics of African industrial policy: The case of the used clothing ban in Kenya, Uganda and Rwanda. *Review of International Political Economy*, *28*(5), 1308–1331. https://doi.org/10.1080/09692290.2020.1751240

Yepanchintseva, S. E., Ashimova, Z. R., & Sakhanova, G. (2023). Modern fashion industry: Trends and prospects for Kazakhstan. *Central Asian Economic Review*, May. https://doi.org/10.52821/2789-4401-2022-6-29-39

Yusupov, E., Khakimov, R., & Rozikov, J. (2021). Issues of competitiveness and results of clustering of the cotton sector entities in Uzbekistan: A review. *E3S Web of Conferences*, (258), 06070. https://doi.org/10.1051/e3sconf/202125806070

Interview

Alemi, A. (2024). Interview. Zoom. 25.03.2024.

Part I

Decentering fashion

1 The impact on fashion of the world's centre of gravity shift

Trade, identity and religion in emerging territories

Chiara Sebastiani

Introduction: From silk roads to fashion roads

In his inspiring book *The Silk Roads: A New History of the World*, Peter Frankopan writes: "We are seeing the signs of the world's centre of gravity shifting – back to where it lay for millennia" (2015, p. 509). The regions that bridge East and West had, in fact, since antiquity been the very crossroads of civilisation. Here, empires were made, and cities bloomed – like Baghdad or Samarkand. We have come to know them only through literature and legends, so fantastic that, as children, we doubted they really existed. Each chapter of Frankopan's book describes one of many historical roads through the region paved for trading between East and West until deep into the second millennium. Though no fashion road features in the list, Frankopan does dedicate a paragraph to fashion in his conclusions with a view to the current global trading situation titled 'The New Silk Road'. 'Western fashion houses' he writes "like Prada, Burberry and Louis Vuitton are building huge new stores and seeing spectacular sales figures across the Persian Gulf, Russia, China and the Far East. [...] Today's ravenous appetites for the most exclusive brands have a rich historical pedigree – and are an obvious indicator of the emerging new elites in countries whose wealth and importance are arising" (Frankopan, p. 517). The archetypal significance of this recent phenomenon does not escape him: He is taking fashion consumption as an indicator of that expected gravity change.

Where Frankopan leaves off, I start: In this chapter, I am detailing the development of a 'road of fashion' between East and West using three quite distinct case studies, which show that this road is far from being only the making of top fashion houses which are serving new elites (Frankopan's 'Uzbek copper magnates' and 'oil moghuls from Kazakhstan'). I am illustrating that fashion's centre of gravity is shifting along the new fashion roads from the West to the East, where they are currently in a more peripheral position. It has – in the case of the first example from the Carpathians, a mountainous region in Central Europe – been paved by a street-level business of thrift shops and flea markets. The idea of flea markets spreading across the old Iron Curtain borderlands is deconstructed: rather, the open borders have been changing

DOI: 10.4324/9781003508076-3

old thrift markets into a new vintage business. In the second example from the plains of Belarus, this road has emerged with brands and designers aiming to meet the demands of new post-Soviet urban middle classes. It stands representatively for other former Union of Socialist Soviet Republics (USSR) countries, where identitarian symbols and post-Soviet ideologies are being played with creatively. The third case, focusing on Turkey, picks up on the thriving online market of fashionable clothes especially designed for Muslim women and increasingly sought after by expanding communities of Muslim migrants and converts in Europe. Turkey is responding to an increasing demand of styles, labelled 'modest', by Muslim women in Western countries as a consequence of post-Second World War migration processes.

Unfolding along these ancient borderlands between East and West, which the three regions straddle, this 'road of fashion' with its many branches draws nourishment, as in the past, from trade, identity and religion – leading to unexplored landscapes of post-globalisation, post-socialism and post-secularism exemplified by fashion. The evolution from second-hand to vintage clothing in the Carpathian flea markets as well as the blending of tradition-inspired Slavic styles and Western-inspired glamour among post-Soviet middle classes and the expansion of Muslim 'modest fashion' led by new urban elites, all demonstrate the impact on fashion of the world's centre of gravity shifting in a southeast direction in the way Frankopan is foreseeing as a more general trend. This is accompanied by the opening of new routes, the blurring of old borders and the merging of cultures and lifestyles.

For the analysis, I am going to concentrate on the impact of geopolitical transformations on an apparently marginal issue like fashion. In the 19th century, in all three regions, fashion consumption was tuned into the way of modern Western individualistic, liberal and formally egalitarian societies (Monneyron, 2006, p. 9). It was dominated by the two great capitals of fashion – London and Paris – which were the undisputed leaders and providers of Western fashion as concept and product. All three regions were, at the time and until the early 20th century, embedded in a major empire: the Austro-Hungarian, the Russian and the Ottoman and each identified with one of the world's great religions–namely, the Catholic, the Orthodox and Islam, respectively. Nevertheless, all three comprised a mosaic of people, cultures and languages. There was none of the cultural and linguistic homogeneity that was being sought by the new nation-states. Thus, in the old imperial territories, dress codes and styles were strongly connected to ethnical identities and social rank (Thompson Ford, 2021), whereas in the new nations, fashion accommodated aspirations of individual self-presentation of members of an empowered bourgeoisie (Sennett, 1977). As a consequence, iconic Western designer fashion styles – luxury commodities produced exclusively in Europe and functioning as social markers of taste, modernity and refinement – travelled from Paris and London to Vienna, Moscow, St Petersburg and Istanbul and from there irradiated to the peripheral provinces where a petty bourgeoisie strived to imitate the aristocracy of imperial courts (as well as depicted in Balzac's *Illusions perdues*, Flaubert's *Emma Bovary* or Thackeray's *Vanity Fair*).

Around the time of the dissolution of the three empires, deep into the second half of the 20th century, a different world emerged, divided into three areas labelled as 'West', 'East' and 'South'. The case studies are situated in settings sitting squarely to those labels. The mountainous Carpathian region became a borderland encompassing a string of countries on the Northern border between West and East. Belarus is a landlocked country in the middle of the Eastern plains. Turkey, meanwhile, continues to bridge East and West across the Bosphorus. In all three countries, republican regimes formally replaced imperial aristocracies with new strata of middle and working classes. Though the latter widely shared the former's appreciation for Western-made fashionable clothes, the new governments' policies differed: whereas in the socialist East, Western fashion was either banned for ideological reasons or scarcely available for economic reasons, in secularised Turkey Western style was encouraged and even imposed (onto men) by the government's modernisation policies. Still, even in the new geopolitical scenario, all three regions maintained a common feature: in each one, the political authorities displayed a keen interest in a matter which in the Western homelands of fashion was considered a frivolous and trivial issue.

Only at the end of the 20th century, following the collapse of the Soviet Union in 1991 does fashion in all three cases become firmly embedded in the free market economy. As the old Iron Curtain borders are being pushed eastwards and more countries are embedded in the new European West, one might expect this to produce a further expansion of Western fashion in these emerging territories. But after close examination, this proves true only in part – the part Frankopan refers to, with old and famous brands accommodating new rising elites with luxury fashion. Quite parallel to this top-down process, a significant bottom-up process is developing, with fashion being reinterpreted in local frames and practices. This is both a symptom and a consequence of the world's centre of gravity rolling 'back to where it lay for millennia' as Frankopan's quote from above predicts.

While along the fashion roads of the last century and a half, raw materials extracted from Eastern regions travelled West to undergo a process of value adding and symbolic branding there, before travelling eastwards again, this dominant process has now been replaced by something that goes beyond "fine fabrics and silks ... being sold back to the place where silk and fine fabrics originated" (Frankopan, p.517). Here, processes of quite a different sort have become pertinent and each of my cases focuses on a specific variable and the reinterpretation of a varied notion, which shows that fashion is undergoing a process of emancipation from traditional Western domination and exporting in turn something new from the East: Second-hand trade, which in post-socialist borderlands makes recycling trendy; national identity, which post-soviet glamour links to sustainability; religion, with post-secular politics making modesty cool. This is a remarkable development: Because it is a general perception that these three variables are unfavourable to the development of fashion – second-hand being perceived as the remains of the day of the fashion feast, national identity as connected to folklore rather than fashion, and religion as linking fashion to vanity – their paving the way to new fashion roads appears quite unexpected.

For the first case, the impulse for the analysis is taken from a novel: 'Taksim' by Andrzej Stasiuk (2011). Stasiuk describes Carpathian flea markets and new trade processes after the fall of Iron Curtain in detail. This fictional description, I contextualise within the literature and data on the new trends in second-hand businesses in the region. The description and analysis of the second case, post-soviet identity in Belarus, are based on regular visits to Belarus between 2013 and 2020 (about three times a year for an average 3–4 days) and informal discussions with a sample of middle-class professionals (doctors and psychologists) ranging from ages between 20 and 60, to whom I was delivering conferences on analytical psychology, on the renaissance of Belarusian culture and its symbolic expression in handicraft. Data collection for the third case, post-secular fashion in Turkey, is based on direct observation (in Istanbul, Bursa and Edirne) between 2005 and 2020 as well as informal discussion with a sample of university-level students and teachers during my lectures in urban studies at Marmara University. In all three cases, the process is based on the methodology of grounded theory (Glaser & Strauss, 2006).

From second-hand to vintage: Flea markets in post-socialist Carpaths

For decades in the 20th century, Western fashions have been the forbidden dream of working classes in Eastern European socialist countries. The mountainous Carpathian region is divided, today, between seven countries, five of which belong to the EU. In the past, it sprawled across the Austro-Hungarian, the Russian and the Ottoman Empires. But for most of the 20th century, it belonged to the geopolitical East and was separated from the correspondent West by a rigid border system known as the Iron Curtain. It was difficult for anybody to cross and generally closed to most forms of trade. From this separation sprang legends, the two worlds spun about each other– one of easy consumption, fashion and luxury, the other of sober and severe ideals – described, for example, by a vast production of Cold War movies[1] ambiguously moving between art and propaganda. Then quite rapidly – almost overnight, following the fall of the Berlin Wall – borders along the Iron Curtain disappeared. And one of the side effects was a second-hand trade that started to move furiously across the new emerging borderlands to become widely available. This impacted on fashion: Western garments had been available mainly to the elites. Thereafter, they had been 'trickling down' by being passed down from the higher to lower social groups. Items were worn and used to the end of their functional life. With the opening of the borders, this ceased to be part of the practice.

The influx of used Western clothes is described vividly and realistically in the novel 'Taksim'. It is an intriguing, fascinating, 'on the road' novel set in a surrealistic land, stretching across Slovakia, Hungary, Romania and Ukraine – in a time around 2010, some 20 years after the fall of the Iron Curtain. The novel describes a world of men always waiting for their big chance, of women always hoping for a lucky catch in regions where urbanisation eats morsels of rural land transforming villages in town outskirts and the borders between East and West are blurred. It is an old peripherical world, of marginal and common people, whose changes Stasiuk describes through the eyes of two flea market peddlers, showing us how such an apparently marginal variable as the trade of second-hand clothes may have a consistent impact on fashion when old borders fall and the world re-centres Eastwards.

The narrator and his friend Wladeck roam the region on their old Ducato, across abandoned border garrisons and through nameless towns and villages, unpacking their heterogeneous arrays of second-hand garments on the village markets. They reminisce about the past: About the time when "there was no second hand, do you remember? Everything worked to the end or you made something else out of it" (Stasiuk, p. 36), dusters had then been made out of old coats and flower-pots out of tyres. Gone are times of the Soviet Union, and even those magical items – silk stockings, that were said could conquer the heart of any woman in Russia – are by now much out of fashion. Second-hand clothes do not seem to attract even the most modest woman of the tiniest village. In the border world described by Stasiuk, the leftovers of mass consumption Western garments now compete with heaps of Chinese sneakers and other plastic items.

In Stasiuk's anonymous small border town, there are "twenty-two thrift shops. A train arrives once a week laden with bales of second-hand clothes. People say all comes from Europe. They say so because Paris, for them, it's always a little treat. Especially for women: they examine dresses under all seams, raise them at arm's length to look at them by light and lay them down, saying: 'Keep it aside for me, I'll come back to-morrow with the money'" (Stasiuk, p. 13, my translation). The train then proceeds on its way towards mountains and borders, to places like Sabinovo or Gönc or maybe Bistrica (in case you don't know, like most of us, these are, respectively, in Russia, Hungary and Slovenia) where they are met by horse teams as well as trucks.

> ... women pay the merchandise by weight but as there is nothing to weigh it on, they quarrel with the wholesalers who swear in five languages ... Bleached blondes extricate one by one the clothes from the bales and shake them under the nose of great big sharks wearing leather jackets shouting: 'What? Paris? France? My ass! This is shit from Turkey!'
>
> (Stasiuk, p. 13)

Against Stasiuk's fascinating albeit decaying background, it is interesting to see that things are changing quickly, and that there is a second part to the story. Well-informed and less romantic business sites give plain figures about the import volume of used textiles, mainly clothing, in the former Eastern bloc countries (Nutall, 2018). Central European consumers wanting to emulate the lifestyle they see in Western countries continue to sustain the market for second-hand clothing that started to thrive in the years of Stasiuk's novel. The expanding middle classes' income made available for clothes and luxury are still below average Western standards: This produces, alongside a greater demand for new consumer goods, an upgrading of flea markets that used to be primarily a source of basic necessities and household goods. The demand shapes a new kind of prospect: These consumers transform the stigma associated with second-hand clothes in poorer countries ('jumble-sale' and charities in the West, 'gipsy' markets in the East) into something both trendy and choosy – that is, fashionable – sustained by competent bloggers. "Quality is an important issue for many second-hand shoppers, who seek out well constructed clothes from high quality fabrics" (Nutall). Under these circumstances, wearing a second-hand item discovered in a flea market is something women coquettishly reveal rather than hide. Second-hand trade is fast expanding from chains still selling in shops by the kilo to online vintage businesses selling single items. Among students, micro-businesses – from flea market findings to social media reselling – are developing, and the 'slow fashion' movement is gaining new adepts (Overton, 2022). A look at the neat diagram depicting the movements of second-hand clothes in recent years (Nutall) reveals that measured by volume the two main trade routes lead from Poland to Ukraine and from Lithuania to Belarus. This is the movement Stasiuk depicts, too, – but in less than ten years, from the beginning to the end of the 2010s, though the routes are the same the merchandise has changed. Eastern Europe is now the destination of top layers, the choicest items of discarded clothes (whereas quality declines as the trade routes move towards Africa). Consequently, flea markets in Eastern Europe are less and less restricted to basic necessities of lower-income population. Also, they now do not feature only plastic sneakers from China and polyester fabrics from Turkey but are becoming more choice and up-market. They increasingly feature a variety of famous brands in good condition.

Yet how long, one may ask, is the second-hand clothes recycling business going to remain really 'sustainable' as Eastern flea markets transform their wares from 'second-hand clothes' to 'vintage items'? Increasingly high prices, supported by an amateur collector attitude among the wealthier strata of the population, and a social media business orientation among younger educated ones, may quickly bring the gentrification of vintage that is already firmly established in Europe (*Grey Journal*, 2021). Post-soviet psychology might make the difference. As I have observed in my work and travel in former socialist Eastern countries, the collapse of the Soviet Union, welcome though it has been by large strata of population, has not involved gleeful acceptance of Western values, in the domain of fashion no less than in general culture and attitudes. According to Prosic-Dvornic (2022), for instance, second-hand shopping involves adding value to high-quality items by "self-made alterations and decorations" (p. 42) as contrasting Western patterns of conspicuous consumption.

Thus, in countries of the former 'Eastern bloc', the evolution of flea markets between high-price vintage items and low-price mass productions might open a space for a return to craftsmanship. Artisanal products and vintage pieces have their uniqueness in common. Moreover, there are at least some kinds of vintage businesses that are just as labour intensive as craftsmanship: Think of small businesses where a single entrepreneur or the members of one family go through all the phases that bring a single item from retrieval to brick-and-wall shops, market stalls or online sites: Sorting, repairing, photographing, advertising, adjusting, delivering, etc. At the same time, craftsmanship items do remain accessible to middle incomes – maybe as special occasion purchases or presents – provided the durability of items in fabric and style balance their price. Perhaps still more importantly, there is the symbolic quality embedded in pieces that may become small family heirlooms designed to keep memories of special events – birthdays, graduations, promotions, engagements, weddings and births. Because of these qualities, handmade fashion items keep an underground connection to those old times when – as Stasiuk's Wladeck narrates – second-hand was still an unknown concept and buying a new pair of boots required a preliminary family council.

Post-soviet glamour and national identity in Belarus

The development of local craftsmanship becoming an alternative to fast fashion and gentrified vintage is supported in the second case by local fashions being shaped by the idea of national identity. The example of Belarus, an independent republic since 1991, shows how the fashionising of tradition is becoming a force in shifting the world's gravitational fashion forces eastwards. Whereas the narrow winding mountainous Carpathian paths trace and sometimes blur borders, the heart of Belarus is a stretch of flatlands connecting the East to the West. The highway running from Minsk to Vilnius is bordered by large alleys and an extraordinary architectural mix that is rivalling Vienna and Paris with imperial pomp and socialist projects, parks and rivers and shopping centres, emblematic monuments like the diamond-shaped Library and the State Circus. But in downtown Minsk, you also find Kastrychnitskaja street – old industrial neighbourhood turned into a community centre with street-artists and pub-crawlers – which challenges in its own way both Soviet nostalgia and post-Soviet glamour.

In contrast to the state of affairs in the former Soviet Union satellite countries in the Carpathian region, on my visits to Belarus, I had seen little evidence of poverty: Not in Minsk, where about 20 per cent of the whole Belarusian population lives, not in the villages where dachas increasingly serve as holiday houses to an increasingly urban population. Complaints from middle classes rather targeted the persisting socialist retribution system, in which manual workers are better paid than intellectual workers, factory workers better than hospital doctors. Younger generations, on the other hand, appreciated the opportunity they were given to pursue higher education and get support in job placement. Official data of The World Bank (2017) document the poverty line as having dropped from the beginning of the millennium to today from over 40 per cent to less than 6 per cent. In 2020–2021, mass protests against president Lukashenko – who controls power since 1994 – were violently suppressed and since 2022, following Belarus' support to Russia in the Russian–Ukrainian war, the borders are closed and what the country looks like now I cannot say.

But when I first visited Minsk, in 2012, the grand appearance of the city coupled in my eyes with the smart appearance of women – including high-heels, tailor-made suits and trendy outfits. The city made me think of Paris, the women's looks suggested Manhattan. Apparently, the "well-dressed people of Belarus" had already struck foreign visitors at the beginning of the second millennium (Bekus, 2004). At that time, post-soviet glamour in public space attire was a means of detachment from the recent soviet past and then, actually, concealed dire poverty. When I first went there, things were already changing. It was not only clothes but also architecture – a touch of glamour characterised new buildings, luxurious apartments and trendy restaurants, to say nothing of the new international Minsk Airport. Belarus being a state economy with Lukashenko as a one-man government these were mainly the results of top-down public policies. But in the domain of fashion, things went somewhat differently: The increasing stress on national identity being something that was widely shared at grassroots level.

Belarus' modern identity has been moulded by the Soviet experience, but an emerging urban bourgeoisie is looking westwards in its consumption patterns and eastwards in its aesthetic standards. What makes the Belarus case interesting is the fact that in the fashion domain, these issues are dealt with differently than in either Eastern Europe or Russia. In Eastern Europe, fashion turns second-hand clothes into something cool and trendy; in Russia, fashion winks at nostalgia. Whereas it is somehow taken for granted, in the general perception, that communism could not have really anything to do with fashion (Bekus, p. 2), in fact, the Soviet regime did pay a lot of attention to fashion: Only it just did not work in the way it was intended (Gronow & Zhuravlev, 2015). In a chapter of her PhD thesis research devoted to 'Fashionable Nostalgia', Ekaterina Kalinina (2014) opposes subcultural fashion practices in Soviet times – which ironically appropriates Soviet symbols as a means of distancing from Soviet ideology – to contemporary Russian fashion brands which make commercial and political uses of the Soviet past in fashion design. 'Nostalgia', she argues, functions as a label with multiple meanings in ascribing political and cultural identities to oneself and others (Kalinina, p. 4).

But in post-Soviet Belarus, second-hand is not that cool and nostalgia is not much at home: Here, the issues being 'national identity' on the one hand and 'economic growth' on the other hand, fashion is being reinterpreted along the above-mentioned lines of combining pre-Soviet identity and post-Soviet glamour. An example of the first – the quest for national identity through fashion – is the Kupala Night fashion event inspired by the Ivana Kupala traditional Slavic holiday, of pagan origins, celebrating the summer solstice. Ivana Kupala holiday is characterised by a rich folklore of night wakes and bonfire jumping, flower-crowned maidens and wood-roaming lovers. In July 2020, the Belarusian Fashion Council organised the Ethical Fashion Show dedicated to the Kupala Night. On the Belarus Fashion Week web-site, the event is depicted in these terms: "All the collections presented are united by the theme of Kupala holiday and will include traditional elements only: Linen, natural colours, flowers and, of course, ethnical symbols widely known among Belarusian buyers. In addition to the theme of ethical fashion, no make-up (or natural make-up) principle will be the main theme of the entire event" (Belarus Fashion Week, 2020). An example of the second – the construction of post-Soviet glamour in fashion – we find in the increasing stress on sustainability that draws inspiration from recent Western trends, but whose products are simmered in Belarusian flavours. The online account of the 2019 edition of the Belarus Fashion Week offers an interesting sample of the post-Soviet Belarus fashion discourse. Devoid of nostalgia for communist sobriety, it also shuns consumerism.[2] But rather than glamourising second-hand recycling, it revolves around the basic concept of 'nature'. The 2019 seasonal Ethical Fashion Show is described as a pageant of collections "in natural colours using the silk-screen printing technique", inspired by "conscious fashion and consumption" or relying "on natural muted colours (green, beige, grey)" (Belarus Fashion Week, 2019). To underscore the back-to-nature note another brand's creations are described as "inspired by nature and the popular Sustainable Fashion Movement" and, as a final touch, "the music of the runway was birdsong of endangered species" (Belarus Fashion Week, 2019). Traditional values of family and motherhood are also invited on the catwalk as designers "prepared a family look – images for the whole family" (Belarus Fashion Week, 2019).

Somewhere in between Eastern folklore and Western glamour comes the rediscovery of textiles, both as fabric and embroidery craftsmanship. This appears as the Belarusian 'third way' in fashion, built on identity embedded in 'material culture'. Recent research shows that textiles "are and continue to be symbols and visual expression of Belarusian cultural identity", they are "a century-long cultural code which is reflected both in current politics and fashion" (LaVey, 2021, p. 175). Typical colours (red, white and pale green) and well-known traditional embroidery patterns are nowadays embedded in the Belarusian craft landscape. Belarusian textiles have been used in politics and art – as recently documented by the University of Michigan online exhibit "The Code of Presence: Textiles in Belarusian Contemporary Art

Before, During and after the Protests" (University of Michigan, 2023) – they are an important part of everyday life as well as of national heritage; today they steer contemporary fashion towards a creative elaboration of identity.

The introduction of new manufacturing technologies and novel textiles has impacted fashion trends throughout history (e.g. Riello & Lemire, 2008, p. 907). What is new, is the fashionising of textiles with symbolic values connected to national identity as in the case of Belarus. The national identity variable, thus, displays a potential for impact on fashion albeit still in a burgeoning phase, characterised by an original mix inspired by nature, tradition and glamour – and strongly signifying the decentering of fashion's centre of gravity. This also implies some distancing from fast fashion: Ethnical identity symbols, though they may become fashionised, can hardly become 'fast' – meaning fast adopted and fast discarded – because of their very nature. At the most, they may be spiced by a touch of nostalgia.

If traditional costumes have been in the past often associated with national identity – in post-colonial or multicultural contexts for instance – they have always been perceived as being opposed to fashion. Turning symbols into fashion is a tricky issue: Normally there is a gain in terms of popularity and a loss in terms of meaning. If this is true for symbols connected to national identity, it is still more true, as we will see in the next chapter, for symbols connected to religion. Nevertheless, this is what is happening in Central Asia's emerging territories. After all, fashion is, among other things, about making pertinent or even glamorous, a set of habits, practices and values that have quite different origins to those connected to public appearance, and turning them into style. This is the role currently played by second-hand trade in the Carpaths, by national identity affirmation in Belarus: Both variables go beyond utility and tradition to produce fashion.

Post-secular fashion: Modesty from Turkey to Europe

The third case focuses on another unlikely seeming variable generating fashion trends: Religion. In a post-secular world, Islam has given life to a thriving fashion and an expanding business, which Reina Lewis has labelled 'modest fashion' (Lewis, 2013). 'Modest fashion' is complying with the Muslim feminine dress code, which has definitely left the 'niche'. It changes from one country to the other, blending the local traditional feminine outfits with innovative design styles, but has by now developed its own international brands and fashion magazines. With a long-established important textile industry, a vibrant metropolis like Istanbul where East and West have been meeting and mixing for centuries, a refined taste among leading classes which is at the same time a heritage of the Ottoman Empire, a product of a rich merchant tradition and its contacts with the Republic of Venice, and the outcome of a modernisation process strongly inspired, for historical and political reasons, by France, Turkey has proven the natural region to assume a leadership role in the promotion and diffusion of modest fashion in the West and important migration processes have supported this trend. Moreover, though post-secular, Turkey remains very liberal in matters concerning dress codes and behaviour in public space, and this also favours the development of fashion.

Turkey underwent a process of secularisation from the 1920s, promoted by Kemal Ataturk and led by a cosmopolitan urban bourgeoisie. This trend was inverted with the rise to power of the AKP party based on Islamic values and beliefs. The post-secular shift played an important role in the development of modest fashion insofar as it liberalised the shariah-compliant dress code: A typical example being women's ability to wear the Muslim headscarf concealing hair and neck in universities, where it had hitherto been banned. Streets in Istanbul and other great cities are full of girls and young women wearing the very characteristic Turkish headscarf, a square piece of printed silk or satin often brightly coloured, draped in the typical 'Turkish hijab style'. Post-secularism as a factor promoting fashion rather than enforcing dress codes may sound strange. Yet, as Elizabeth Bucar (2018) noted in her field research nowadays for Muslim women "it is considered important to select a modest outfit and headscarf that is visually pleasing in public; this allows women to represent Islamic piety in the best way possible, as well as to avoid the harsh critiques of the secular elite that veiled women are ugly and unfashionable".

But there are other factors as well that have played a role in making Turkey a fashion trendsetter and they have to do, as discussed in the former cases, with the new geopolitical developments. We have seen the impact of the fall of the Iron Curtain and the dissolution of the Soviet Union on fashion; in the case of Turkey, the impact is a result of the new Schengen borders. The creation of the Schengen area – which Turkey is outside of, while being a candidate to inclusion – has made the country a popular destination for those people from the Mena region as well as Eastern Europe and Central Asia wishing to travel for leisure or shopping, but meeting increasing difficulties to access the Schengen space because of visa restrictions. This is the case, for instance, of Tunisian women who have had a long tradition of shopping in nearby Sicily to buy a bride's wedding trousseau and have now turned to Turkey as the new Mediterranean wedding outlet.

According to Bucar, "visions of femininity in Istanbul take their lead chiefly from the West, not the East". Turkish fashion does show the unmistakable mark of French tradition not only in the silk foulards but also in slim waists, neatly fitting tailored lines, carefully chosen accessories. Yet, it is a long time since these have been appropriated and made indigenous and a highly prized textile tradition has helped the process. Moreover, nowadays not only "strict secularism is no longer the aspiration" but a fast-developing modest fashion is meeting the demands of Muslim women in non-Muslim countries increasingly looking for something different than outfits that are merely a blend of religious dress code and local traditional costumes. As Istanbul is promoting itself as "the new capital of prêt-à-porter" (Miller, 2013) and Turkey is seeking to promote its designers abroad, fashion explicitly aiming at compliance to Islamic precepts has long become an important business trend and Turkish chains offering items that conform to pious fashion are expanding westwards: For instance, the 'Hijab Paradise' store in Bologna, named after a Turkish chain, represents the first modest fashion store in Italy. And the fast expansion of online shopping has also helped in the westward expansion of Turkish shariah-compliant feminine outfits.

In contemporary Turkey – where there are no enforced dress codes and in the streets of the big cities one may find black chadors, but also, at times, coloured mini-skirts – fashion inspired by religious values and claiming conformity to religious dress code probably represents the most original product between traditional Muslim outfits (widespread in poorer neighbourhoods as well as in Anatolian rural areas) and Westernised modern styles (at times more cool than pious). It combines religious values with an important textile tradition based on natural fabric (Alkaya & Demirer, 2013) and a rich variety of prints and colours, the promotion of Indigenous cloth and embroidery, drawing motifs from the Ottoman tradition (and its revival in popular TV series) are all parts of its success. As a highly promising trend in an increasingly flourishing market, Turkey's exportation of fashion accommodating the requests of an expanding Western-based clientele gives a vivid account of new 'fashion roads' from East to West. A recent report on the state of today's modest fashion market (Bianchi, 2024) makes the case of Istanbul-based e-tailer Modanisa brand which, selling "both private label and third-party brands to customers in dozens of countries around the world, was a pioneer" (Bianchi). The fashion style that seeks compliance – more or less strictly – with Quranic norms nowadays does not limit its markets to Muslim countries alone any more. If on the one hand "more and more Western labels, fast-fashion giants and luxury ready-to-wear top brands are embracing this growing modest sector as it moves from niche to mainstream" (Bianchi), on the other hand, start-ups like the 'Hijab Paradise' store in Bologna are the realm of young female Muslim entrepreneurs addressing to young and low-income strata of Muslim clientele in non-Muslim countries. In this case, a style is travelling from East to West. Religion in post-secular realms is having an impact on fashion, not only in emerging territories of the East but also in the – somewhat stagnating – territories of the West.

Conclusion: From East to West

In spite of difference of contexts, history and culture, all three variables of trade, identity and religion are paving the way of new 'fashion roads'. In the new geopolitical order in which borders have fallen (new ones have arisen, but this is another story), collective identities are being rediscovered and religious practices are spreading in novel ways, new 'fashion roads' are emerging on the remaining traces of the old silk roads. Not only the major geopolitical shift of the current millennium has an impact on fashion but it also leads us to think that fashion is not so marginal after all from a world history viewpoint. Unsurprisingly, the impact of this historical shift is showing itself to be very different from one region to another. Each one of our three cases is dominated by one variable which has a particular influence on fashion. In the first case, trade flows made possible by the collapse of the old Iron Curtain borders resulted in the upgrading of second-hand attire. In the second case, the emergence of a newly independent state and its quest for national identity results in the glamourisation of traditional products and crafts through their recognition as symbols of national identity. This means the development and consumption of styles from local production and is exemplary for other post-Soviet countries. In the third case, the liberalisation and support of religious practices following a shift in political majorities results in the fashionisation of religion-compliant 'modest' attire. The gaining of traction of any one variable, which undermines the dominance of Western fashion influences – trade, identity and religion – is obviously determined by the specific conditions and cultural, geographical and historical features of each region. Yet all three variables are part of the same picture – the new geopolitical order, the evidence of a shift of the world's centre of gravity and its impact on fashion. Moreover, the impact, though yielding different material products – Eastern vintage fashion in the Carpathian region, ethnical sustainable fashion in Belarus, and modest fashion in Turkey – supports in all three cases the same trend: Emancipation from Western fashion leadership and promotion of fashion trends originating in Eastern regions and travelling westwards.

This raises some new questions. In the first place: If this is happening, might it not be because fashion – considered a typical product of modernity, cutting loose from traditional patterns and values – is but the external phenomenon of deeply rooted human and social processes? Maybe we should revise our too-limited definition of fashion and see in it a manifestation of a more general symbolical and archetypal phenomenon rooted in the realms of ancient civilisations which are now being re-discovered together with their cultures and traditions, arts and crafts, people and lifestyles. Undoubtedly, we are to some extent dealing with the gentrification of thrift, the glamourisation of folklore and the fashionisation of religious dress codes. Nevertheless, these are probably epiphenomena. The impact of the world's centre of gravity shift on fashion appears to be the product of more structured variables – trade, identity and religion – which connect both to the domain of economics and the domain of ideas. If it is so, then a second question might concern the impact that fashion, in turn, from emerging territories can exert on a wider scale, involving new models of production and consumption, new social relations and values.

We are witnessing, writes Frankopan describing the turmoils of emerging territories, "the birthing pains of a region that once dominated the intellectual, cultural and economic landscape" (2015, p. 509). Migrants are pressing on the new Eastern borders of the enlarged EU, post-Soviet republics are theatres of identitarian conflicts and clashes between contending secularist and religiously inspired visions of the world are endemic in the Middle East. Fashion, now journeying from East to West on new fashion roads that trace ancient Silk Roads, to some extent makes all this visible.

Notes

1 Probably the most famous of these is 'Silk Stockings' (Mamoulian, 1957), the love story between a fascinating American producer and a beautiful but austere Russian agent.
2 The rejection for consumerism among educated younger generations one also finds in Russia (Reiter, 2012). But whereas in that case the values are good taste and social ethics, in Belarus the attitude is linked to tradition and environment ethics.

References

Alkaya, E., &Demirer, G. N. (2013). Sustainable textile production: A case study from a woven fabric manufacturing mill in Turkey. *Journal of Cleaner Production, 65*, 595–603. https://doi.org/10.1016/j.jclepro.2013.07.008
Bianchi, C. (2024). The state of today's modest fashion market. *Istituto Marangoni*. https://www.istitutomarangoni.com/en/maze35/industry/the-state-of-todays-modest-fashion-market
Bekus, N. (2004, May 26). The well-dressed people of Belarus. *Eurozine*. https://www.eurozine.com/journals/arche/ (Retrieved January 29, 2024)
Bucar, E. (2018, February 1). How Muslim women use fashion to exert political influence. *The Atlantic*. https://www.theatlantic.com/international/archive/2018/02/muslim-women-fashion-political-influence/550256/
Frankopan, P. (2015). *The New Silk Roads*. London: Bloomsbury.
Glaser, B., &Strauss, A. L. (2006). *The Discovery of Grounded Theory: Strategies for Qualitative Research*. Aldine Transaction.
Grey Journal. (2021). The dark side of thrifting: The thrift store gentrification phenomenon. *Grey Journal*. https://greyjournal.net/play/style/fashion/the-dark-side-of-thrifting/ (Retrieved January 23, 2024)
Gronow, J., &Zhuravlev, S. (2015). Fashion meets socialism: Fashion industry in the Soviet Union after the Second World War. *SKS, Helsinki, Finnish Literary Society, 20*, 303. https://doi.org/10.21435/sfh.20
Kalinina, E. (2014). *Mediated Post-Soviet Nostalgia (Doctoral Dissertation)*. Huddinge: Södertörn University.
LaVey, A. M. (2021). Reading Belarus: The evolving semiosis of Belarusian textiles. *Journal of Belarusian Studies*,*11*(2), 175–205. https://doi.org/10.30965/20526512-12350011
Lewis, R. (2013). *Modest Fashion: Styling Bodies, Mediating Faith*. London: Tauris Academic Studies.
Monneyron, F. (2006). *La Sociologie de la Mode*. Paris: PUF.
Nutall, C. (2018, December 20). Castoff clothing a 770-million-dollar business in Eastern Europe. *bneIntelliNews*. https://www.intellinews.com/castoff-clothing-a-770mn-business-in-eastern-europe-153726/
Prosic-Dvornic, M. (2022). 'Twice is Nice': Second-hand clothing in today's global world. *Glasnik Etnografskog Instituta, 70*(1), 19–52. https://www.researchgate.net/publication/361454331_Twice_is_Nice_Secondhand_clothing_in_today%27s_global_world

Overton, A. (2022, November 4). The gentrification of charity and vintage shops. *The Courier*. https://www.thecourieronline.co.uk/the-gentrification-of-charity-and-vintage-shops/
Reiter, A. (2012). Young, educated and shopping: Clothing, consumption and difference among the educated young in Krasnodar, Russian Federation. *Emecon – Employment and Economy in Central and Eastern Europe*,*3*(2), 1–14. https://emecon.eu/index.php/emecon/article/view/28/18
Riello, G., &Lemire, B. (2008). East and West: Textiles and fashion in Eurasia in the early modern period. *Journal of Social History*, Summer, 887–916. https://wrap.warwick.ac.uk/190/1/WRAP_Riello_Final_Article.pdf
Sennett, R. (1977). *The Fall of Public Man*. New York: Alfred A. Knopf.
Stasiuk, A. (2011). *Taksim*. Arles: Actes Sud.
Thompson Ford, R. (2021). *Dress Codes: How the Laws of Fashion Made History*. New York: Simon & Schuster.

Sources

Belarus Fashion Week. (2019, October 17). Ethical fashion show, women fashion brand, Nelva by Huawei, Jovanas Couture. https://www.bfw.by/en/news/belarus-fashion-week-ethical-fashion-show-women-fashion-brand-nelva-by-huawei-jovanas-couture.html#print
Belarus Fashion Week. (2020, July 6). NGO Belarusian Fashion Council is organizing Ethical Fashion Show #3. https://www.bfw.by/en/news/etichnaya-moda-v-formate-onlaj.html
Istituto Marangoni. (n.d.). The state of today's modest fashion market. Retrieved May 20, 2024, from https://www.istitutomarangoni.com/en/maze35/industry/the-state-of-todays-modest-fashion-market
Mamoulian, R. (Director). (1957). *Silk Stockings* [Film]. Metro-Goldwyn-Mayer.
The World Bank. (2017, October 17). Poverty reduction in Belarus. https://www.worldbank.org/en/news/feature/2017/10/17/poverty-reduction-in-belarus
Miller, A. D. (2013, March 31). Fashion: Istanbul is the new capital of prêt-à-porter. *Turkish Forum*. https://www.turkishnews.com/en/content/2013/03/31/fashion-istanbul-is-the-new-capital-of-pret-a-porter/#gsc.tab=0
University of Michigan. (2023). The code of presence: Belarusian protest embroideries and textile patterns, online exhibit curated by Sasha Razor. https://apps.lib.umich.edu/online-exhibits/exhibits/show/code-presence

2 Responsible fashion in Central Asia

Aika Alemi

Manuscript

The word 'responsible' is abstracted from 'responding' and 'being able to respond'. In the field of fashion, there is certainly an expectance of the industry to take responsibility for and respond to the critical issues which plague it. In the Central Asian countries – Kazakhstan, Uzbekistan, Kyrgyzstan, Turkmenistan and Tajikistan –, however, the fashion industries, at the moment, mainly respond to challenges of meeting their basic needs such as economic stability, growth and development. They also respond to a search for identity after long years of oppression by Russian colonialism and Soviet totalitarian rule. To understand the current state of affairs and assess the potential of this region's fashion, some context needs to be established about the past. The five countries' cultural background of a nomadic way of life and the Silk Road cities connecting East and West, Russian colonial rule starting from the late 18th century until the Revolution of 1917, which gave it a continuation under the communist regime, 70 years of the Soviet period in the 20th century and 34 years of post-communist post-colonial independence all condition this story. In this chapter, I am exploring these issues on the basis of my insights and impressions as a fashion designer and entrepreneur in Kazakhstan. I am also presenting cases of entrepreneurs infusing the Central Asian fashion scene with a new dynamism and situating sustainability at the core of their work to illustrate how individuals are driving the development and are creating networks to support others, too.

Backstory

The former Central Asian republics of the Soviet Union became independent states after the USSR was dismantled in 1991. Their economies, each in their own distinctive way, started transitioning from the command model of centralized governance to market economies. The Soviet experiment had lasted for 74 years, and the transition back to basic freedoms of expression, religious beliefs, movements and liberalized economy has not been easy, linear or straightforward. It was probably rather the opposite of all that. At that very

DOI: 10.4324/9781003508076-4

time when countries such as the United Kingdom, the United States, Germany, France, Japan and other G7 countries were starting to discover and adopt a new paradigm of the 'creative economy' – moving away from physical assets to ideas and concepts as key value generators – Central Asian countries along with other former Soviet Union states were busy dealing with abandoning the communist paradigm. They were swapping communism for capitalism and were simply swamped with a tectonic geopolitical transformation and macro-economic reforms. An important factor defining the current situation for fashion in Central Asia is the structure of the respective economies: They ail from the so-called 'Dutch disease' or the 'resource curse' – a heavy dependency on natural resources and raw materials, which undermines economic growth and development of a country (Auty, 2001).

In thrall of this effect, Kazakhstan like other Central Asian countries has been choosing paths of lowest resistance and the easiest strategies to export abundantly extracted raw materials such as oil, gas, metals and uranium – but also domestically produced raw materials like wool, cotton, etc. – without processing them and adding value locally (Aliev, 2015). Being a raw material extraction appendix of the developed world has been hindering sector diversification and developing non-raw material extraction industries and precluding innovation, knowledge-based, intellectual property-based creative and innovative industries (Ondagash et al., 2014). Extraction and export are still important drivers of economic growth in Kazakhstan. Any other type of production that had existed during the Soviet period declined and was very often destroyed completely. The same counts for intra-sectoral ties between former Soviet Union republics which had all become independent states.

> Despite efforts to diversify the economy, Kazakhstan's exports have become increasingly concentrated on mineral products, especially oil. [...] From 2001 to 2014, before moderately declining in 2018, the average annual growth rate for mineral products was 21.6 per cent, while that for manufactured products was 11.1 per cent.
>
> (UNCTAD, 2020, p. 15)

This growth presents an obstacle to diversification of the economy and a strong government with the public sector as a major employer and impedes the success of small enterprises (UNCTAD, p. 16).

There were several incidences of oil-price drops (including the one induced by the Covid-19 pandemic; Czech & Niftiyev, 2021) and also reduced demand from China and the Russian Federation, which had devastating effects on economic stability and caused inflation in Kazakhstan (UNCTAD, 2020, p. 16). The crises forced the resource-rich countries of Central Asia to adjust. In fact, in Kazakhstan, a National Fund (NRFK) has been installed by presidential decree in 2000 funded by oil revenue to counter the effects of oil price changes. However, it is not managed to perform sufficiently when needed (Dautova, 2020). The most important solution remained and remains diversification of the economy, which meant developing deeper processing industries and creating higher value-added products, services and works based on intellectual property, creativity and innovation (UNCTAD, pp. 17–35). So, the crises rather emphasized further the need to direct attention to what was traditionally overlooked in the post-Soviet paradigm of hard, tangible, physical assets – intellectual property and creative ideas and concepts. Here, the appreciation of the creative economy is only slowly growing, as the habit of ascribing more value to tangible entities like land, buildings, equipment rather than ideas, concepts, innovation is still quite strong (Assaniyaz, 2023). The pandemic crisis initiated a push to look for new sources of economic growth in the creative industries sector, too: Scaled and accelerated by digital technology fashion and crafts as part of creative economy offered a new alley for exploration (Assaniyaz). This trend is now at the centre of agendas not only in Central Asia, but in all post-Soviet countries, especially in Russia, Ukraine, Georgia and Azerbaijan.

Responsible fashion in Central Asia today

In Central Asia, besides this region having the potential for being a strong contender for alternative economic growth and innovative and diversified economy, responsible fashion ideas are still considered somewhat premature, non-essential and sort of 'nice to have' developments which can be afforded only by rich countries. Nevertheless, responsible fashion already exists and is albeit slowly and gradually evolving, because in the age of globalization and digitalization a country or a region cannot really fence itself away from the rest of the world. There are several responsible fashion directions now starting to develop in Central Asian countries which have a multi-faceted, complex effect economically, socially and culturally both short-term and longer-term.

Revival of crafts

Central Asian crafts originated from and were integral to the rural areas until the 20th century. But during the time of Soviet industrialization and urbanization, around 70% of crafts and folk, ethnic and indigenous artisanal were abandoned and the knowledge of them lost (Social Innovation Central Asia, nd.; also, Kurzt, 2023). They were measured against the more profitable serial production and their economic performance. Rural life – and the rural lifestyle as a paradigm – were transformed altogether by the pull of cities. The young Soviet state embraced technological progress as it was eager to present the new communist ideology as superior and substantiate the need for centralized supply and demand management, censorship and oversight of cultural values and formulaic moulding of peoples' and country's identity. In a quest to convert an agrarian country into an industrialized one, destroying rural traditions and 'freeing' peasants as an economic class through disenfranchising collectivization the totalitarian regime drove the USSR to famine catastrophes in the 1920s and in the 1930s. In Kazakhstan, since cattle were the only source of income and population in rural areas was predominantly dependent on nomadic cattle grooming, the effect of such famine was the starvation of up to around 40% of the then population (Volkava, 2012; Pianciola, 2001). During the Soviet period, it was the national policy to suppress identities of all the ethnic groups living in the country to cut roots with the pre-Soviet past (Martin, 1998). It was partially a new form of colonialism whose tradition the Soviets successfully continued in Central Asia after the Czarist rule was overthrown in 1917. Also, identity suppression was ideologically charged to instil the new order of communist equality values and the new world for the poor.

In this setting, crafts became a battlefield between village and city, agrarians and industrialists, natural and artificial, manual made or machine manufactured, original and serial (Fitz-Gibbon, 2004). From this perspective, the revival of crafts 30 years after the Soviet experiment ended in defeat of its values and political and economic failure today the renaissance of decorative folk arts and preservation of the artisanal heritage and crafts are part of a larger context of creative industries. Crafts as part of creative economy are a catalyst for a circular fashion development and offer economic growth solutions with a diversity of immediate and longer-term impacts. I see crafts as being ingrained with a sensitivity to nature because they are rooted in traditional life which was moulded in close contact to nature and in tune with the ecosystem. Artisanal techniques and crafts are organically directed at zero or lower waste from processing and production. For instance, patchwork techniques – fabric, cut into strips and sewn together – are an effective example of zero waste practices. They find use in fashion and as well as interior design. Patchwork craft is also ideal for redesign and upcycling of pieces: The pieces are disassembled into original stripes of fabric and then sewn into new styles, decor elements and objects. Another example is the traditional felting technique when layers of discarded wool tops are made into a felt fabric which is then cut out in the form of negative-positive ornament appliqués leaving no cut-out waste as any wool leftovers are reused with the application of wet felting techniques as new textures, objects and elements are created from felt leftovers.

Craft and hand-made techniques that are committed to the traditional way of production are eco-friendly. They employ natural dyes from grass, flowers, bark, leaves and hot water for wet felting and for rinsing and natural sun drying. Traditional nomads in Kazakhstan and Kyrgyzstan used natural materials to obtain natural colours of a broad spectrum of shades inspired by the shade grades of clouds, rain, sky, earth, rivers, hills, mountain snow tops and other manifestations of the Earth's beauty and eternity. Traditional craft techniques such as felting, patchwork, embroidery, goldsmithing and stone, bone and wood carving require manual labour, many hours and a lot of energy. The cost of resulting pieces is quite high, but they represent perfect examples of true slow fashion with longer-lasting styles, keeping consumption at reduced levels and minimizing fashion being thrown away and reaching landfills. Of these products, Aigul Amirjanova says in an interview, I conducted with her in 2023 as part of my research into the scene: "It's eternal fashion that can be handed over to our daughters. It's beyond trends and it lasts forever!" (interview Amirjanova, 2023). Amirjanova is CEO of *Viled luxury* (Viled, nd.) a group based in Almaty, Kazakhstan, which promotes and sells emerging Kazakh and Central Asia responsible fashion labels. *Viled* constitutes a portal for customers verifying the products and, thereby, it supports the nascent local fashion industry providing a market for their ideas and designs.

Ancient manual techniques like *biz keste* and *suzani* embroidery, *kiiz basu* felting, *quraq* patchwork and other handmade techniques represent the multitude of hours and the energy that went into making them. But they can create high margins and new employment opportunities for creators. Traditional crafts have a positive economic and social impact creating employment and commercial opportunities in rural and remote areas for women, handicapped, marginalized, unemployed people and young talents. *Born Nomad* (nd.) promotes craftspeople, boosts crafts and handicraft businesses and revives crafts in Central Asia. More than 2,000 craftspeople from all five Central Asian countries are to take part in the project consisting of education program to help craftspeople commercialize their products as well as an incubator to help launch craft peoples' start-ups and also a pitching session to investors and a festival to showcase the stories and products by local craftspeople. Laura Hays (2022) from the Economic Section of the Embassy of the United States of America to Kazakhstan was an early supporter of *Born Nomad*. As an economic development professional, she advocates the economic empowerment of craftswomen and female fashion designers through commercial capabilities building in particular and accentuates the fact, that most of the craft entrepreneurs are women. In an interview I conducted with her in November 2021, she stated that she believes that "where women thrive, countries prosper".

Design skills create new jobs and help women start businesses and make a living. This contributes to reviving the economic activity in underdeveloped areas and eventually helps to bring people back and provide gainful employment which also makes a contribution to mitigating ecological problems. This is very pertinent in Central Asia, because, during the Soviet period, the significant increase in agricultural production in the lowlands of the basin, led to the construction of large-scale storage and irrigation infrastructure and massive diversion of water away from its natural course. This contributed to a drop in the level of the Aral Sea of more than 20 meters since 1960, causing the sea to shrink from the third largest lake in the world to 10% of its size and split into four water bodies by 2011, the Southern Aral Sea and the Northern Aral Sea and degrading the land area around the water basin (Micklin, 2014, p. 2). Ecological activism addressing the natural environment coupled with initiatives to coach local craftspeople in remote areas of ecological disaster such as Semey, Kazakhstan and Aral in Uzbekistan and Kazakhstan helps create sustainable crafts and fashion design. In Karakalpak region of Uzbekistan, a non-governmental organization *Golden Heritage of Aral* trains craftspeople in ancient techniques of carpet weaving and embroidery as well as computer literacy in order to create jobs, launch craft businesses and ultimately revive the Aral Sea area which in the aftermath of the environmental water crisis was deserted and depressed not only ecologically, but also economically and socially. *Golden Heritage of Aral* works with international organizations as well as Uzbek government to create sustainable crafts and design opportunities programs for craftspeople in Aral Sea area. Gulnar Egemberdieva, the NGO's founder, lives in the Aral Sea area and deals with the challenges of the ecological catastrophe aftermath by trying to re-educate the local craftspeople and help them earn a living here to prevent mass exodus of young talent and workforces on a day-to-day basis. She shares her story:

> I was upset that our *muinak* embroidery, the samples of which are kept in many prominent museums, is considered simply a dead art. I started to teach women the embroidery and carpet weaving techniques and how to sell and receive income from the crafts.
>
> (Egemberdieva, 2022)

Fashion design

Central Asian designers are an integral part of the global fashion industry. As in all post-Soviet territories they are dealing with an interesting challenge connected to the Soviet design tradition (Krasnyanskaya & Semenov, 2021). Fashion design in the realm of authoritarian communist ideology was not primed on original thinking, free creative expression, fresh new ideas or diverse creativity nor was teaching students the essential skills of building a brand or ensuring commercial aspects of marketing, selling, costing and seeking profits a goal. Rather, it censored and limited anything that was outside the main direction of prescribed aesthetics. During Soviet times the sector was not even referred to as 'fashion' but as 'light industry' (versus heavy machinery industries of planes, tractors, motors and equipment) (Gronow & Zhuravlev, 2015). It can be said, that, in that period, garment technology universities did not groom designers (Sauvage, 2018) or commercial managers, but pattern makers, technologists, manufacturing managers, equipment technicians and materials experts. One would think that this approach should have changed in 30 years after the USSR collapsed, but the Soviet experiment which had lasted for more than three generations still lives on in the mentality and the way of thinking, teaching, learning and creation of fashion.

After Central Asian countries became independent and as soon as they started to get out from under the Soviet and Russian rule they were subjected to other, not less incessant influences: The United States, China, Turkey and Arab countries endeavoured to impose their values into the ideological space freed up after the Iron Curtain fall and the Kremlin had relaxed its grip on these territories. But Russia didn't loosen its hold on them completely, either, and its politics, ideology, culture and language are still quite powerful and ubiquitously felt. As a result, apart from high production costs and logistics challenges, local fashion designers in Central Asia are dealing with an eroded identity. It is my impression, that in the process of rediscovering it, they (and, in fact, all other creatives) are either looking too much into the past, are dreaming about a future they cannot, yet, quite imagine and are not living enough in the present in which alien and foreign concepts abound.

Kazakh fashion designer Aizhan Zhubay solved the lack of orientation in terms of identity, laid out above, for herself through philosophy and self-reflection. In an interview, she shares the following insight about how fashion carries meaning and can signify identity: "The word 'brand' and its semantic meaning imply an audience that buys the right to share your state of mind, philosophy and mental conclusions. Clothing reveals information about and represents a person" (Zhubay, 2024). Local designers need offline and online stores and platforms that carry and promote Central Asian designers who position themselves self-confidently like Zhubay and take the lead in imbuing their work with meaning. Teplo Store (nd.), a multi-brand store in Tashkent, Uzbekistan, is one of them and promotes local designers by giving them space in their store.

Apparel factories and plants

State of affairs and conditions for local production of fashion differ from country to country. However, the common circumstance in all five Central Asian countries is that the neighbouring China with its 1.4 bn population and numerous factories producing products for all segments is churning out cheap and fast fashion at much lower costs, higher volumes and with shorter delivery times than most other producing countries. In the wake of Western sanctions against China, trade between China and Kazakhstan has reached new heights, causing some disquiet among Kazakhs (RFE/RL staff, 2024). Chinese produce makes it difficult or impossible for domestic producers to stay competitive especially in the affordable and mass production segments. This challenge common to all five 'stans' has its own variations in each country and government policy regarding supporting fashion producers is different in each country, too. But there are some success stories. Fazliddin Sirojiddinov, CEO of UzTex, is a seasoned garment manufacturing professional whose company grows, processes and exports cotton to 45 countries while heeding sustainability goals, for example. It is a leading producer with advanced and sustainable production processes and employs 10,000 people in Uzbekistan. Sirojiddinov explains in an interview that he created his company "to guarantee ecological and economically viable production" (interview with Sirojiddinov, 2023). In Uzbekistan in 1991, only 7% of the cotton grown in the country was processed to add value by producing textiles domestically (Aris, 2023). Today, in 2020, this factor has risen to nearly 90% and Uzbekistan is even being rated as a possible future rival cotton product exporter to Chinese (Preuss, 2022). In Kyrgyzstan, the apparel production industry amounts to 3% of all processing industries. In Kazakhstan, the fashion production sector employs 22,000 people working in 1445 companies and only 30 of them are exporters (Kapital.kz, 2024; Prime Minister of the Republic of Kazakhstan, 2019). Being confronted with challenges not only in terms of competitive production costs but also in terms of consumer market readiness, local producers of fashion are on a steep and continuous learning curve. For example, the use of child labour in Uzbek cotton fields has been addressed after the country has come under the pressure of international human right organizations (ILO, 2022). They are also faced with the need to adapt best practices on how to build capacity in brand management, branding and visual communications, product development, marketing, online and offline wholesale and retail sales as well as protection of trade-marks and logistics quickly. Local production of fashion being an uphill battle in many senses is thus limited by the numerous objective factors described above. For the moment, this situation does not create the threat of overproduction, but needs to be monitored to be able to react should the circumstances change.

Digital fashion

In parallel with crafts, a responsible and sustainable fashion is manifesting itself via digital design such as 3D design, virtual and augmented reality applied to fashion design. Instead of physical clothes, accessories and shoes, the companies, which are invested in this, produce digital pieces that are sold at a fraction of the price to those who want to show the digital fashion only on social media, not in real life. This opens an alley not only for reduced carbon effect, responsible consumption, but also for a different kind of creative thinking and a path to new meanings and approaches. *Drape 3D* company with offices in Almaty and Moscow is one such venture which can help customers to apply 3D designed clothing, accessories, jewellery on their photos. "We are looking for inspiration everywhere: in Sci-Fi, fantasy, mythology. If in life we cannot afford to wear bold and bright colours, in digital world we can wear anything we want" thinks Olga Comissar, a founder of *Drape 3D* digital atelier and digital wear store which is focused on creating digital fashion which designers can design over your photo or video (interview Comissar, 2022)

Vintage and second-hand retailers and platforms

Following the sustainable development trends around the globe a small, but growing percentage of (mainly younger) consumers adopted eco-conscious consumption practices. They abandoned cars and hopped on their bicycles, bought multi-use coffee cups, started to sort rubbish and stopped using plastic bags. The era of fast consumption is, if not coming to an end, then definitely bringing people to question the effect fashion consumption has on the planet. In this vein, apart from flea markets that existed even in Soviet times and maybe even before that to extend the life cycle of garments, shoes, accessories and jewellery, to streamline and reduce consumption, second-hand and vintage shops started to pop up in the last five to seven years: in Almaty, Kazakhstan *Rebirth* (nd.), *Asaý Júrek* (nd.), *Momo Reuse* (nd.), *Sandyq Store* (nd.) and *La Luxe* (nd.). In Bishkek, Kyrgyzstan: *Kitsch for All* (nd.). In Tashkent, Uzbekistan: *Human House* (nd.) and *Vintage Tashkent* (vintage_tashkent, nd.). In Dushanbe, Tajikistan: *Craft Store* (nd.), *Noor Art Gallery* (nd.). Regular garage sale fairs and events are organized so people can exchange and sell unneeded fashion and give it a second chance to be worn differently or redesigned. For instance, the eighth edition of *Garage Sale* (nd.) in Almaty is being organized in May 2024. There are also several others such as *Garage Sale Bishkek* (nd.) and *Garage Sale UZ* (nd.).

Rebirth Vintage, a family business co-founded by Mira Tastemirova and Serik Joldasov, is a vintage store and atelier emerged from a love of searching and collecting vintage fabrics and garments all over the world. They believe that

> upcycling or remaking of old pieces in a new manner being an ancient tradition is not just a trend today but a conscious choice reflecting that all is cyclical and takes us to the roots. Rethinking the old meanings and introducing the new ones, upcycling is a necessary dictated by the time.
>
> (Interview with Tastemirova & Joldasov, 2024)

Lola Saifi, founder of *Human House*, links sustainability and preservation of traditional crafts into one. For many years, she has been working with vintage textiles from Uzbekistan and came up with an innovative way of preserving rare traditional Uzbek *suzani* embroidery: Instead of using the actual embroidery she photographs it, prints it out on a new fabric and uses it for a garment while keeping the vintage original embroidery in her archive. In an interview, Saifi says: "I am very passionate about zero-waste and creating exciting garments from fabric cut outs and leftovers. We are trying to be sustainable from various angles: restore old fabrics and give them a new life even if they have holes" (Interview Saifi, 2024).

Global fast fashion chains and Chinese knockoffs

A responsible fashion advocate would think that *Zara*, *H&M*, *Mango*, *Bershka* and many other mass-market fast fashion brands entering the Central Asia market and opening the stores in major cities wouldn't help the sustainable consumption and protection of the environment. However, fast fashion does not come as cheaply in Central Asia as in Europe. This is a result of the high logistics costs due to the distances the imported merchandise has to cover to reach these land-locked countries. Additionally, customs duties apply and a relatively low profitability per unit for relatively high rent rates for the shop versus relatively low population density in these markets. If you add to this a relatively lower income per capita numbers versus, e.g. European countries and relatively low competition and unsaturated local markets, it becomes obvious, that fast fashion brands not being as affordable for local consumers does not yet constitute irresponsible consumption problem (Sakurova, 2021; Kurbonov & Dzhanzakov 2024).

At the same time, cheap knockoffs from China, which the vendors elegantly call 'replicas' of catwalk trendy fashion, and similar no-name products flood the market with short-lived discardable garments. In the settings this creates, shopping can be carried out as an inexpensive hobby, a constant pastime that consumers turn to every week or more often, and which, ultimately, jams landfills with subsequently discarded items. The issue is aggravated by the fact that Central Asia also serves as a transit zone for cheap fashion counterfeit goods going to Russia, Ukraine, Azerbaijan, Georgia and other countries of the former Soviet Union. The solution to this problem is simply beyond the scale that five Central Asian countries have vis-à-vis China even collectively for economic and geopolitical reasons.

I see international fast fashion brands as constituting a positive influence. They help educate not only consumers as the unsaturated market gradually develops and becomes more sophisticated. They also coach local fashion designers and retailers by leading the way and acting as role models to imitate how to effect monitoring of trends, visual merchandising, branding and visual communications, to develop product lines, packaging, to design stores both online and offline, to care and serve customers and many other aspects of the fashion industry. H&M also leads with their recycle and used clothes trade-in campaigns.

Respond to past, present and future

As responsible fashion means 'fashion being able to respond' to what is happening economically, socially, politically, philosophically and otherwise, it is not necessarily only the accountability of the industry, not something burdensome that the industry needs to do to balance out the moral and physical costs of doing business, using the resources and making profits. Being responsible is also about being open, sensitive, compassionate and inclusive, about being able to listen and understand all stakeholders and to enable them to act together to address crucial issues. Overall, responsible fashion in the Central Asian countries of Kazakhstan, Kyrgyzstan, Tajikistan, Turkmenistan and Uzbekistan brings with it a relatively new concept and has various undercurrents of creativity, technology and commerce. The responsible fashion agenda is still not very high on the list of priorities of the societies and the governments in Central Asia. Oftentimes, it is only spoken about because of the initiatives and at times the demands of the international organizations, projects and markets.

The reason that responsible fashion values are not, yet, being genuinely and sincerely practiced by the citizens, companies and governments of Central Asian countries is that the countries are immediately concerned with more basic issues, urgent challenges and more mundane problems such as increasing the GDP per capita and income levels, accessibility of lending resources and diversification of economic growth. Thus, main stakeholders and actors act as if sustainable development is an issue that is of relevance only far away. Furthermore, these countries still have vast natural resources, untapped and unused, and this creates an illusion that they still have the luxury of not to have to worry about climate change and circular economy development challenges. Being part of sustainable developments, responsible fashion may still be viewed as something external and foreign. It may look as if Central Asians only pay lip service to sustainable development and ethical fashion concerns.

It is my hope that the independent countries of Central Asia – now having more control of their destinies, each in their own and unique way and also collectively, on their common path – even in the face of the pressing issues of the everyday survival will find space and time for being able to respond to these important and inevitable challenges of a connected and interdependent world. The need to care for the planet and the environment in order to be fair to their traditions and heritage, for people to find themselves in the present moment and to pave way for the future generations preserving their identity, dignity and freedom along the way.

References

Aliev, T. M. (2015). Kazakhstan: Resource curse or Dutch disease? *Problems of Economic Transition*, 57(10), 1–28. https://doi.org/10.1080/10611991.2014.1119558

Aris, B. (2023, April 11). *Uzbekistan's multi-coloured textile revolution.* bne IntelliNews. https://www.intellinews.com/uzbekistan-s-multi-coloured-textile-revolution-227890/

Asaý Jurek (nd.). asayjurek. Instagram. Retrieved May 24, 2024 from https://www.instagram.com/asayjurek?igsh=ejlnZDBjdnU1a2F6

Assaniyaz. A. (2023, December 31). Kazakhstan steps up creative economy development. The Astana Times. Retrieved from https://astanatimes.com/2023/12/kazakhstan-steps-up-creative-economy-development/

Auty R., 2001. *Resource abundance and economic development.* Oxford University Press. https://doi.org/10.1093/0199275785.001.0001

Born Nomad (nd.). Bornnomad.kz Instagram. Retrieved May 21, 2024 from https://www.instagram.com/bornnomad.kz?igsh=YXUxYzZobHh3b2Ez&utm_source=qr

Comissar, O. (2022). Founder of creative agency Glyph. https://glyphcompany.com/en

Czech, K., & Niftiyev, I. (2021). The impact of oil price shocks on oil-dependent countries' currencies: The case of Azerbaijan and Kazakhstan. *Journal of Risk and Financial Management*, 14(9), 431. https://doi.org/10.3390/jrfm14090431

Craft Store (nd.). craftstore.dyu. Instagram. Retrieved May 24, 2024 from https://www.instagram.com/craftstore.dyu?igsh=MWFqZ21mamk0enJzZQ==

Dautova, I. (2020). *Avoiding Dutch disease in the oil industry of Kazakhstan*. Eurasian Research Institute. https://www.eurasian-research.org/publication/avoiding-dutch-disease-in-the-oil-industry-of-kazakhstan/
Fitz-Gibbon, K. (2004). Something borrowed, something red: Textiles in colonial and Soviet Central Asia. Textile Society of America Symposium Proceedings, 442. Retrieved from https://digitalcommons.unl.edu/tsaconf/442
Garage Sale Bishkek (nd.). garage.sale.bishkek. Instagram. Retrieved May 24, 2024 from https://www.instagram.com/garage.sale.bishkek?igsh=a2pvaDFzcWR3MW9y
Garage Sale (nd.). garagesale.ala. Instagram. Retrieved May 24, 2024 from https://www.instagram.com/garagesale.ala?igsh=MTZzb3dzdTZ6a2Q4NA==
Garage Sale UZ (nd.). garagesale_uz. Instagram. Retrieved May 24, 2024 from https://www.instagram.com/garagesale_uz?igsh=MTF6cXZ1Mno4aGRrNQ==
Gronow, J., & Zhuravlev, S. (2015). Fashion meets socialism: Fashion industry in the Soviet Union after the Second World War (Vol. 20). Finnish Literature Society. https://www.jstor.org/stable/j.ctvggx2cr
Human House (nd.). humanhousegallery. Instagram. Retrieved May 24, 2024 from https://www.instagram.com/humanhousegallery?igsh=NnhhZXBrNm94bm52
ILO. (International Labor Organization) (March 1, 2022). *Uzbek cotton is free from systemic child labour and forced labour*. https://www.ilo.org/resource/news/uzbek-cotton-free-systemic-child-labour-and-forced-labour
Kapital.kz newspaper (2024, April 21). Referencing the press service of Ministry of Industry and Infrastructure Development of Kazakhstan: https://kapital.kz/amp/economic/114999/ob-yem-proizvodstva-legkoy-promyshlennosti-v-kazakhstane-vyros-na-37-8.html
Kitsch For All (nd.). kitschforall. Instagram. Retrieved May 24, 2024 from https://www.instagram.com/kitschforall?igsh=aWgwdWhlMjBobXlu
Krasnyanskaya, K., & Semenov, A. (2021). Soviet design: From constructivism to modernism 1920-1980. Scheidegger & Spiess, Zurich, Switzerland.
Kurbonov, Z. & Dzhanzakov, T. (2024, March 1). Zara opened a shop in Tashkent. Why - Photo Report. Kursiv Uzbekistan newspaper. https://uz.kursiv.media/2024-03-01/zara-otkryla-magazin-v-tashkente-chto-pochem-fotoreportazh/
Kurzt, J. (2023, December 6). Tengri worldview: Kazakhstan's cultural heritage. Smithsonian Center for Folklife and Cultural Heritage. Retrieved from https://festival.si.edu/blog/tengri-worldview-hkazakhstan-cultural-heritage
La Luxe. (nd.). _laluxe. Instagram. Retrieved May 24, 2024 from https://www.instagram.com/_laluxe_?igsh=ZXV6bmUwcnh0aXFj
Martin, T. (1998). The origins of Soviet ethnic cleansing. *The Journal of Modern History*, 70(4), 813–861. https://doi.org/10.1086/235168
Micklin, P. (2014). The Aral Sea. Springer, Berlin, Germany.
Momo Reuse (nd.). momo_reuse_store. Instagram. Retrieved May 24, 2024 from https://www.instagram.com/momo_reuse_store?igsh=b2Z2Njhvd2UxNWVw
Noor Art Gallery (nd.). noor.art.gallery. Instagram. Retrieved May 24, 2024 from https://www.instagram.com/noor.art.gallery?igsh=MTFzYWd0eTltYTM0bw==
Ondagash, A., Elemesov, R., Makasheva, K., Movkebayeva, G., & Gubaldullina, M. (2014). Assessment of value of resource curse concept for a practical solution of the problem of industrial and innovative development of Kazakhstan. *Middle-East Journal of Scientific Research*, 22(11), 1596–1602. https://www.idosi.org/mejsr/mejsr22(11)14/1.pdf
Pianciola, N. (2001). The collectivization famine in Kazakhstan, 1931–1933. *Harvard Ukrainian Studies*, 25(3/4), 237–251.
Preuss, S. (2022, July 1). Cotton from Uzbekistan: Comeback after boycott, potential alternative to China. FashionUnited. https://fashionunited.com/news/business/cotton-from-uzbekistan-comeback-after-boycott-potential-alternative-to-china/2022070148422

Prime Minister of Republic of Kazakhstan (2019, December 23). *Overview of the state of the light industry of Kazakhstan: Import substitution, export and state support.* The Official Information Resource. https://primeminister.kz/ru/news/reviews/obzor-sostoyaniya-legkoy-promyshlennosti-kazahstana-importozameshchenie-eksport-i-gospodderzhka#:~:text=B

Rebirth (nd.). rebirth_vintage_shop. Instagram. Retrieved May 24, 2024 from https://www.instagram.com/rebirth_vintage_shop?igsh=YnVpaWFyOHgwMHd4

RFE/RL staff (2024, April 30). China-Kazakhstan trade hits record high. OilPrice.com. https://oilprice.com/Geopolitics/International/China-Kazakhstan-Trade-Hits-Record-High.html

Sakurova, A. (2021, November 17). Mass-market at the price of the luxury: why is so expensive only in Kazakhstan. Liter.Kz newspaper. https://liter.kz/mass-market-po-tsene-lyuksa-pochemu-tak-dorogo-tolko-v-kazahstane/amp/

Sandyq Store. (nd.). sandyqstore. Instagram. Retrieved May 24, 2024 from https://www.instagram.com/sandyqstore?igsh=MXJqbXdyN3JkZXU3aA==

Sauvage, M. (2018, February 4). Soviet Union fashion. Fashiongton Post. Retrieved from https://fashiongtonpost.com/soviet-union-fashion/

Social Innovation Central Asia (nd.). Revitalizing Kazakhstan's cultural legacy: USAID champions the preservation of Kazakh traditional arts. Retrieved from https://socialinnovationca.org/success-projects/revitalizing-kazakhstans-cultural-legacy-usaid-champions-the-preservation-of-kazakh-traditional-arts/

Teplo Store (nd.). teplostore_2022. Retrieved from May 21, 2024, from https://www.instagram.com/teplostore_2022?igsh=bHdsdnN1M3JwMWsw

UNCTAD (2020). Challenges, policy options, and the way forward. Economic diversification in selected Asian Landlocked Developing Countries (Bhutan, Kazakhstan, Mongolia, and Turkmenistan. United Nations. https://unctad.org/system/files/official-document/aldc2020d1_en.pdf

vintage_tashkentt (nd.). Instagram. Retrieved May 24, 2024 from https://www.instagram.com/vintage_tashkentt?igsh=M3hoNHh3dnJwdGYy

Viled (nd.). About. Viled. Kz. Retrieved May 24, 2024 from https://viled.kz/en/news

Volkava. E. (2012). *The Kazakh Famine of 1930-33 and the politics of history in the Post-Soviet Space.* The Woodrow Wilson Centre for Scholars, Washington, DC, United States. https://www.wilsoncenter.org/event/the-kazakh-famine-1930-33-and-the-politics-history-the-post-soviet-space

Interviews

Amirjanova, A. (2023). CEO, Viled Luxury Retail Group based in Almaty, Kazakhstan [Interview].

Egemberdieva, G. (2022). Founder of Golden Heritage of Aral NGO, Uzbekistan [Interview].

Hays, L. (2022). Economic Section of the Embassy of the United States of America to Kazakhstan. Astana, Kazakhstan [Interview].

Saifi, L. (2024). Founder of Human House, Tashkent, Uzbekistan [Interview].

Sirojiddinov, F. (2023). CEO, UZ TEX Group, Tashkent, Uzbekistan [Interview].

Tastemirova, M. & Joldasov, S. (2024). Co-founders, Rebirth. Almaty, Kazakhstan [Interview].

Zhubay, A. (2024). Kazakh fashion designer. Astana, Kazakhstan [Interview].

3 Cultural identity and memory in clothing design in Kazakhstan (with sketches by Aishabibi Zhanabilova)

Assiya Ruslanovna Nurdubayeva and Gulnar Dzhambulovna Bekibayeva

Introduction

The study of cultural identity in Kazakhstan in fashion and costume design requires a dedicated process of exploration by everybody involved: students, designers, producers, and craftsmen. In this visual medium, identity is created as a blend of traditional elements with modern aesthetics and situating cultural heritage at the core of a unique and recognizable visual Kazakh style. This chapter introduces processes of deconstruction with which elements of cultural heritage are analyzed and dissembled with the aim of enabling a rethinking of established symbols and evolving them in synthesis with elements of different cultures and thereby promoting cross-cultural dialogue. This approach provides the freedom to experiment with form, structure, and materials. The authors' vision of cultural identity is reflected in the resulting scope for design the goal of which is the creation of unique personal art objects, forming a metaverse of images and intersecting points of view of the local observers as well as keeping international observers in mind. This means, it is taking into account the effects of both local and international dynamics around Kazakh identity.

Various research methods were employed for this study. A phenomenological approach was used to get an intimate grasp of experiences and also decode the meanings of design elements at an individual level and to learn how these shape personal and collective identity. The method analyses the structures and meanings in the experience of vibrant cultural phenomena that are produced within the dynamic sphere of culture in Kazakhstan. Additionally, the semiotic method provides the means to analyze cultural signs and symbols in fashion and to identify the cultural, social, and historical meanings in them. This is particularly important as fashion design is a language rich in complex ideas and formulations of identities. The deconstruction method makes it possible to analyze various design elements that convey messages, associations, and that can be used separately or in combination with others. Deconstruction becomes a tool for exploring expressions of cultural identity, making it especially valuable in the search for and support of ethnic uniqueness. Deconstruction is an important method

DOI: 10.4324/9781003508076-5

for modernizing traditional designs and paves the way for creating a new figurative language.

The purpose of the study is conceptualizing the ethnic core of ideas in fashion design that is creating new impulses. It shows how design practices have moved on from previous periods of design in Kazakhstan in a systematic and conceptual search for cultural identity at a universal level. The focus is on incorporating and processing traditional and regional elements in the designs that fulfill a connecting function and transcending any divide even between the elite and the mass. It provides a new grammar for the language of designers of the new generation.

Fashion and costume design in Kazakhstan

Globalization and integration have homogenized lifestyles across the world and all areas of human life. In Kazakhstan, in the realm of fashion and costume, this is countered by an increasing interest in seeking ethnic identity. Ethnic identity had become particularly relevant after the experience of total acculturation in the 20th century during the Soviet era. In the 21st century, the country is still engaged in the task of identifying form and content of its national identity. As for its cultural heritage, parts of it, like Kazakh petroglyphs, nomadic dwellings, musical instruments, folk crafts, dances, and ritual practices, have been put on UNESCO's list of Masterpieces of the Oral and Intangible Cultural Heritage of Humanity. In the garment industry, references to these traditional forms have the potential to be made into widely recognized brands. Designers, manufacturers, and retailers could collaborate to contribute to a creative and innovative environment attractive to the global market. This hasn't happened, yet. But there are some distinct trends building on utilizing traditional elements in productive ways in design:

- Traditional elements are not only implemented and preserved in fashion design and stage costume, but they are also transformed. Traditional costume and the interpretation of traditional motifs, and historical types of fabrics and textures are key points in the rethinking of cultural heritage at the level of material implementation – velvet and felt fabrics, silk materials, etc. Also, richly decorated embroidery, accessories, and the characteristic silhouette of Kazakh clothing – a straight, fitted, A-line, and a form-fitting girlish silhouette – are commonly part of the dress for special occasions or wedding ceremonies. These are also deconstructed and reassembled in virtual representations, expanding their potential in the digital environment, widening their visual impact and resonance, and leaving traces even in global styles.
- The 'exotic' effects of Kazakh traditional culture and ethnically specific crafting techniques are used as a strategy for the integration into the world fashion scene. Furthermore, some authors (Prabhata et al., 2023) suggest that there is a revived interest in ethnic motifs, forms, and historical

technologies, which, in our opinion, is becoming part of the mainstream of modern fashion and art. This can be understood as a counter-movement to globalized homogenized trends.

- The interest in 'forms' and their role in shaping ethnic identity in the garment industry is perceivable. The relationship between costume and body and their interaction in shaping both conscious and unconscious perceptions of physicality blurs the line between the tangible and intangible aspects of fashion.

Costume is, here, considered from a philosophical and anthropological perspective, rethinking the concept of what the physically clothed body is. This is relevant to the practice of presenting the communicative body in fashion shows, which thus opens up to the world, displaying its visual and cultural texts. Studying traditional cultural practices and spiritual matters and the scope of implementation in fashion and costume can stimulate innovation in design, generating unique and meaningful work. Without adequate comprehension, the designer will struggle to integrate these elements into current trends in ways that are both inventive and respectful. The relationship of the theatrical effect of ethnic costume and fashion has been considered by different authors and from different angles (Milman, 1998; Bakerkina, 2012; Chuprina et al., 2021). The effect of these clothes as costume also shapes the general understanding of material culture of the public. In Kazakhstan, a national costume holiday has been established to celebrate the New Year in the spring – *navryz*. The government could extend its support for experimental and culturally meaningful designs even more. That might inspire fashion designers to explore how identity (in its specificity to localities and historical periods) can inspire designs and thereby foster a deeper understanding of cultural heritage. Folk craftsmen are expert at embracing historical garments and adjusting them in their work to make them relevant for current times, thereby, integrating traditional designs into everyday culture.

Through the clothes they wear, individuals express ideas, beliefs, and feelings that they have about themselves, producing values and showing preferences. Garments are part of the identity work people do, representing social role, gender, and ethnicity in present-day Kazakhstan.

Here, contemporary clothing is being interwoven into cultural heritage and has distinctly been moved on from the practices of the Soviet-era. This transformation is a product of the complex interplay of individual development and cultural evolution, highlighting clothing as a powerful expression of both personal identity and collective heritage.

During the times of the USSR, Kazakhs' clothes, hats, shoes, and accessories were designed to express their identity as being modernist and progressive. Their designs had focused on forms that were simple to read, they relied on the use of decorative elements, operating with established stereotypes. They aimed at visual and cultural uniformity in the same way they attempted to streamline thoughts and feelings: It suggested an innate cultural and civilizational correspondence of the construct of a new nation with the external attributes of the previous nation of 'Kazakhs'. However, it solely remained as ever the same ornaments embellishing all conceivable garments. We now call this approach 'old school' in fashion design, referring to the time when the Soviet ideologeme 'national in form, international in content' reflected the cultural policy of the USSR. The prominence of uniformity in Soviet fashion was aimed at maintaining a unified collective identity and followed the established cultural policy, allowing only superficial diversity.

This concentration on ornament in ceremonial national costume has led to a dead-end in fashion design. Soviet-style suits can be seen as precursors to postmodern practices in fashion, which played with forms and contexts to engineer a homogenized social identity. Differences between Belarusians, Kazakhs, Russians, etc., were minimized, simply indicated by minor modifications of headdresses and other details and otherwise homogenized. This depersonalization through emblemization is still endlessly employed on the catwalks of Kazakhstan. But in contemporary fashion and costume design, a variety of style elements are implemented.

The following examples show how inspirations from Kazakh cultural heritage, identity, and references to nature are worked into fashion designs and create a nuanced language of representation:

A 'natural print' characteristically consists of contrasting colors of Earth and Sky (see Figure 3.1), which are thought to be the emblematic frame of the Kazakh landscape. In their symbolic dimension, they are referring to the people living in this landscape – signifying a deep connection to nature and their historical roots as nomads. 'Nature' constitutes the framework in which the nomads settled in the vastness of the universe. 'Natural prints' go beyond a simple visual portrayal, but represent the complex interactions between the individual and the environment and the immediate connection of an individual with nature. They are part of a continuously existing historical landscape. Visual metaphors like 'the face of the sky', a bluish color, and 'the face of the earth' a brownish color display hidden mythological and cultural heritage in garments worn in every-day contexts. The landscapes depicted on these costumes represent a geographical determinism that is immediately recognizable even to non-Kazakhs who might be unfamiliar with them.

This stylistic expression can be read like a map that outlines the presence of the Kazakh community in the region, affirming their unique local identity. It's a visual narrative that merges individual and environment, showing their identity as interwoven with the natural world. Beyond the visual effect, this is producing, this is addressing a deeper human need to feel intrinsically connected to nature and the local environment.

Animals, which are listed in the *Red Book* as endangered (Simwa, 2020), are sometimes referenced in designs to capture elusive meanings and forms, which signify cultural processes. They are identified as textural and semantic traces – shifting and adapting: Hybrid images of people-animals symbolize

Figure 3.1 'Natural print' design with contrasting colors from the 2010 collection by Camila Kurbani. Sketch by Aishabibi Zhanabilova. Copyright: Zhanabilova.

human migrations with animals as well as the very understanding of nomadism and its traditions by sedentary cultures. This use of magical configurations in fashion garment design combining traditional aesthetics with modern fashion trends aimed at giving modern clothing rich cultural motifs.

This approach can also be seen as an attempt to emphasize cultural identity in a globalized world, in which traditional clothing is at risk of being overshadowed by dominant Western fashion norms (Zakin & Zeng, 2019). The universal motifs featured in this garment conception are the interwovenness of nature with nomadic culture, extending to the entire universe. In this capacity, the practice of Kazakh fashion design meets the Western gaze head-on with non-Western symbolism, since the exoticism is the hallmark and basis for the perception of Western fashion, bridging the regional and the fashionable in all cultures and historical moments. In other words, there is a convergence between Western and non-Western fashion.

Turning to one's own culture in the sense of an ontology implemented with a rational and pragmatic interest in the world can be seen as a 'tool'. But at the bottom of this animal representation in garments and the reference to magical realms lie the animalistic and natural images known in the nomadic culture of the Kazakhs, which represent a syncretic consciousness. They point as precursors to other spiritual practices that heed the effect man has on the environment and the complete interwovenness of man and nature.

Also, when designs were presented, in the show, the models performed abrupt actions leading to the continuous reproduction of spatial forms, with the trajectory and signs of the animal world: the clatter of horses' hooves, the cry of cats and movements with the angularity of the knee joints of argali. Exoticization, here, constitutes a strategy which points to the sacred which masks as the supernatural. In this show, the large beast signified represents the universe of nomads, as a branching of the beginning of the structure of the World in the worldview of the ancient Turks. Because in the visual language of the Kazakhs, space is represented by a large beast. In an Old Turkic dictionary, it says that the space of the outskirts or corner of the World Order is *buçyaq*. This means two things: (1) The four cardinal directions and (2) an animal skin with four limbs. *Buçyaqlan* is what is angular, i.e., the corners of the cardinal directions are semantically superimposed onto a space. These verbal constructions highlight the body-centric grasp of space in nomads' thinking. Space is seen for example as a 'folding of legs', which can be understood to be the first spatial transformation – the folding of the outer layers of the cosmos, by modeling the materiality of the world with angles. This is also evident in the collection of the *Red Book*. This book provides a resource for designers wanting to refer to the 'big beast' that symbolizes the culture of the nomads in animal form. The syncretism of the images of the 'big beast' remains as a technique that plays with the image outsiders have of Kazakhs. In fact, the use of this intertextual imagery in designs makes them recognizable as Kazakh.

Another theme in the search for visual identity is the spatiality of the nomads' dwelling – *kiiz ui* (yurt). It is impossible to understand the construction of meanings without identifying the foundations and provisions of the predestination of the first spaces. Such a key is the very organization of the nomadic dwelling kiiz ui, in the immense element of open spaces, as the primary exploration of the World, reconstructed by the final result of such ideas – aesthetics.

Form and structure as spatial expressions are explored ethnographically by fashion designers as a way to understand the uniqueness of nomadic culture. This works similarly to the semiotic method of identifying form, which was laid out above. The dwelling (the yurt) and its internal structure, texture and outline in particular become the object of the designers' study of form. Just as the body is a place of interaction and influence, so the home – as in the example of the yurt – is an extension of bodily existence (see Figure 3.2).

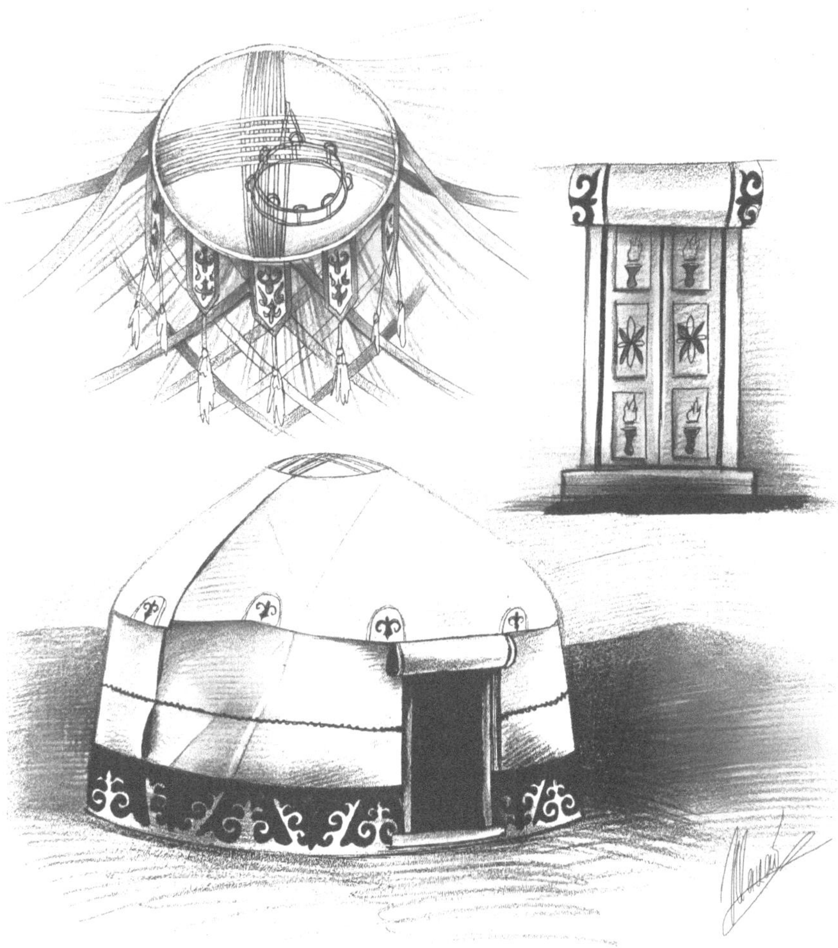

Figure 3.2 The yurt and its internal structures influence designers' thinking about form. Sketch by Aishabibi Zhanabilova. Copyright: Zhanabilova.

In the collection 'The nomad' by A. U. Zeynollaeva, representations of the human body are dissolved. The fragmented spatial bodies of nomadic dwellings take the scene and their 'organs' penetrate the bodily outlines of the subjects. In the process of a personification of the dwelling of the human body is deconstructed. An important part of this is the distinct shape, the hemispherical silhouette, in the open space the dwelling is situated in. Reflection on the body of the dwelling and the human being is the hermeneutical key to understanding the 'post-nomadic', 'post-humanistic', which, in turn, leads the authors to various philosophical, artistic, and scientific positions. In Jean-Luc Nancy's book 'Corpus' (1999), the human body is presented as alien, entirely oriented toward show and externality. This implies that a person, in fact, does not have 'their own body' and the feeling of its perception and sensation occurs only during its reconstruction. Also, the body, in his opinion, is located at the borders, but also perhaps, at the outer layers of the universe.

Some of the forms implemented in the collections create meaning beyond their material manifestations. For example, all Kazakhs understand that an open lattice design as visible on a sweater (see Figure 3.3) refers to the conceptual connection between the dwelling and the human body. This design also highlights the unconventional representations of the body with the use of surfaces that conceal the bodily form. This is a play on our anxiety about the lack of a readable silhouette of the human body, which we know is constantly being rearranged and changing, like a nomadic dwelling that is dismembered and reassembled in a new place.

The most interesting thing, according to the philosopher E. Petrovskaya, is also the process of 'thinking with the body'. For this aspect, the dwelling is paid particular attention in fashion design to work out semantic relations and values. The body and the dwelling are deeply intertwined and shape each other. In this sketch, the bodies of the models are merged with the surroundings creating a hybrid of human-object-dwelling: The external outline is streamlined and layered within a multitude of rope red ropes and decorative ribbons connecting the dwelling, as elements of the dwelling clothing. Wrapped in several canvases, a sphere is formed, which expands from its core – the human body.

Structural features in costumes are often a reference to the aesthetics of the home. In the case of references to nomads' dwellings this is often done by picking out just an element from the whole. The most recognizable element of the yurt – the wooden poles that make up its walls – is repeated in the form of an oblique lattice. This oblique weave is implemented as an ornament in clothing as a topical motif in the form of the texture of knitted sweaters (see Figure 3.4).

Transformation of the historical and social image of girlish costume

The increasing rejection of the tight-fitting girlish silhouette in designs is evidence of the transformation of the social perception of girls in contemporary Kazakhstan (see Figure 3.5). The silhouette is adjusted to different ideals in

Figure 3.3 Course project by A. U. Zeynollayeva, supervisor Bekibaeva, G. Sketch by Aishabibi Zhanabilova. Copyright: Zhanabilova.

Figure 3.4 Sweater by Zeinollayeva, A. Diploma work, supervisor Bekibayeva, G. Sketch by Aishabibi Zhanabilova. Copyright: Zhanabilova.

Figure 3.5 The A-shaped silhouette of the Kazakh traditional girl's costume. Sketch by Aishabibi Zhanabilova. Copyright: Zhanabilova.

line with other dominant trends: Without an emphasis on the waist, but a lush bottom from the traditional silhouette, and the pigtails now hang down the back like decorative ribbons. The transformation of the image and perception of the possibilities of the social role of a girl is also confirmed in the preferences of the modern generation, which has experience of Kazakhstan's Soviet history, when the role of women as builders of industrial society was entrenched in the masculinity of images.

In some cases, artists in Kazakhstan are aiming to deconstruct the dichotomy between masculinity and feminity in their search for what identity can be. In this case, the image of the female presents a liberated symbol of femininity in national identity. The element of leather in the form of a biker jacket brings modern masculinity to the image of an Amazon girl, constituting multiple references to different historical periods, merging female steppe culture and the modern independence of women. It also introduces a motif of their military inclinations, which is not consistent with the official state narratives that often prioritize male characters in this context. Femininity is thereby transformed into a weak peripheral sign, while what could be conceived as the essence of femininity retreats. Form-making and body signs try to explain to the outside world their aesthetic experience and the socialization of gender, which, in fact, does not exist in such models, but signs of historical roles remain.

Synthesis of world and local discourse

The tried and tested method of synthesis of image and style direction is firmly rooted in global practice, providing beginners with a universal language to represent local territorial independence and cultural uniqueness in their designs. They can combine traditional motifs with modern aesthetic principles, reflecting the cultural heritage of Kazakhstan. Aida Kaumenova uses graphics of camels, the 'ships of the desert', on her costumes to convey her sense of belonging to the world community, corresponding to their view of Kazakhstan. The use of national symbols and signs, such as images of camel, ram, and bull, are both decorative and informative. The designer uses the style of Henri Matisse and, thereby, builds on its global recognizability to create a visual identity that is instantly familiar to the Western observer. This way a neo-colonial discourse between tradition and modernity is created.

Ethno-signs are featured in most shows. They are also found in traditional costumes with high headdresses, like the *saukele*, to wedding costumes that elevate the mood and transport viewers into a world of illusions and fairy tales. This concept de-sacralizes the symbol of the bride in everyday life.

Another trend is constructivism and the consideration of viewpoints from both inside and outside of Kazakhstan. Here, the expectations of the encounter with an unknown culture are in focus (see Figure 3.6). This approach is characterized by the construction of paradoxical forms and

Figure 3.6 Design of trousers made of a *tuskiiz (ceremonial carpet)* by Aya Bapani. Sketch by Aishabibi Zhanabilova. Copyright: Zhanabilova.

combinations of textures, reminiscent of the Kazakh technology of assembling a carpet *kurak* – from the remnants of small pieces of fabric. This is a bricolage – characteristic of patterns of mythological thought.

Claude Lévi-Strauss described mythological thinking as the ability to create of the new on the basis of the existing old (Lévi-Strauss 2013). The model wears a garment made of a *tuskiiz (ceremonial carpet)*, a wall hanging, which traditionally holds a place of honor and plays a sacred role in the traditional interior of a nomad's dwelling. The designer using this material for sewing pants, which cloth the body below the waist, affronts the perceptions of a person familiar with these meanings – the insider – and their understanding of the sacral role of the carpet. The designer deliberately profanes the item, thus transforming established values. They assume the role of an uncomprehending observer – from the outside –, who is not aware of the absence of traditional narrative in the reproduction of textures, perceiving only their decorativeness. This setting becomes a frame for something else: This design has freed itself from any connection with its culture, since a kaleidoscope of new impressions can be created by an external observer. The ornament that appears on the surface of the costume is that lost construct of the special 'speaking text' of the traditional world and information about the inner sacredness of the thing on which it is located. Visual symbolism is used in a way that renders their traditional significations irrelevant, making the design a carrier of aesthetic messages not for the internal consumer, but addressed to external ones.

In workshops of the department of 'fashion and design of the *Kazakh National Academy of Arts* the theatricalization of everyday life as a way of visualizing cultural identity is being experimentally developed. This is evidenced in the above-mentioned student works. Also, another trend of theatricalization by Associate Professor Muslim Zhumagaliev, who developed the theater 'Arlan Zhete', which reproduces the special ceremonial costume of Kazakhs, complementing it with stage action.

Thinking about everyday life from the perspective of the theatrical provides additional research tools for comprehension and analysis of both individual cultural facts and the cultural situation as a whole. It shows up the connection between such phenomena as fashion, theatricalization of life, costume jewelry and cultural identity.

Conclusion

The Soviet era's modernist design principles were concentrated on rational form, schematism, and progressive narratives, which might have integrated ethnic elements of ceremonial costumes and derive at products, which are 'national in form and socialist in content'. In fashion design, this was realized in the language of quickly and functionally communicable ideas that were meant to underline the national economic achievements. Aesthetic purity and 'originality' were perceived as universal and the only reference to anything 'national' would be delivered through use of ornaments. The postmodern period, in contrast, favors a playful mix of signs and styles, giving preference to external stylization, blending irony with high and as well as mass culture. All the while, this has not diminished the desire for purity and originality but has ultimately led to an eclectic and fragmented approach to fashion design. This often results in the diversion of form and meaning of garments, presenting ethnic images as disjointed and sometimes contradictory.

On contemporary catwalks, principles of meta-modernism are notable. This means that designers are engaging in a dialogue with postmodernist designs and their adaptability regarding form while also revisiting modernist ideals. Their activities extend into the digital realms where far-reaching transformations are implemented. Also, the multi-layering of garments allows the creation of innovative forms of clothing items that re-transform the shape of past styles and can combine authenticity and nostalgia with innovation. This fusion transfers the dialogue of form and content toward creating new meanings and the stirring of increasing interest among the wider population (Podoroga, 1995, p. 8).

To understand the transformation of form and content in fashion design, we study the relations between modernism, postmodernism, and meta-modernism in this field. Here, we identify how the ongoing explorations and redefinition of form and content are reflecting broader cultural shifts and technological advances. In fashion, we read garments as if they are constructed like texts. Striking elements like rich costume jewelry – which can be observed throughout all historical periods – can be implemented and fed into the narrative of traditional elements, like quotes from another text. Artifacts preserved in the historical photographic collections and museums, the metatexts, serve as reference points for this.

The ever-changing designs suggest that ethnicity is thought of as an internal text and a dialogue with an external observer, which makes it possible to return to the original – traditional culture. Thus, in the visual realm of fashion design, bright designers create culture-trading prerequisites and suggest the focus of vision of the current scene from external observers on a large scale. They set the stage for a theatrical presentation of cultural identity that engages with both historical and modern texts, creating a complex intertextuality.

Lastly, we would like to note, here, that there seem to be two important metatexts of what a Kazakh should be. One contains that of a classic traditional Kazakh with 'correct' behavior and the other involves a unique visual portrait of a synthetic hero of our time. They don't conflict with each other, but reflect the state of the current scene of cultural identity for Kazakhstan and many variations between them. They provide a spectrum of interpretation that swings like a pendulum in designers' collections. An 'external observer' might provoke a more exotic formation of what a Kazakh's dress should be like, while an 'internal' observer might be happier to concede a more nuanced and facetted design which allows for transformations in the sphere of symbolic communication of dress design.

References

Bakerkina, O. A. (2012). *Fashion and theatre: Facets of interaction*. RGPPU: Ekaterinburg.

Chuprina, N. V., Remenieva, T. V., Frolov, I. V., & Tereshchenko, O. H. (2021). Design of contemporary garments based on the transformation of stylistic and artistic-compositional characteristics of traditional decorative art. *Art and Design*, 3(3), 30–44. https://jrnl.knutd.edu.ua/index.php/artdes/article/view/897

Lévi-Strauss, C. (2013). *Myth and meaning*. Routledge: London and New York.

Milman, A. L. (1998). Fashion as a form of theatricalization of life: Aesthetic aspects of costume design. Dissertation. Moscow. https://rusneb.ru/catalog/000199_000009_000212746/

Nancy, J.-L. (1999). *Corpus*. Ad Marginem: Moscow.

Podoroga, V. (1995). *Phenomenology of the body: Introduction to philosophical anthropology*. Ad Marginem: Moscow.

Prabhata, T., Susanto, I., Savira, P., & Murwonugroho, W. (2023). Local culture synchronization in global contemporary fashion style breakthroughs. *Mudra: Jurnal Seni Budaya*. https://doaj.org/toc/2541-0407

Simwa, A. (2020, May 7). Animals of the Red Book of Kazakhstan: A comprehensive list. Legit.ng. https://www.legit.ng/1327765-animals-red-book-kazakhstan-a-comprehensive-list.html

Zakin, V., & Zeng, Y. (2019, January 12). Trousers turn ... into protest. *Time Newspaper Kazakhstan*. https://time.kz/articles/grim/2024/01/12/bryuki-prevrashhayutsya-v-aktsiyu-protesta

4 The contemporizing of Uzbek traditional textiles through collaboration and entrepreneurship

Karan Khurana and Annick Schramme

Introduction

Uzbekistan is the second largest and most populous country in Central Asia (Pikalov, 2014). It looks back on an ancient history of textile production. The "Queen of Textiles," Silk, has been produced in the Fergana Valley region since the 4th century, originating from the Zaravshan River and the southern part of the country. Uzbek weaving masters in this region have established a state-of-the-art technique of thread weaving, turning Fergana Valley's Margilan silk into one of the most worthwhile textiles. B.C. Kikuta (2009) details that many kinds of handicrafts such as silk, cotton textiles, paper, and pottery were developed in the Fergana Valley region. An example of the unique Uzbek craft product is the *suzani*, a decorative and embroidered tribal textile material and carpets. The oldest surviving examples date from the late 19th century Bukhara (Kalter & Pavaloi, 1997; Izrailova, 1998; Wentz, 2022). Popular design motifs of the embroidery include sun and moon disks, flowers (especially tulips, carnations, and irises), leaves and vines, fruits (especially pomegranates), and occasional fish and birds. The colored *ikat* (made of silk or cotton), *doppi* embroidery, Bukhara golden embroidery, and Karakalpak embroidery are further unique types of traditional textiles of Uzbekistan (Mentges, 2012).

Uzbekistan is an agriculturally driven economy and cotton output contributes significantly to the socio-economic progress (Djanibekov & Finger, 2018). The country is the sixth-largest producer of cotton (762,000 tons) and the third-largest producer of silk (2037 metric tons) in the world (Djanibekov et al., 2012). Since its independence in 1991, the country has focused on exporting raw materials to enhance its trade potential. According to Orzu (2015), the country exported to Russia 36.8% cotton yarn, fabrics, knitted fabrics, and ready-made garments-knitwear; to Turkey 18.8% cotton yarn, knitted fabrics, and finished products; to China 16.2% cotton yarn; to the EU 15.3% cotton yarn and to South Korea 5% cotton yarn and fabric. The economic performance is evident from the export volumes; however, concentration on exporting only creates a major vulnerability for the domestic economy. Currently, the demand is satisfied by imports of Turkish

DOI: 10.4324/9781003508076-6

and Chinese brands. Interestingly, the raw materials these countries need for their textile productions are supplied by Uzbekistan, and in turn, the consumer must pay a higher price making fashion inaccessible for the masses in the country. This has left a huge gap in the domestic sector as the country is not able to benefit from the growing workforce capacity its steadily increasing population provides. On January 21, 2022, the President of Uzbekistan signed Decree No. UP-53 "On measures to stimulate deep processing, production, and export of finished products with high added value by textile and sewing and knitting enterprises." Geographically, historically, and commercially the Silk Road holds immense potential for the creative crafts of the country. A balanced combination of rich culture and availability of raw materials should open doors for local designers and manufacturers to exploit the hidden potential of domestic and foreign markets. The growing economy of Uzbekistan and globalization have had a positive effect on consumer buying behavior (Karimov & El-Murad, 2019), and the new generation (like some of the millennials) has higher purchasing power and is more fashion-conscious than the older consumers. However, global online fashion giants such as the UK platform *Farfetch* and *Trendyol* now deliver all kinds of fashion merchandise in all fashion segments to Uzbekistan which is an increasing threat to the local brands, designers, and cultural crafts, who can't export their fashion products. Academic literature (Khurana & Ataniyazova, 2020; Khurana, 2021) shows that the local fashion brands are more rooted in traditional crafts and have not, yet, explored making desirable fashion products that are attractive to young generations as well as to consumers in other countries. Even though Uzbekistan has cheap labor and easily available raw materials, it was found in the research that the existing merchandise is of very low quality in garment construction and finishing. The buying power of the Uzbek middle class has increased over the last decade and it has become increasingly important to reach out to them through various distribution channels. However, the lack of marketing and distribution channels makes it impossible to upscale and turn into a profitable brand.

One of the possible routes to break this traditional way of working is to connect the different stakeholders in the fashion and textile value chain toward the concept of successful product development and collaboration. One of the recent examples of successful product development in an emerging economy comes from India. During and after the pandemic, one of the biggest challenges for producers there were several economic challenges for the manufacturing houses (garment exporters); as the volume of orders shrunk, the exporters had to sustain their infrastructure and labor contracts. In conversation with a representative of one of the leading exporters in India, we learned that in this export crisis, they had reacted by starting producing labels that were directed toward the domestic Indian market (Sinha & Sainy, 2021). This involved product development for a broader range of consumers. This even turned out to make them stronger than before. Expanding beyond mainly exporting, they are now more prepared for economic disruptions such as pandemics or foreign brands entering the domestic market (Sinha & Sainy, 2021). With this insight in mind, this chapter deals with the following research questions:

Research question 1: What are the current hindrances to traditional textiles of Uzbekistan to become the basis of successful fashion brands?
Research question 2: What would be possible strategies to enhance the performance of traditional textiles to achieve their place in domestic markets and possible internationalization?

Theoretical background

Uzbek crafts' status and their problems

The increasing commodification of indigenous textiles around the world has threatened the preservation of traditional, eco-friendly methods of textile production (Ramkumar & Dias, 2023). The case of Uzbek traditional textiles is very similar to that of other emerging economies. Artisans in developing countries are mainly independent workers and can sometimes be classified as social and small enterprises (Steiner & Teasdale, 2019; Ciambotti et al., 2023). Historically, numerous problems have existed for traditional textiles/handlooms and have hampered their growth nationally and globally. Until the independence of Uzbekistan, the artisans in the textile sector had limited access to foreign markets, which constituted a great barrier to the expansion and trade of textiles. Academic literature (Pomfret, 2000; Ruziev et al., 2007; Ibragimovna, 2020) states that the new economic and foreign policy reforms after independence in the nineties have opened up several opportunities to all industrial sectors in the country. The changing of economic policies (taxes, regulations, etc.), agricultural reforms (banning of Uzbek cotton (2009–2022); water shortages, etc.), and governance (formation of cotton clusters) have had a very deep impact on the socio-economic conditions of the artisans working in the textile sector (Shtaltovna & Hornidge, 2014; Babadjanov & Petrick, 2023). Furthermore, as the Uzbek domestic middle class tends to buy more fast and trendy fashion from global retailers or brands, it becomes very difficult for artisans to preserve and commercialize their craft and ancient skills and to turn them into a profitable business. The traditional crafts still serve high-end Western brands that outsourced their production to low-wage countries such as Uzbekistan. However, the artisans themselves remain part of the supply chain of Western fashion brands and are based on a system of exploitation. Another reason is that the market is flooded with counterfeit goods that arrive from China. Previous research (Ibañez-Tirado & Marsden, 2022; Chand & Fei, 2021; Khan et al., 2021) has highlighted that there is a substantial increase in the consumption of counterfeit goods in emerging markets, especially Asia, which has negatively impacted the marketability of artisans' goods. These issues create a huge impact on the economic situation of the artisans and hence, the upgrading of infrastructure and innovation in the regions of Uzbekistan has been a critical issue for decades now. Van der Straeten & Obertreis (2022) have explored in various cases in their research how technology is a key element to the progress of various industries in Central Asia. Obsolete technology is the key aspect that affects the productivity of these handloom artists or embroiderers and, hence, the desired quality and quantity don't reach the domestic and international markets. Technology upgradation can help increase productivity, quality, and consistency in supplying the products to the markets.

Finally, there is no adequate support from the government for these artisans working in the textile sector. In emerging economies, often support from the government is limited to financial support. This is important, because, of course, financial security is a major factor in the success of artisans (Dalal et al., 2023). However, we observe that the government should valorize the artisans more and help the artisans and other stakeholders in the clothing value chain to develop entrepreneurial solutions for ease in business operations nationally and internationally.

Product development and the Uzbek fashion sector – what kind of product development strategy is needed?

Since 2019, business in the fashion sector has also been hindered by several political crises and pandemics (Black, 2020; Blancheton, 2021; Khurana, 2022). In the past years, the challenge of climate change and sustainability has pushed the value chain stakeholders (raw material manufacturers, garment producers, distribution channel members, and government bodies) to look for innovative solutions. For instance, achieving sustainability (Brydges et al., 2020) and sustainable supply chain management (Wren, 2022) have become the biggest challenges for fashion brands to encounter unprecedented shocks in the fashion sector. This leads to a very interesting argument to not only focus on an aesthetically viable product but also on more sustainable business models for artisans producing traditional textiles to contribute to a more robust value chain.

In this vein, strategies in new product development (NPD) have been discussed in the last few years by several academics. Although the problem of artisans has different dimensions, in this article we want to focus on the strategy in NPD as a possible solution for the survival and possible growth of artisans' potential to increase their trade in Uzbekistan. Fashion product development is the strategic planning of goods using the key areas of the value chain, as there are the creative and sourcing, the technical innovation, the production, marketing/promotion, and distribution of fashion products and is recognized as a potential strategic weapon for corporate performance (Choi et al., 2005).

Parker-Strak et al. (2022) have stated in their article that NPD already exists for all fashion segments; however, for traditional and handicraft products such strategies have not been developed yet. Here lies our area of work and contributions to the field of research. This study on the existing literature leads us to understand what kinds of product development models are feasible for traditional textiles to be developed in emerging economies like Uzbekistan.

Methodology

This research involves both primary and secondary sources. First, we performed a systematic literature review (SLR) to investigate the problems of the Uzbek traditional textiles sector and, then, we carried out an in-depth study on the relevance of NPD for the members of the fashion value chain. van Dinter et al. (2021) argue that SLR studies aim to identify relevant primary papers, extract the required data, and analyze, and synthesize results to gain further and broader insight into the investigated domain. After a comprehensive exploration of the literature, we were able to investigate qualitatively an Uzbek designer in a case study. The chosen designer – Kamola Rustamova (Brand-AzukarMoreno) – has worked with Uzbek traditional textiles for around 10 years and provided information that is relevant to the research question and aims of the study. AzukarMoreno is one of the first Uzbek brands to seriously think about conscious consumption and "slow" fashion, the main goal of which is to create clothes that pass from generation to generation and are produced with the least environmental harm. The brand produces different types of clothes from ikat: chapans (warm jackets), shirts, dresses, trousers, bags, shoes, and accessories. The raw materials are chosen mostly from artisans in Uzbekistan.

Data were gathered through a semi-structured interview with qualitative open-ended questions that were based on the topic list, including the following themes.

- Assortment breakdown
- Fashion product development process
- Use of digitization and AI
- Human resource and skill development
- Collaboration with key players
- Future product extensions and prospects
- marketing and communication; target groups

The data collected from the interview were then analyzed and recommendations were proposed using Collaborative NPD. The authors also visited the brand during their stay in Uzbekistan in the framework of the Responsible Fashion Series (March 2023).

The collaboration of local designers and cultural crafts – the new product cooperations amongst small and medium-scale enterprises

From our data, we can observe that, for instance, the *ikat* print was used in similar colors in a traditional chapan (Uzbek overcoat for men and women) or the *suzani* embroidery on jackets for several years. No change in garment patterns or textile production techniques has taken place as no one is ready to take the risk of NPD. And logically, if the changes occur more on the side of artisans, they fear financial instabilities and overstocking. As a result, the domestic consumer does not consume large quantities of Uzbek national textiles or products made from them. Simultaneously, the garment's silhouettes differ in size type, or quality from international standards. An L-size t-shirt may be XXL in European size. This also limits online trading possibilities and future global expansion strategies. The designer should be an entrepreneur as well and assume an initiative-taking part of designing the fashion and lifestyle merchandise that not only uses available Uzbek traditional textiles but also provides ideas for innovative textile production. The textile artisans need help from the designer-entrepreneur and they should be able to order more custom-made fabrics and accessories for their garments. This increases the potential for Uzbek traditional products to demand a premium price in the domestic and possibly in the international markets. The craftsman's self-sufficiency should be accompanied by two additional features: the first is understanding consumer preferences, which allows them to achieve a higher level of customization; the second is being connected to the social and territorial environment where the artisan operates, which allows the development of expertise and provides a unique identity to the product. This can only happen when the designer-entrepreneur and artisans have a bond between them. In this vein, the designer could also venture into new lifestyle products such as home furniture and other interior merchandise. In the in-depth interview, the owner of the brand mentioned that she would also like to introduce new products, and for a brand, it's important for the brand identity to offer a diversification of multiple products in the same style.

Creating digital enterprises through collaboration and communication

To ensure practicable communication and collaboration between the various stakeholders (the designers, entrepreneurs, and artisans), the implementation of suitable technology can also play a key role. Denaro (2020) argues that new technologies regarding design, textile innovation, and the digital world have become instruments for craftsmen in small and medium-scale enterprises, which they can and must use to upgrade their skills and to find a position within the industry 4.0 market.

According to the proposed Collaborative NPD model, the designer must collaborate and discuss the creation with the artisans and then begin to design new products. Such processes must be documented and can be digitally transported/transmitted between each other. It should be noted that in emerging economies, the implementation of digital product development can be a pressing issue; therefore, easier ways of communication have to be used. In the case of Uzbek fashion companies and our case, Telegram Messenger is very widely used and has a lot of basic features that are essential for maintaining a constant level of communication. Further in this area, fashion design education should also train the artisans to understand basic design software that is very user-friendly and increases overall efficiency. Priyono et al. (2020) suggest that partners with exceptional digital skills help those with limited computer literacy in the value chain collaboration process and transmit the required knowledge to them. Hence, collaborating digitally is the first step to strengthen the value chain. It is often pointed out in academic literature (Khurana & Ryabchykov; 2017; Gopura et al., 2019) that the fashion design education system in emerging economies is either very restrained or doesn't exist. For instance, in Uzbekistan, there is no fashion design school, so we find that all established designers are self-taught, and starting a label and therefore scaling up for them remains a big challenge. Furthermore, in conversation with the designer, she highlighted that the workers and artisans needed a lot of skills to produce a qualitative product.

Sustainability – A key building block and entrepreneurship

Sustainability and traditional textiles have a compelling connection. One of the aims of Collaborative NPD is to "preimmunize" (Ritson, 2009) the traditional textile so that they do not need to sell enormous quantities, which increases the scope for creativity and reduces inventory at all levels. A premium product is commonly referred to as higher-priced, innovatively designed, selectively distributed, and exceptional quality merchandise (Huang and Huddleston, 2009). The model proposes a conscious production and consumption strategy for the crafts to maintain premium standards across fashion segments in both companies that deal on a "business-to-business" basis and those that deal on a "business-to-customer" basis. Furthermore, crafts are a highly sustainable activity (Gobattoni et al., 2015); contribute positively to job creation (Sánchez-Zamora et al., 2014); and sustainable tourism development (Bellver et al., 2023). Sustainable development of communities and local artisans is one of the key pillars of Collaborative NPD. It proposes to foster entrepreneurship in the regions of emerging economies and thus reduce unemployment. Here, the need for collaboration between the fashion and tourism sectors in a more sustainable way arises. According to Ona & Solis (2017) and Fletcher et al. (2019), indigenous entrepreneurship that includes crafts, attractions, and activities can provide a large range of experiences for tourists. Karakul (2019) adds that tourists usually express interest in the local traditional crafts of the areas they visit, promoting heritage conservation and restoration activities in line with the UNESCO Convention on the Safeguarding of Intangible Heritage. Another important area of collaboration and uplifting entrepreneurship is the women's workforce in the sector. Women drive the global artisan craft sector, the second-largest employer in developing countries (Chappe & Jaramillo, 2020). Still, only a few studies are found in the literature on the benefits of artisan entrepreneurship for women (Edgar, 2023). Through our model, there is a need for strong policy and government support for establishing women entrepreneurs in Uzbekistan. Training and educating the women workforce would be an essential initiative in this area. Lastly, according to researchers (Woodeside et al., 2008; Peirson-Smith, 2013), premium brands must have a strong creative storytelling process that talks about the creative process of brand formation. In the case of Uzbek artisans and designers, their entrepreneurial journey and historic relevance of merchandise shall provide impactful storytelling to the local and global consumer.

Discussion

In this section, the authors discuss the proposed NPD strategy in an explorative way. The case study constituted an in-depth analysis of a fashion brand that exists in Uzbekistan and uses traditional textiles as raw materials for its products.

In our research, we found that there is a significant amount of disruption in the value chain of traditional textiles of Uzbekistan. The element of integration and collaboration must be strengthened for a larger stakeholder profitability (Jones & Wright, 2018).

Based on the empirical evidence and literature review we suggest a new methodology for the traditional textiles and craftsmen that can be termed as Collaborative NPD. For small and medium-sized companies in the value chain collaboration in decision-making for product development will prove to be a very productive methodology (Theyel, 2013). In this practice, the Uzbek fashion designers, craftsmen, traditional textile production and fashion entrepreneurs, and retailers will benefit majorly (Uzbek multi-brand stores like Teplo store, Matera, and Human house); as well as shops for tourism, and local digital platforms (Uzum, social media selling platforms). The main source for this methodology is inspired by the Collaborative Planning, Forecasting, and Replenishment (CPFR) technique and model of Boujut & Laureillard (2002) which focuses on product and process integration and cooperation and has been widely discussed in recent years (Jain et al., 2009; Sari, 2008; Wang et al., 2010; Derrouiche et al., 2010; Irani & Kamal, 2014). In this methodology, the retailer collaborates directly with the artisans, to reduce inventory levels and risks across the value chain. Through our empirical research, we find out that designers are best placed to play a central role in managing the different stakeholders within the value chain as they understand the creative product as well as the business side of fashion. They keep also the capability of creating new and innovative products. Therefore, the designers-entrepreneurs are kept as the beginning point of the Collaborative NPD. In the interview, the owner, Kamila Rustomova stated that creativity as a commonality is still a missing element in the raw material manufacturers and current business operating models. To clarify, further, until the artisan produces not a creative/innovative textile which is an influential part of the final product development, the final product can't be exclusive.

Conclusions

Geographically and commercially, the concept of the Silk Road and its rich cultural heritage holds immense potential to the creative crafts of the country. Currently, the fashion sector in Uzbekistan is increasingly struggling with the monotony and hegemony of fast and ultra-fast fashion. A lot of consumers from the growing middle class, too, are in search of merchandise that is a unique fashion product. With an estimated population of 35.5 million, Uzbekistan has the potential needed to become a regional economic fashion powerhouse: a dynamic, literate, and entrepreneurial population – the largest in Central Asia; a relatively good infrastructure; and the largest potential consumer market in the region. Uzbekistan's cotton industry and rich natural resources such as gold and natural gas offer also attractive opportunities for investors.

In this research, we explored the following questions: What are the current hindrances to traditional textiles of Uzbekistan and what would be the right product development strategy? The Uzbek fashion and textile value chain is very fragmented and thus there is a visible gap between the different stakeholders (the artisans, designers and entrepreneurs). The artisans suffer from a variety of hindrances such as lack of financial support, marketing support, business management, and entrepreneurial skills, networking with raw material suppliers, and lack of supporting institutions, at times, low craft quality, and access to business information and digital skills (Synovate, 2012; Walonzi, 2014). Collaboration among the stakeholders to bring a product successfully to the domestic and international markets will be essential to accelerate the progress of the sector and to develop new fashion enterprises. Lastly, the role of technology will be pivotal, however, the implementation of technology in the value chain must be very easy for enhanced efficiency. This study was based on one case study and was therefore explorative by nature. Further research is needed to investigate the thresholds and challenges of NPD, marketing, entrepreneurship, and implementation of AI and digitization in the fashion industry in Uzbekistan as an exponent of Central Asian countries and their emerging economies.

References

Babadjanov, J., & Petrick, M. (2023). Uzbekistan's cotton clusters in the context of the industrial policy debate. *Eurasian Geography and Economics*, 1–30. https://doi.org/10.1080/15387216.2023.2267093

Bellver, D. F., Prados-Peña, M., García-López, A. M., & Molina-Moreno, V. (2023). Crafts as a key factor in local development: Bibliometric analysis. *Heliyon*, 9(1).
Black, S. (2020). Fashion in a time of crisis. *Fashion Practice*, 12(3), 327–330.
Blancheton, B. (2021). French fashion and textile during COVID-19: Once again, flying to high quality and innovation to survive. *Fashion and Textiles*, 8(1), 1–13.
Boujut, J. F., & Laureillard, P. (2002). A co-operation framework for product–process integration in engineering design. *Design Studies*, 23(6), 497–513.
Brydges, T., Retamal, M., & Hanlon, M. (2020). Will COVID-19 support the transition to a more sustainable fashion industry?. *Sustainability: Science, Practice and Policy*, 16(1), 298–308.
Campbell, S., Greenwood, M., Prior, S., Shearer, T., Walkem, K., Young, S., ... & Walker, K. (2020). Purposive sampling: Complex or simple? Research case examples. *Journal of Research in Nursing*, 25(8), 652–661.
Chand, V. S., & Fei, C. (2021). Self-brand connection and intention to purchase a counterfeit luxury brand in emerging economies. *Journal of Consumer Behaviour*, 20(2), 399–411.
Chappe, R., & Jaramillo, C. L. (2020). Artisans and designers: Seeking fairness within capitalism and the gig economy. *Dearq*, 1(26), 80–87.
Choi, W., Powell, N. B., & Cassill, N. L. (2005). New product development and its applications in textiles. *Journal of Textile and Apparel, Technology and Management*, 4(4), 1–28.
Ciambotti, G., Zaccone, M. C., & Pedrini, M. (2023). Enabling bricolage in resource-constrained contexts: The role of sense of community and passion in African social entrepreneurs. *Journal of Small Business and Enterprise Development*, 30(1), 167–185.
Dalal, A., Bhattacharya, S., & Chattopadhyay, S. (2023). Hurdles to handicraft marketing for artisan entrepreneurs in an emerging economy. *Journal of Small Business and Enterprise Development*, 31(1), 74–94.
Denaro, G. (2020). Industry 4.0 and new artisans: Between hand-crafted design and digital production. *International Journal of Design Management & Professional Practice*, 14(3), pp. 1–7. https://doi.org/10.18848/2325-162X/CGP/v14i03/1-7
Derrouiche, R., Neubert, G., Bouras, A., & Savino, M. (2010). B2B relationship management: A framework to explore the impact of collaboration. *Production Planning & Control*, 21(6), 528–546.
Djanibekov, U., & Finger, R. (2018). Agricultural risks and farm land consolidation process in transition countries: The case of cotton production in Uzbekistan. *Agricultural Systems*, 164, 223–235.
Djanibekov, N., Van Assche, K., Bobojonov, I., & Lamers, J. P. (2012). Farm restructuring and land consolidation in Uzbekistan: New farms with old barriers. *Europe-Asia Studies*, 64(6), 1101–1126.
Edgar, S. (2023). Artisan social enterprises in Zambia: Women leveraging purpose to scale impact. *Social Enterprise Journal*. Advance online publication. https://doi.org/10.1108/SEJ-10-2022-0095
Fletcher, C., Pforr, C., & Brueckner, M. (2019). Factors influencing Indigenous engagement in tourism development: An international perspective. *Sustainable Tourism and Indigenous Peoples*, 24(8–9), 34–54.
Gobattoni, F., Pelorosso, R., Leone, A., & Ripa, M. N. (2015). Sustainable rural development: The role of traditional activities in central Italy. *Land Use Policy*, 48, 412–427.
Gopura, S., Payne, A., Bandara, D. C., Buys, L., & Seneheweera, L. (2019). Fashion education in Sri Lanka: The nexus between formal and informal education. *International Journal of Fashion Design, Technology and Education*, 12(1), 23–34.
Huang, Y., & Huddleston, P. (2009). Retailer premium own-brands: Creating customer loyalty through own-brand products advantage. *International Journal of Retail & Distribution Management*, 37(11), 975–992.

Ibañez-Tirado, D., & Marsden, M. (2022). Trade 'outside the law': Uzbek and Afghan transnational merchants between Yiwu and South-Central Asia. In S. Fehlings & H. H. Karrar (Eds.), *Informal markets and trade in Central Asia and the Caucasus* (1st ed., pp. 135–154). Routledge: London & New York. https://doi.org/10.4324/9781003259886

Ibragimovna, R. S. (2020). Reforms in the field of medicine in Uzbekistan during the years of independence. *Medical Care*, 24(46), 73–7.

Irani, Z., & Kamal, M. M. (2014). Intelligent systems research in the construction industry. *Expert Systems with Applications*, 41(4), 934–950.

Izrailova, A. (1998). Suzani vernacular: Technique and design in the Central Asian dowry embroideries. *Textile Society of America Symposium Proceedings,* 177. https://digitalcommons.unl.edu/tsaconf/177

Jain, V., Wadhwa, S., & Deshmukh, S. G. (2009). Revisiting information systems to support a dynamic supply chain: Issues and perspectives. *Production Planning and Control*, 20(1), 17–29.

Jones, S., & Wright, C. (2018). Fashion or future: Does creating shared value pay? *Accounting & Finance*, 58(4), 1111–1139.

Kalter, J., & Pavaloi, M. (Eds.). (1997). *Uzbekistan: Heirs to the Silk Road.* Thames and Hudson: London.

Karakul, Ö. (2019). The effects of tourism on traditional craftsmanship for the sustainable development of historic environments. *European Journal of Sustainable Development*, 8(4), 380.

Karimov, F., & El-Murad, J. (2019). Does country-of-origin matter in the era of globalisation? Evidence from cross-sectional data in Uzbekistan. *International Journal of Retail & Distribution Management*, 47(3), 262–277.

Khan, S., Fazili, A. I., & Bashir, I. (2021). Counterfeit luxury consumption: A review and research agenda. *Journal of Consumer Behaviour*, 20(2), 337–367.

Khurana, K. (2021). Uzbekistan: The Silk Route of Handloom. In M. Á. Gardetti & S. S. Muthu (Eds.), *Handloom sustainability and culture: Entrepreneurship, culture and luxury* (pp. 281–294). Springer, Singapore. https://doi.org/10.1007/978-981-16-5967-6_13

Khurana, K. (2022). The Indian fashion and textile sector in and post COVID-19 times. *Fashion and Textiles*, 9(1), 15.

Khurana, K., & Ataniyazova, Z. (2020). Insights and future forward for fashion and textile value chain in Uzbekistan. *Research Journal of Textile and Apparel*, 24(4), 389–408.

Khurana, K., & Ryabchykov, N. (2017). Fashion education as a form of sociocultural capital to developing economies. *The International Journal of Social Sciences and Humanities Invention*, 4(3), 3394–3403.

Kikuta, H. (2009). A master is greater than a father: Rearrangements of traditions among Muslim artisans in Soviet and post-Soviet Uzbekistan. In D. C. Wood (Ed.), *Economic development, integration, and morality in Asia and the Americas (Research in Economic Anthropology, Volume 29)* (pp. 89–122). Emerald Group Publishing Limited: Leeds.

Mentges, G. (2012). The role of UNESCO and the Uzbek nation building process. In B. Bendix & L. Bortolotto (Eds.), *Heritage regimes and the state* (pp. 213–231). Universitätsverlag Göttingen: Göttingen.

Ona, J. G., & Solis, L. S. L. (2017). Challenges and opportunities for the development and promotion of Ibaloy crafts as tourism products. *International Journal of Culture, Tourism and Hospitality Research*, 11(4), 593–607.

Orzu, D. (2015). The export potential of Uzbekistan's textile industry. *European journal of economics and management sciences*, (2), 11–14.

Parker-Strak, R., Boardman, R., Barnes, L., Doyle, S., & Studd, R. (2022). Product development, fashion buying and merchandising. *Textile Progress*, 54(4), 247–403.

Peirson-Smith, A. (2013). Wishing on a star: Promoting and personifying designer collections and fashion brands. *Fashion Practice*, 5(2), 171–201.
Pikalov, A. (2014). Uzbekistan between the great powers: A balancing act or a multi-vectorial approach? *Central Asian Survey*, 33(3), 297–311.
Pomfret, R. (2000). The Uzbek model of economic development, 1991–99. *Economics of Transition*, 8(3), 733–748.
Priyono, A., Moin, A., & Putri, V. N. A. O. (2020). Identifying digital transformation paths in the business model of SMEs during the COVID-19 pandemic. *Journal of Open Innovation: Technology, Market, and Complexity*, 6(4), 104.
Ramkumar, B., & Dias, R. M. (2023). Sustaining traditional textile art among the Indigenous Nongtluh women of north-eastern India: An interpretative phenomenological analysis. *Fashion, Style & Popular Culture*, 10(4), 485–512.
Ritson, M. (2009). Should you launch a fighter brand? *Harvard Business Review*, 87(10).
Ruziev, K., Ghosh, D., & Dow, S. C. (2007). The Uzbek puzzle revisited: An analysis of economic performance in Uzbekistan since 1991. *Central Asian Survey*, 26(1), 7–30.
Sánchez-Zamora, P., Gallardo-Cobos, R., & Ceña-Delgado, F. (2014). Rural areas face the economic crisis: Analyzing the determinants of successful territorial dynamics. *Journal of Rural Studies*, 35, 11–25.
Sari, K. (2008). On the benefits of CPFR and VMI: A comparative simulation study. *International Journal of Production Economics*, 113(2), 575–586.
Shtaltovna, A., & Hornidge, A. K. (2014). A comparative study on cotton production in Kazakhstan and Uzbekistan. Bonn: Center for Development Research (ZEF).
Sinha, P., & Sainy, R. (2021). How can Indian small-scale fashion retailers survive COVID-19 disruption? A brand portfolio optimization perspective. *Journal of Retailing and Consumer Services*, 62, 102633.
Steiner, A., & Teasdale, S. (2019). Unlocking the potential of rural social enterprise. *Journal of Rural Studies*, 70, 144–154.
Synovate, I. (2012). Market research on handicraft products in East Africa—Tanzania. *Belgian Development Agency (BTC)*.
Theyel, N. (2013). Extending open innovation throughout the value chain by small and medium-sized manufacturers. *International Small Business Journal*, 31(3), 256–274.
van der Straeten, J., & Obertreis, J. (2022). Technology, temporality, and the study of Central Asia: An introduction. *Central Asian Survey*, 41(2), 211–222.
van Dinter, R., Tekinerdogan, B., & Catal, C. (2021). Automation of systematic literature reviews: A systematic literature review. *Information and Software Technology*, 136, 106589.
Walonzi, B. (2014). The benefits of tourism handicraft sales at Mwenge handicrafts centre in Dar es Salaam, Tanzania (p. 46). Tempere University of Applied Sciences. https://urn.fi/URN:NBN:fi:amk-2014120818869
Wang, K. J., Jha, V. S., Gong, D. C., Hou, T. C., & Chiu, C. C. (2010). Agent-based knowledge management system with APQP: Implementation of semiconductor manufacturing services industry. *International Journal of Production Research*, 48(10), 2913–2936.
Wentz, M. R. (2022, June). Suzani cloth silk embroidery on cotton. *Mayo Clinic Proceedings*, 97(6), 1215–1216.
Woodside, A. G., Sood, S., & Miller, K. E. (2008). When consumers and brands talk: Storytelling theory and research in psychology and marketing. *Psychology & Marketing*, 25(2), 97–145.
Wren, B. (2022). Sustainable supply chain management in the fast fashion industry: A comparative study of current efforts and best practices to address the climate crisis. *Cleaner Logistics and Supply Chain*, 4, 100032.

Part II

Crafting decentred and responsible fashion

5 (Re)Felting the future

From ancient craftsmanship to contemporary fashion design

Kim Poldner, Galina Mihaleva, and Agnes Evangelista

Felting: A journey to modernity

The art and practice of felting have mastered a long and arduous journey, pre-dating the times of the Silk Roads. Felted material would be carried on the backs of horses of nomadic pastoralists[1] throughout Central Asia, serving the peoples of the region being both of practical and symbolic value. Despite the construction techniques being very old and established before wool spinning and all other early textile techniques, it is still often made the same way as it was thousands of years ago. Felt is a non-woven textile made mostly of sheep fleece, but also of other animal fibres, like camel hair, by beating and pressing the animal fibres into a compact mass (Laufer, 1930; Zhukenova et al., 2016). Due to its natural composition, the material itself has been subject to erosion over time and few historical specimens remain. Thus, it is difficult to pinpoint its precise historical origin (Muhetaer, 2020). Unlike the historical specimen, the practice has stood the test of time and is making a resurgence in modern-day Kazakhstan, the same ancestral techniques coming to use (Zhukenova et al.). There are techniques that create beautiful intricate designs – history, symbology, and meaning are woven into its fabric and represent tradition and its impact. It's a remarkable and unique story, given the fluidity and movement of nomadic lifestyles, that this attribute of their culture has stood the test of time (Bunn, 2010).

Historical perspective

No pinpoint origin of the practice of felting is known. It can, at least, be traced back to 2300 BCE China, where a mummy, 'the beauty of Loulan', was discovered wearing a preserved felt hat (Burkett, 1977; Muhetaer; Mair, 2012). Although felt began travelling before the Silk Roads were established, it is likely this further helped spread the material to many regions. Today, it can still be found in its traditional capacity in many areas, for instance, in Uyghur regions of China with bustling felt markets in the same province of Xinjiang where Loulan was located (Muhetaer). Among other areas, the traditional form of the practice also thrived in Turkey

DOI: 10.4324/9781003508076-8

Figure 5.1 Kazakh Yurt. Reprinted from Wikimedia commons (Ekaterina) cc-by-sa-2.0.

and Kazakhstan (Muhetaer). The various travels and cultural aspects of each region have resulted in different forms of felting. Felting lent itself well to nomadic pastoralists. They travelled with herds of sheep and were, thereby, consistently at the source of the material. But, also, the textile was warm (Erdener, 2017), relatively lightweight, had medicinal properties[2] (Marhabo, 2023), and in use for yurts (felt houses, see Figure 5.1) which provided natural insulation that could be rolled up and compacted (Zhukenova et al.). Imagine being able to fit your house on the back of a horse! The spread of yurts evolved during the 11th century as cultural exchange along the Silk Roads was lively (Muhetaer). Kazakhstan as a nation-state is still very young as it only gained independence after the fall of the Soviet Union (Schreiber & Tredennick, 2010). However, current practices trace back through time, weathering sometimes difficult conditions and felting thriving throughout its rich history[3] (Schreiber & Tredennick).

Techniques and artistic styles

Due to felt's diasporic emergence in varying cultural contexts, several distinct techniques have been developed from the basic one. Although machinery and other appliances for felting have been invented, in Kazakhstan, the intricate handmade practice has been preserved, with the range of patterns, techniques, designs, and even motifs remaining largely consistent since at least 500 BCE (Bunn). The two main construction methods are dry and wet felting; however, within these categories exists a myriad of techniques, assembly, symbolism, and artistic executions. In dry felting, wool is repeatedly pierced using special needles so that the fibres bind together to produce a dense material (Bunn; Zhukenova et al.). This form of felting was and is still used to make three-dimensional products, like toys and jewellery (Marhabo). Wet felting is predicated on wool fibres having two layers and using steam and warm water to hook the fibres together. This is usually done through wet soaking and executed with friction (Marhabo). This is commonly used for making flatter products like rugs, clothes, or panels that can be sewn together to form yurts and other products (Erdener).

Within the spectrum of dry and wet felting a plethora of other techniques exists, with which single uniform coloured felt or an array of vivid colourful felt products can be created. In the past, colours were produced using natural elements like walnut shells, indigo plants, pomegranate peel, saffron, or charcoal to produce beautiful and vivid works of art (Erdener; Sun Productions, 2015). Nowadays, artificial dyes are most often used although natural dyeing is becoming more popular again. *Syrmak* is the term given to decorative felt pieces that hang in yurts, see Figure 5.2 (Zhukenova et al.). *Syrmaks* design techniques are divided into mosaic, application, stitched, and mixed designs. Contemporary felting in Kazakhstan utilizes not only these techniques but has popularized a merging of techniques with other ones, like a Japanese one called *Nuno* (Zhogova & Sheromova, 2014; Erdener). For *Nuno* felting, loose fibres, mainly of sheep's wool, are bonded to produce a translucent fabric resulting in a very light felt material (Erdener). The contemporary adaptation often employs patterns and motifs from the region's rich history, with two often solid but distinct colours utilized, creating vivid designs. These have gained international interest in the upscale fashion scene (Erdener; Sun Productions; Marhaboy).

Symbolism and meaning

These beautiful works of art don't just signify an extraordinarily rich history, but also give us a glimpse of culture through symbolism. In felting in Kazakhstan today, and historically for the nomadic pastoralists at the root of this practices, ornamental elements are important. This form of imagery can be dated to at least 500 BCE (Erdener) and continued to stay prominent alongside the spread of Islam in the 6th century as images of living creatures were mostly prohibited in Muslim art. Ornamental decoration features consistently in Kazakhstan and other nations with a predominantly Islamic population[4] (Dzhelbuldin & Jeteyeva, 2014).

The practice of felting is coined by a deeply engrained symbology. For example, in Kazakhstan, white felt is seen to signify wealth and prosperity (Sun Productions). It frequents Kazakh traditions and customs: a yurt covered in white felt is seen as wealthy and prosperous, a ceremony of

Figure 5.2 Syrmak. Reprinted from Wikimedia commons.

placing a child's crib on white felt carpet is assumed to stimulate well-being and wealth for an infant's future and when a wife appeared in her new husband's home, she would be seated on white felt (Sun Productions; Mamynova et al., 2014). As in many customs, white is seen as sacred purity, symbolizing innocence, justice, and a high social status (Mamynova et al.). Felting and its symbolism are ingrained in Kazakh culture and traditions. The *Tuzkiiz* is a decorative felt mat that is placed in the centre of the Yurt, entrenched in rich tradition it serves as good luck and was often used as a dowry with names of the maker and gift receiver embroidered (Erdner; Zhukenovaa et al.). This felt is traditionally gifted to a bride, unfinished, who is then meant to finalize it according to her own style (Sun Productions; Zhukenovaa et al.). The *Tuzkiiz* was also passed down generationally, meaning many Yurts featured more than one *Tuzkiiz*, one inherited and one produced as part of the dowry tradition (Dhamija, 2004). Another recurring symbol in the Kazakh and other felting cultures is the semantics of the World Tree (Zhukenovaa et al.). This symbol is seen to represent the underlying world order, each compositional layer is seen as important in Kazakh tradition as it could symbolize fertility, endless life, and wealth. The Yurt, too, is seen as an embodiment of the world tree; the felt floor protecting from the underworld border, and the dome symbolic of ancestral spirits (Zhukenova et al.,). These symbolic meanings are profoundly characteristic of nomadic people, providing a sense of consistency that is still in evidence today, in an otherwise ever-changing context.

The art and practice of felting is central to Kazakhs' ethos, interwoven into the culture and customs. Felting crucially involves community in its social and collective capacity as the traditional and laborious method involves a group of women working together on one felt (Muhetaer; Sun Production). It is often accompanied by traditions, songs, and rituals, which can also be seen mirrored in the Uyghur felting custom with washing rituals and prayers spoken before the production process to ward of any bad luck (Muhetaer; Sun Productions). The Kazakh ideographs used in felting carry some of the oldest meanings through combined shapes and colours (Kunanbay, 2001). Not only do they try to bring meaning to the universe through ornamental compositions in their felt, but they also attempt to organize the natural world. This deep meaning and the establishing of a connection to nature is strong as each ornamental composition represents the cycle of life (Kunanbay; Zhukenovaa et al.). Connection to nature is further extended with the cultural history of the material having been created from the hair of nomads' hand-reared flocks in accordance with the natural world around them. Even the architecture of the felt-covered Yurt was designed to work in line with nature, comprised of four sides (the cardinal directions East, West, North, and South). In this conception, the Yurt forms its own world that obeys and celebrates nature's laws, for example, the entrance is placed facing the East so that the inhabitants will be greeted by the rising sun in the morning (Samuratova & Akhmetova, 2016). Clearly, nature is not just celebrated in felting practices, but the techniques and symbolism used are a homage to it.

Female empowerment

The practice of felting has great potential to enrich the lives of women in Central Asia. Historically, the spreading of the technique into different parts of central Asia resulted in different levels of female involvement depending on the region they were situated in.[5] Felting in Uyghur and Turkish tradition is handed down to men doing the more physical aspect of the laborious process of making felt, where women and children are more involved in the design aspects (Muhetaer). In Kazakhstan, this differs as tradition is steeped in felting as a more female practice. Historically women would have worked together to produce the materials for their homes and their hosting abilities were often judged by their felting abilities (Sun Productions). Perhaps this can be attributed to the fact Kazakh culture utilizes felt in far more diverse ways; women would have made felt furniture covers, bags, storage, kitchen cloths, and a broad range of felt products for the home – which was also made from felt (Erdener). Herein lies an opportunity for female entrepreneurs in Kazakhstan today: their entrepreneurship in this regard is more appreciated than in other areas, as in the public's view 'it keeps tradition alive' as will be reviewed in the following section.

Contemporary felting in Kazakhstan

In the 21st century, the traditional art of felting brings diverse opportunities. The government of Kazakhstan has designated the textile industry as a key future investment as they see the great potential in local development and international interest that the industry attracts (Erdener). In a more globalized fashion industry, the Kazakh government is investing in its textile production as a form of strategic development which provides opportunities for women. The strong tradition of women in felting ultimately means a large investment in female entrepreneurs. There is also increasing global interest due in part to the environmentally friendly properties of felt. Although it was not its primary design, traditional felting techniques are well suited for ecological sustainability. The natural material has a longer use life, insulating properties, it is light, uses fewer resources, is biodegradable and its handmade production methods have a far better ecological impact than other textiles (Erderner; Zhukenova et al.). Furthermore, the non-woven technique of felting is being hailed as having the smallest ecological footprint of all textiles (Palamutcu, 2017). The potential for the materials sustainability application has therefore gained attention globally.

Trashure: From textile trash to couture treasures

After this historical contextualization of felting as a practice, now, two case studies are introduced to illustrate how felting is adapted to be brought to global catwalks while contributing to a more sustainable fashion industry. Every year, around 300 million kilogrammes of textiles are discarded in the Netherlands – enough to fill 122 Olympic sized swimming pools! No mainstream commercial use has been identified or deemed profitable enough to secure the necessary investments for reducing this number. Consequently, collectors of textile waste do not have the capacity to absorb such a large amount and over half of discarded textiles end up as residual waste, mostly incinerated.

This is what the first project presented here, *Trashure*, aims to address. It is its ambition to contribute to systemic change in the fashion industry, focusing on dealing with textile waste. So far, only 1% of clothing consists of recycled textiles, while the goal of the Dutch government for 2030 is to increase the application of recycled textiles up to 50% of all produced (textile) products. The goal is to arrive full circle with 100% circular textiles by 2050, requiring drastic changes in our consumption and production patterns and approaches, notably addressing the expanding textile waste mountain.

Textile waste volume keeps increasing; more is produced, consumed, and discarded, while not enough is re-used, repaired, and recycled. Textile sorters emphasize how traditional business models of discarded textiles are not working and besides technical issues, the demand for recycled textiles is limited. Recycled textile comes with a higher price tag but lacks overall appeal and is considered 'not attractive' enough for fashionable, high-quality products. Therefore, existing business models are not capable of providing profitable solutions, thus, the demand from factories to manufacture products from recycled fibres is also limited as they don't see the business potential. Achieving the Dutch government's ambitions requires contemporary business models that optimally balance supply and demand.

The Hague University of Applied Sciences (THUAS) partnered up with three SMEs (small-medium enterprises) to research innovative and profitable business models that reach 'mainstream' target groups. *i-did* is an innovative and inclusive Dutch company that transforms textile waste into felt. Internationally acclaimed fashion designer Ronald van der Kemp (RVDK) is a pioneer in sustainable haute couture and he dresses celebrities such as Michelle Obama and Emma Watson. *Sympany* is a textile collector and sorter (by colours/qualities, etc.) that provides the raw materials for the textile innovations RVDK creates. Together they aim to raise awareness around revaluation of textile waste and offer attractive fashion items made from this felt: from trash to treasure!

Collaboration between the partners led to the visibility of this project in (inter)national (social) media, especially when RVDK launched conversation pieces crafted from felt during fashion weeks. *Trashure* caught the attention of celebrities and has been featured in global magazines such as *VOGUE* and *Harper's Bazar* as well as the *Dutch Financial Times* as well as national television. *Trashure* was also presented twice during Dutch Design Week (DDW) and included in a DDW exhibition as well as a digital magazine. In addition, a limited-edition designer tote bag collection was launched which sold out on the *i-did* webshop within 24 hrs. The partners have secured follow-up funding to further develop the business case as well as technological innovation of the felt material. Altogether, *Trashure* has shown the value of design as a catalyst for transitioning from a linear to a circular textile economy (see Figures 5.3–5.6).

Figure 5.3 Ronald van der Kemp during launch of tote bags Amsterdam Fashion Week (September 2021). The tote bags being produced in *i-did* workshop and modelled by the seamstresses. The partners from *i-did*, Sympany, and The Hague University of Applied Sciences during the launch. Copyright: Poldner.

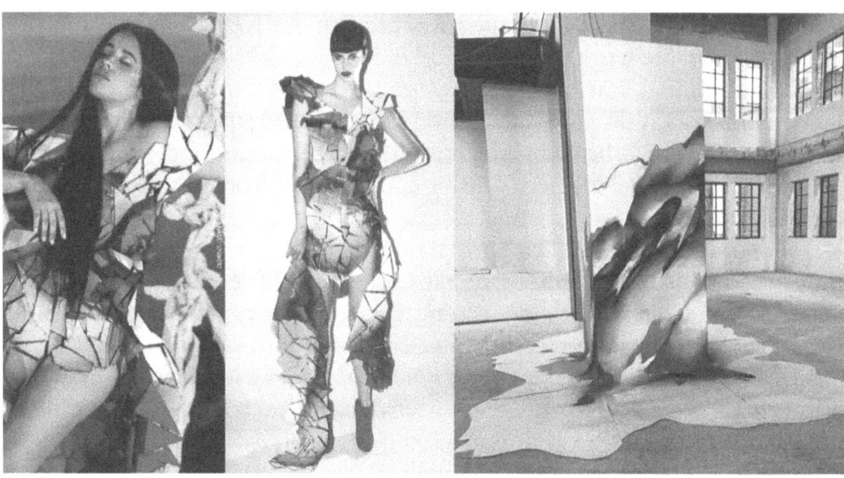

Figure 5.4 Singer Camila Cabello wearing RVDK *Trashure* couture (April 2022) crafted from *i-did* felt, spray painted by a graffiti artist during Amsterdam Fashion Week (September 2021) and shown during Paris Couture Week (January 2022). Copyright: Poldner.

Figure 5.5 Sketches by RVDK for creating wearable felt (September 2023). Copyright: Poldner.

Luxury meets sustainability

Another research project, committed to ethics and the wellbeing of the planet by applying circular design principles is *Luxury Meets Sustainability*. It is invested in eliminating waste and pollution, circulating products and materials, and regenerating nature. This project explores and questions the possibilities for a world in which luxury, elegance, and sustainability can coexist.

The underlying foundation of this project is the aspiration that a world where luxury, elegance, and sustainability coexist is not only possible but is deemed to be extremely glamorous. This is underpinned by the power of creativity, innovation, new technologies, and what these can achieve in a

Figure 5.6 The very first prototypes crafted from wearable felt (September 2023). Copyright: Poldner.

changing world: innovative fabrics and luxurious garments made from them. In parallel with the big brands, there are many small artisan companies and innovative start-ups capable of creating new fabrics from the most disparate materials. It is extraordinary to acknowledge that connoisseurs of style and elegance can adapt to an increasingly ethical and green approach to our planet. What was formerly seen as waste material, can be reimagined and infused with a little bit of magic.

Essentially, this project is driven by the same harsh realities of the current unsustainable nature of the fashion industry as outlined in the *Trashure* case study above. It is clear the fashion industry is one of the leading culprits of environmental pollution, responsible for over 92 million tons of textile waste every year (Perleberg, 2023; Ruiz, 2023; Fisher, 2024). Due to the fast pace of the fashion industry between 80 and 100 billion, new garments are produced globally (Perleberg; Ruiz). The warning of environmental disaster looming larger every year, the industry must overhaul the existing model in all phases of development (Fern Green, 2022). While the Netherlands are considered pioneers in circular practices, Italy is considered a leader in the luxury fashion world. Italy sets high standards, making it an interesting case study in the implementation of sustainable practices in the fashion context. Italian fashion has a long tradition of craftsmanship that has always given high value to the quality of fabrics. It is lauded internationally due to the unmatched passion and expertise self-evident through a high degree of specialized craftsmanship. Big luxury brands set the stage as sustainable fashion and ethical consumption are becoming increasingly trendy.

To get to the root of the fashion industries disastrous impact on the environment it is evident that consumers' relationship to clothing must be re-examined. For a piece of clothing to be sustainable it has to have a long use-cycle. This means, it has to withstand the test of time while also remaining stylish and attractive. Felting, with its lessons and traditions that span across a long history, can provide this (Wool, 2018; Life Gate, 2020; Perleberg, 2023). Wool is a great example of a naturally durable fibre that has a potential of 20–30 years of active life (FernGreen). Because of its ability to be remoulded and reshaped using techniques such as dying and felting (Sapkota, 2018), wools versatility lends itself perfectly to exploring this, which is what the *Luxury Meets Sustainability* research project from Arizona State University aims to do.

Consumer goods such as sweaters and jackets made of wool can often get damaged and sport holes that are difficult to mend. Ultimately, this results in otherwise long-lasting materials going to waste arresting the material in its second life (Wool, 2018). To extend the life of the material, an innovative approach has been developed that serves to remedy this issue by adhering to the circular system of the garments life. Luxury wool jackets are often lined with silk, and when they are deconstructed and both materials run through an industrial dry felting machine together where the fibres bind together they create a very durable surface. An entirely new garment can be sculpted by creating new shapes, adding more dyed wool, and applying embroidery techniques. The jackets selected for this project were originally made in Italy, purchased second-hand in America, and redesigned with Kazakhs method of felting described in the first part of this chapter. An innate sense of elegance, excellent tailoring, the choice of fine materials, and a constant search for innovation are far removed from the logic of Fast Fashion. Italy is fortunate to still maintain all the phases of fashion manufacturing within its borders, from raw material products such as yarns, feathers, and fabrics, to designers and dressmakers. In the higher-end fashion market, the result of this is valuable and durable garments that do not wear out in one season and therefore have a lighter environmental impact. Nowadays, however, all of these factors are not enough: the label *Made in Italy* must also encapsulate the logic of sustainability and evolve to meet it in all of its phases, not just an extended use life. Italy is the world's leading producer of luxury fashion, and the entire Italian fashion industry is now moving towards increasingly ethical and green production. Thanks to its leadership role and respected position in the market, it has the power to drive this vital change. Moreover, sustainability has become a critical competitive lever to meet the approval of an increasingly environmentally conscious public.

The initial jackets resulting from this project can be seen depicted in Figures 5.7 and 5.8. The conceptual capsule collection of jackets was shown at *5-V*: vignettes vibrant volumetric view vogue in San Francisco in December of 2022 and in Albuquerque at a charity event, *Pennies for the Homeless*, in November 2023.

The organization *Dress for Success* made use of a large haul of thrifted sweaters, which were donated to the project for a show. To maximize the material, the sweaters were deconstructed to use in a collage, additional dyed wool was then applied to create a surface ready to be redesigned. By adding a layer of new wool to the thrifted sweaters and running them through the dry felting machine, the holes were mended in the wool and added a decorative touch. Inspired by the Kazakhs' traditional dry felting techniques, we applied the new wool in a swirling motion to mimic painting strokes.

'Sustainability' in fashion can be considered a fairly recent movement, but recently, the term has become a buzzword. Unfortunately, this has led to several fast fashion companies greenwashing themselves, attempting to appeal to this demographic. Furthermore, due to the lack of proper funding and research for sustainability-led projects in fashion, these factors have resulted in garments that are recycled or upcycled being viewed as lower quality or cheap. Meanwhile, the luxury world, widely known as an unsustainable industry, associates with an upper-class, high-society demographic has always been very exclusive.

The main colour choices deployed in our sustainable felting project were vibrant colours such as yellow, purple, and red against darker background colours such as violet and black. Purple and red exemplify royalty and power, while yellow resembles gold or wealth. The colour symbolisms connect back to the idea of luxury, enforcing the concept behind this project as 'Sustainability in the Luxury Fashion World', showing that luxury fashion and sustainability can be intrinsically connected. The finished material serves to highlight further felting's potential in sustainable fashion. It was produced to create a series of dresses featured in a fashion show in collaboration with photographer and artist Chris Loomis, shown on 5 and 6 January 2024 at an exhibition space in Phoenix, Arizona.

The fashion experience served as a poetic metaphor and an artistic interpretation of consumerism pushed to its limits, culminating in a speculative biological future, framed symbiotically by the constructed environment. The

Figure 5.7 Deconstructed, felted, and embroidered jacket; back view. Copyright: Mihaleva.

project began with important factors like assessing environmental impact through assessing the life cycle of a product in its entirety. Products made from natural fibres were selected. Wool was mainly used, selected for its renewable recourse and characteristics such as being breathable, durable, long lasting, non-flammable moisture absorbent, having natural elasticity, and mainly lending itself to being easily recycled or reused. The collected products in their *first life* were made from pashmina, mohair, cashmere,

Figure 5.8 Models posing with luxurious redesigned, felted garments. Copyright: Mihaleva.

and pure merino wool in the form of sweaters, vests, tops, and dresses. They were carefully sorted according to their textures and colours and then deconstructed and put together into a colourful collage and combined with raw wool by needle felting. Drawing from the practices that stretch back centuries (Shepherd's Dream, 2022), felting became the technique used to create new materials from existing products, thereby allowing them to enter their *new life* (see Figures 5.9 and 5.10).

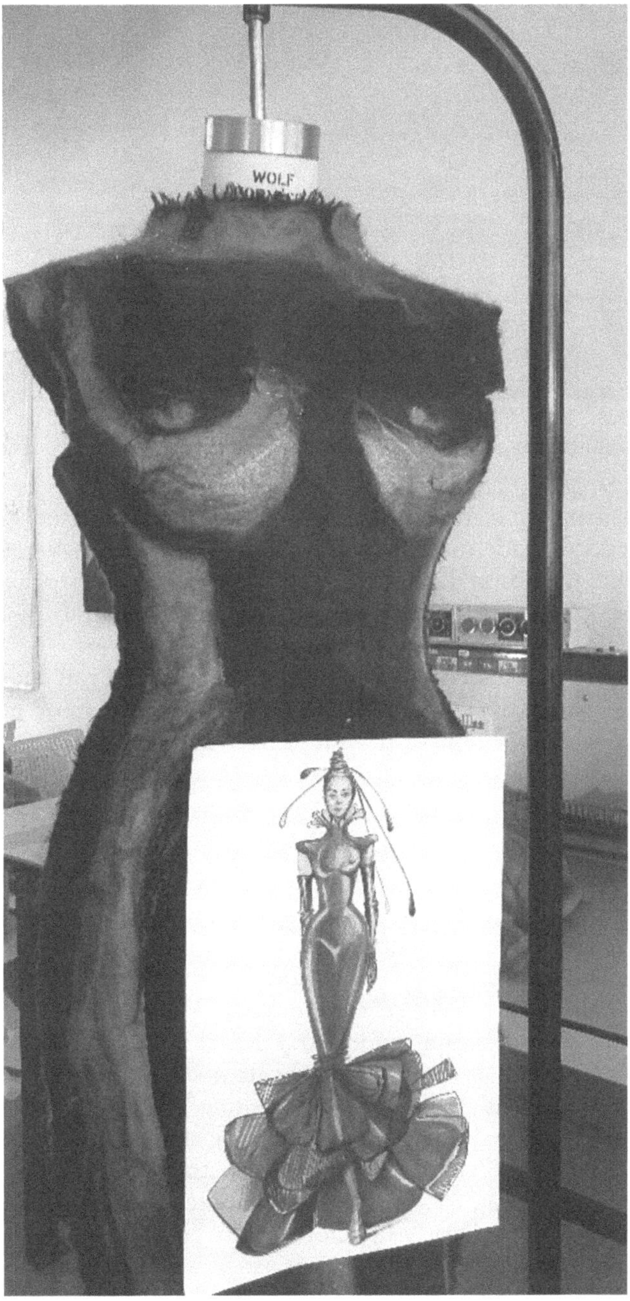

Figure 5.9 Collection Development; Felt experiments. Copyright: Mihaleva.

Figure 5.10 Embedding chia seeds into the felt using feltloom. Copyright: Mihaleva.

To emphasize the metaphor of the circular life of the garment, chia seeds were embedded inside the wool, using felting techniques. When the seeds sprout within the fibres, the protein in the fibre serves as an organic fertilizer and nutrient source for the seeds making the garment entirely biodegradable at the *end of its life*.

The process of the seeds growing inside the wool is symbolic for an end of a cycle – ending the cycle of wasting energy to create more product in a waste-filled world, to replace it with using what we already have through nature.

Conclusion

The practice of felting encapsulates a profound journey through time, traversing the vast landscapes of Central Asia and weaving itself into the cultural fabric of nomadic communities. Its origins showcase a resilient tradition that has endured the challenges of erosion and time. The practice has experienced a remarkable resurgence in modern-day Kazakhstan, employing ancestral techniques that continue to produce intricate designs.

The techniques and artistic styles of felting reflect the diverse cultural influences and regional adaptations that have shaped this craft. From the meticulous needle-piercing in dry felting to the steam and warm water bonding in wet felting, each method contributes to the creation of three-dimensional toys, jewellery, rugs, clothes, and even yurts. The vibrant palette of natural dyes, echoing the ancient use of walnut shells, indigo plants, and saffron, has evolved to include contemporary adaptations, such as the Japanese-influenced Nuno felting.

The case studies of *Trashure* and *Luxury Meets Sustainability* highlight the global evolution of felting as a sustainable and innovative practice in the fashion industry. The *Trashure* project in the Netherlands transforms textile waste into designer felt, showcasing its potential to contribute to a circular economy. Meanwhile, the *Luxury Meets Sustainability* project at Arizona State University reimagines discarded wool garments inspired by Kazakh felting methods, aligning luxury fashion with sustainability goals.

In a world grappling with the environmental impact of fast fashion, felting emerges as a beacon of hope. Its inherent qualities of durability, versatility, and sustainability align with the growing global interest in ethical and green practices. As the fashion industry endeavours to redefine its relationship with clothing, felting stands poised to be a catalyst for change – a bridge between tradition and innovation, culture and sustainability. The journey of felting, from ancient nomadic practices to contemporary global runways, is testament to its enduring relevance and transformative potential in shaping a more sustainable and meaningful future.

Notes

1 Pastoralists are, here, defined as groups of people who maintain livestock and move periodically in search of more pasture.
2 Felting material was used for healing broken bones.
3 For instance, during the Kipchak confederacy, felting was a common practice.
4 The prayer-mat used in Kazakh and other Islamic cultures, too, was made of felt.
5 Historically the felt clothes first made were often genderless, with men and women wearing the same traditional outfits that served for primarily practical purpose, the gendered aspects appeared later.

References

Bunn, Stephanie. (2010). *Nomadic felts*. British Museum Press. London, England.

Burkett, M. E. (1977). An early date for the origin of felt. *Anatolian Studies*, 27, 111–115.

Dhamija, J. (Ed.). (2004). *Asian embroidery*. Abhinav Publications. New Delhi, India.

Dzhelbuldin, Y. & Jeteyeva, D. (2014). *Traditions and customs of Kazakhs*. Authorhouse. https://doi.org/10.4018/978-1-5225-1865-5.ch016

Erdener, C. B. (2017). Fashion fusion in Kazakhstan: Advanced technology converges with the past. In *Advanced Fashion Technology and Operations Management* (pp. 363–376). IGI Global. Hershey, PA. https://doi.org/10.4018/978-1-5225-1865-5.ch016

Fern Green. (2022). *Wool, wool felt & sustainability*. Fern Green Designs. NL. https://ferngreendesigns.com/blogs/news/wool-wool-felt-sustainability

Fisher, E. (2024). *Sustainability*. FeltLOOM. Sharpsburg, KY. https://www.feltloom.com/pages/sustainability

Kunanbay, A. (2001). *The soul of Kazakhstan*. Easton Press. New York,

Laufer, B. (1930). The early history of felt. *American Anthropologist*, 32(1), 1–18.

LifeGate. (2020, November 16). Felt, the history and sustainability of a versatile designer fabric. *LifeGate*. https://www.lifegate.com/felt-sustainability

Mair, V. H. (2012) (ed). The 'Silk Roads' in Time and Space: Migrations, Motifs, and Materials. *Sino-Platonic Papers,* (228). https://docslib.org/doc/4998196/silk-roads-in-time-and-space-migrations-motifs-and-materials

Mamynova, B., Anessova, U., Satkenova, Z., & Shalabay, B. (2014). Symbolism of white and black colours in Kazakh culture. *Life Science Journal*, 11(10), 300–303.

Marhabo, Kamalova. (2023). One of the types of craft is the art of felting. *EPRA International Journal of Research and Development (IJRD)* 8(4), 217–221.
Muhetaer, Mukaidaisi (2020). Economy and identity: Felt making and marketing in Kashgar region and Konya. *Uluslararası Uygur Araştırmaları Dergisi, Sayı*, 8(16), 224–232. https://doi.org/10.46400/uygur.828616
Palamutcu, S. (2017). Sustainable textile technologies. In S. S. Muthu (Ed.), *Textiles and clothing sustainability: Sustainable Technologies* (pp. 1–22). Springer. Hong Kong. https://doi.org/10.1007/978-981-10-2474-0_1
Perleberg, T. (2023). *Elevate your needle felting experience: Discover the eco-friendly advantages of a wool felting cushion.* Bear Creek Felting. Nome, ND https://bearcreekfelting.com/blog/elevate-your-needle-felting-experience-discover-the-eco-friendly-advantages-of-a-wool-felting-cushion.html/
Ruiz, A. (2023). *Is felt biodegradable and is it eco-friendly?* theroundup.org. https://theroundup.org/is-felt-biodegradable-and-eco-friendly/
Samuratova, T. & Akhmetova, G. (2016). The symbolic image of the yurt in Kazakh applied arts. *Acta Histriae*, 24(2), 427–447. 10.19233/AH.2016.17
Sapkota, A. (2018). Felt as a sustainable and environmentally friendly material. *Woollyfelt - The Felt Studio Handmade Felt Products.* https://woollyfelt.com/felt-as-a-sustainable-and-environmentally-friendly-material/
Schreiber, D. & Tredennick, J. (2010). *Kazakhstan: Nomadic routes from Caspian to Altai.* Odyssey. Hong Kong.
Shepherd's Dream. (2022). The practical magic of wool felting. *Shepherd\'s Dream.* https://shepherdsdream.com/blog/eco-sustainability/the-practical-magic-of-wool-felting/
Sun Productions. (2015). Decorative arts and crafts of Kazakhs-felt making. [video]. Accessed on 17 October, 2023. https://www.youtube.com/watch?v=gdrua8WP0Q4
Wool (2018) *About sustainability.* WoOL Amsterdam. https://woolamsterdam.nl/stories/about-sustainability/
Zhogova, M. & Sheromova, I. (2014). The synthesis of technologies and traditions in the modern fashion industry by the example of felting in clothes design. *Modern Problems of Science and Education*, 9(4), 118–126.
Zhukenova, Z. D., Soltanbaeva, G. S., & Izhanov, B. (2016). Traditional Felt in the Kazakhs Folk Art. *International Journal of Environmental and Science Education*, 11(10), 3719–3729.

6 Social enterprises support textile artisans and designers in Afghanistan

Sharifa Jamaldin

As part of the Responsible Fashion Series looking at the Silk Road, I researched the rich cultural heritage of Afghan textiles and fashion. Afghanistan's place in the history of the Silk Road and its complex textile and fashion history is of personal significance to me, given my Afghan ancestry on my mother's side. The study explores social enterprises, designers, and individuals who support and promote brands, artisans, and homeworkers, across the Afghan diaspora to preserve the craft of embroidery. Their heroic effort to preserve and revitalize traditional craftsmanship in face of a fundamentalist regime that is curtailing basic human rights amounting to gender apartheid is showcased. My research led me to the MOMU fashion library and various online textile archives. Through the artistic initiative of DOEK VZW formed around textiles, I met and had conversations with Afghan embroiderer Nadia Mohmand living in Antwerp, who provided me insight into Afghan textile heritage and culture. The trend and increased appearance of Pashtun dresses on social media and in publications brought Afghan embroidery to light. The context of women's rights violations in Afghanistan under the Taliban regime, even though men's rights are also impeded in innumerable ways, entered the picture.

Introduction

Afghan embroidery and textile crafts are crucial to the community of artisans and designers across the Afghan diaspora, who stand up to an austere regime through social entrepreneurship and creative initiatives. The objective is to bring to light and to focus on the social, cultural, political, ecological, and economic significance of the Afghan embroidery. Embroidery and the textile economy in Afghanistan are reliant on women's creative skills and talent, yet the Taliban's recent edicts hinder women's right to education, self-sufficiency and to earn an income (Feminist Majority Foundation, 2021). A woman must be accompanied by a man to sell their products and is not allowed to speak and negotiate with male counterparts at the market (Aram, 2023). The challenges are multiplied when facing social inequities, insufficient resources, and reduced mobility (Feminist Majority

DOI: 10.4324/9781003508076-9

Foundation, 2021). To circumvent the Taliban stranglehold, women have turned to online opportunities and started creative initiatives and social enterprises, seeking a global market (Aram). On social media platforms, thousands of posts show Afghan influencers, wearing the Pashtun dress, some using the hashtag #DoNotTouchMyClothes as a digital rally cry. Expressed simply, Afghan women are fighting back by showing they can wear whatever they want. Afghan women are reclaiming their own narrative to counter the suppression of their human rights. They do not have to wear the Burqa prescribed by an irrational dress code. Afghan women choose to promote the Pashtun dress, not a flashy fashion statement, but rather as acts of bravery and a cultural beacon to other women. Zooming in on the Pashtun dress: embroidery features prominently.

In the ebb and flow of history along the passage of the Silk Road, embroidery plays a significant part in the intangible cultural heritage of the Pashtun people and of Afghanistan.

In the context of the 21st century, embroidery has a role to play in a purpose-driven economy on the one hand and a role to play in sustainable fashion on the other. Specifically, social enterprises have developed to counter austere social injustice and human rights violations to support embroiderers in and outside of Afghanistan.

Afghan traditional garments

Traditional garments of Afghanistan worn today date back to even the pre-Islamic era. The basis of the Afghan dress is the *shalwar-kameez* (a long tunic over trousers, worn by women, men, and children, with regional differences. Notably, the same silhouette is found along the Silk Roads, Tajikistan, Uzbekistan, and beyond to Iran and Turkey (Paine, 2006, p.10). Accessories include loose headcovers or shawls for women and turbans for men. The garments are embroidered and often decorated with beads, coins, and mirrors. Embroidery patterns vary across Afghanistan. Afghan embroidery decorates all sorts of objects: "tent hangings, purses, bags for kohl or tobacco, small cloths, covers for bicycle saddles, telephones, and guns, and especially caps in a great variety of styles for men and children" (Paine, 2010, p. 42). Embroidery work is generally under the providence of women.

The *hijab*, which covers the hair and neck, is the most common headwear for women in Afghanistan. Although synonymous with the Afghan dress code, the *burqa*, *chadari* in Afghans, is a foreign phenomenon that entered the culture through Persia around 200 years ago. The *burqa* covers the face and entire body. The ongoing debate in Islamic discourse about how women should cover their hair, face, and body is a point of contention (Aziz, 2011). Under the fundamentalist Mujahideen and Taliban regimes, who follow a strict interpretation of the Quran and Hadith, the wearing of the *burqa* has been imposed. In the pre-Islamic period and further, face veils appeared and were often worn by women in upper classes. Headcovers and face veils appear across a variety of religions, cultures, and classes. Most Islamic scholars agree that face covering is not mandatory, modesty being the key point. Prior to the Islamic era, Afghans had followed Hinduism, Zoroastrian, and Buddhism.

Garments are made from cotton, silk, or rayon raw materials and often contain velvet (Paine, 2006, p. 16). Afghanistan's mountainous region supplies gemstones. Roundels, decorated circular, or triangular patches adorn the shoulder area. An overview of traditional Afghan textiles and attire is available on the Textile Research Centre's Leiden Online Exhibitions (Vogelsang & Vogelsang, 2017).

The Pashtun dress (Kuchi)

The Pashtun dress, generally worn for special occasions, has a fitted bodice, wide sleeves, full skirt, or a long wide shift, worn with baggy pants with drawstring (see Figure 6.1).

Figure 6.1 Pashtun or Kuchi dress, decorated with beads, buttons, coins, including gul-i pirahan circular discs Late 20th century Courtesy Textile Research Centre, Leiden', TRC 2008.0248b (Vogelsang & Vogelsang, 2017).

Figure 6.2 Detail of Kuchi Dress Panel, Full-length, 1950s.
Source: UNT College of Visual Arts + Design, 2014.

The terms Pashtun dress and Kuchi dress appear in documentation and are commonly interchanged, although some differences exist. For instance, the embroidered dress is worn for special occasions by the Pashtun people, the majority ethnic group that reside on both sides of the Afghanistan and Pakistan border along the Durand line of 1896. The Kuchi, the nomadic tribe of Pashtun, wear the dress every day. Most Afghan people do not identify as Kuchi but consider themselves Pashtun (Tapper, 2008). The terms are related and at times cross-pollinate and cross borders. Today, both the Pashtun dress or Kuchi dress feature their own regional differences. A long loose headscarf is standard. The headwear is bejeweled with dangling beads, stones, and frame the face. Dramatic amulets, chokers, necklaces, and chest jewelry are added for special occasions. Deconstructing the Pashtun dress highlights the creativity of embroidery. Unique to Pashtun dresses are elaborate and colorful embroidery on a front panel of the bodice (see Figure 6.2).

The shape of the Pashtun dress is constant, like a uniform. What varies are the motifs and patterns of the embroidery and here lies its sophistication and potential application in slowing down fashion. It has been gaining in popularity throughout the Afghan diaspora, particularly on social media platforms like Instagram, Facebook, TikTok, as well as articles in magazines and exhibitions as exemplified by the artwork of Mashid Mohadjerin, a photograph of university student, Maria Mahmond, reconnecting to her Afghanistan roots (see Figure 6.3).

Figure 6.3 Maria Mahmond by Mashid Mohadjerin.
Source: Mohadjerin, 2019.

The hashtag #DoNotTouchMyclothes is a form of protest against the Taliban dress code. Vogue US featured Instagrammer Lema Afzal, one of many for popularizing the Pashtun dress (Satenstein, 2021). As we transition to a responsible and regenerative fashion system, creative hand embroidery will be an effective replacement to the candy aesthetics of fast fashion.

Afghan fashion and textile history in the context of conflict

Afghanistan is seen as a country of constant conflicts, lesser known for its rich fashion and textile history, and its adoption of regional and global styles. Rather, Afghanistan is wrongly associated with the strict Islamic dress code imposed by the Taliban. In analysis of the Pashtun dress, Afghans exhibit a strong attachment to their traditional garments as an expression of their identity. In the first half of the 20th century, reforms empowering women were implemented by progressive leaders that impacted the dress code (Ahmed-Ghosh, 2003). During the reign of King Amenallah Khan along with Queen Soraya Tarzi, who was the founder of the first women's magazine and political figure in Afghanistan and her father, Mahmud Tarzi, considered the father of journalism advocated for Women's rights and education and campaigned against polygamy and the veil (Time Staff, 2020). Even Western dress (short dresses, shirts, and pants) was adopted in the major cities. In the 60s, Kabul was called the Paris of Central Asia. In the 70s, the Marxist-Leninist communist party PDPA (People's Democratic Party of Afghanistan) pushed for women to enter the workforce to bolster the economy. Archival photographs show women wearing short skirts, chic scarves, and beehive hairdos, while men sported blazers and striped shirts (Grall, 2019).

But traditional Afghan dress styles were also picked up globally by the hippy movement. For instance, John Lennon popularized the embroidered Afghan coat, wearing it on the album cover, *Sgt. Pepper's Lonely Hearts Club Band* in 1967. The country's fashion industry flourished in the 1960s (Aubrey, 2010). For instance, Designer Safia Tarzi, a descendant of Soraya Tarzi, appeared in the *Vogue UK* in a 1969 edition, and fashion shows were held in Kabul (Vigne, 2020, p. 47). The Afghan goat-skin coat appeared in the *Vogue UK* in the December 1969 issue, *Afghan Adventure*. Afghanistan attracted travelers, artists, writers to what is referred to as the 'Hippy Trail.'

Many artists and writers were attracted to Afghan textile aesthetics. Alighiero Boetti was drawn to Afghan embroidery, discovering it in 1971 (Bennett et al., 2012). Boetti is famous for his embroidery artworks, where he engaged Afghan embroiderers to execute freeform designs. His *Mappe* and *Order and Disorder series* are wonderful examples of the creative possibilities of embroidery as a medium of art. Boetti challenged the elitism of art, by creating art that elevated craft, craftspeople, and textiles. After the Soviet invasion in 1978 and later, he could not meet with the women embroiderers, so he worked with them long distance through their male counterparts (Marescalchi & Bennett, 2011).

Textile academics and historians play a role in creating cultural appreciation to the general public with links to museums. Sheila Paine traveled to remote parts of the world to get first-hand stories about textile traditions, even during the unsafe times of the Taliban rule (Pitt Rivers Museum, 2016). Her detailed study and collections of textiles and embroidery, which includes Afghan garments, are invaluable today as a log of history (Paine, 1994).

The decades fluctuate with phases of women choosing to cast aside their head-covers and face-covers and those of women being compelled to wear them again. In 1992, the Mujahideen took over Kabul and declared Afghanistan an Islamic state. "In 1992, women were increasingly precluded from public service. In conservative areas in 1994 under the Taliban, many women appeared in public only, if dressed in a complete head-to-toe garment with a mesh covered opening for their eyes" (United States Department of State, 1995). In 2001, a US-led coalition ousted the Taliban regime, giving Afghans a moment of reprieve (Maizland & Robinson, 2023). However, another iteration of the Taliban resurfaced. In August 2021, the Taliban retook the country and enforced over 50 decrees to restrict women's education and movement (Chalabi, 2023).

Today, Afghan women face unimaginable human rights violations, with the Taliban set to completely disempower women. The Ministry of Women's Affairs was closed down and replaced with the Ministry for the Propagation of Virtue and Prevention of Vice. In strict regimes, people are controlled by violence, brutality, fear, and imprisonment (Amnesty International, 2022). Afghan women are limited to doing what is deemed women's work, such as sewing and embroidery. Yet, a fashion resistance exists inside and outside propelled by social enterprises supporting Afghan entrepreneurs.

Social enterprises provide income and hope

The rise and evolution of social enterprises in the world economy is a positive trend. The Social Enterprise Alliance outlines a social enterprise as a business that has a social and environmental purpose (Social Enterprise UK, 2018). In the dangerous situations that prevail in Afghanistan, where women have to navigate every step they take or risk being attacked, social enterprises have formed to support women embroiderers. The act of embroidery takes on the form of resistance, activism, and self-preservation in all its complexity. It takes weeks to produce a special Pashtun dress. The topics of fair pay, fair trade, fair fashion, women's rights, and cultural heritage enter the discourse. Hand embroidery, machine embroidery, and the act of sewing tend to be labor intensive and form a viable strand of the economy. Consequently, embroidery work has vital economic function, sometimes the sole means to earn an income. It is worth noting that textile workers and artisans fall under two definitions in policy or employment category. In an ILA report, workers can be defined as home-based work or as independent workers (International Labour Organization, 2015). Home-based work is informal work done mostly by women. They are paid directly or indirectly by an employer, like subcontractors, generally on a piece rate. Self-employed independent sellers make and market their products themselves.

The following case studies, many work with sustainable fashion practices including ecological materials, seasonless collections, fair wages, valuing people and planet over profit, and preserving cultural heritage, are examples of how Afghan entrepreneurs are creating social enterprises and at the same time working to promote the Pashtun dress, Afghan embroidery, and traditional craft (Brismar, 2014).

Rangini Hamidi – The Kandahar Treasure

Rangini Hamidi is an Afghan American writer, scholar, social entrepreneur, and former Afghanistan Minister of Education. In 2003, Hamidi, who grew up in Virginia, decided to return to Kandahar to help Afghan people, taking up a leadership role in the Women's Income Generation for Social (Kandahar Treasure, 2017). She served as the manager of the Women's Income Generation Project for Afghans for Civil Society, an organization dedicated to social development in Kandahar province of southern Afghanistan.

She manages to withstand the political machinations of the Taliban regime, especially navigating the suppression of women's rights of movement, education, civil liberties, and employment. She observes that after having been forced to leave the workforce *en masse*, women often find solace in embroidery. Her platform Kandahar Treasure, which supports and promotes female embroidery artisans, works to empower women and help them gain financial independence in a volatile unsafe landscape since 2012:

> The revival of Khamak embroidery focuses on the untold story of the pioneering women of Kandahar Treasure, an artisan organization in a conflict-battered Kandahar, a city considered the home of the Taliban movement in southern Afghanistan… Kandahar Treasure provides work for culturally homebound women, an important first step in securing economic independence. One-third of the women working with Kandahar Treasure are widows or heads of households.
>
> (Hamidi & Littrell, 2017, p. 26)

Kandahar Treasure elevates the art of Khamak embroidery and other techniques practiced in the region. "Despite their cultural significance in Afghanistan, Khamak textiles are little known outside the country. Kandahar residents describe the Khamak embroidery style as old" (Hamidi & Littrell, 2017, p. 27). It is structured as a non-profit organization with initial foundation support from Thunderbird Group of Economics and BPeace, an organization that provides business skills to SMEs in crisis-affected communities (Kandahar Treasure, 2017). Profits gained from selling hand-crafted embroidery products online and at the International Folk Art Market are used to pay artisans and administration and to provide financial aid and training.

Zolaykah Sherzad – Zarif Design (Paris)

Afghan Swiss Designer and former Architect Zolaykah Sherzad created Zarif Design in 2004 to reframe how Afghan culture is perceived by highlighting its beautiful textiles and artistry. In 2005, Sherzad organized the first fashion show in 30 years in Kabul, which was unthinkable under the Taliban regime. Her mission is to help restore cultural heritage lost due to decades of wars and to revive traditional textiles in a modern fashion design context and to make a case for the artistic qualities of Afghan textiles. Conscious of the destruction caused by the conflicts, Sherzad, whose family had been Afghan political refugees, decided to return to Kabul from Lausanne after the fall of the Taliban in 2002 and founded the School of Hope, to help rebuild the broken infrastructure. Soon after under Zarif Design, Sherzad used her creative know-how to empower embroiderers, weavers, and tailors in her ateliers giving her team agency over their financial independence. Her designs are now conduits to the rest of the world. In the exhibition and book *Textile as Resistance*, authored by writer Samira Bendadi and photojournalist/artist Mashid Mohadjerin, the work of Zolaykah Sherzad is featured as a visionary example of resistance against the oppressive governments (see Figure 6.4).

Figure 6.4 Zolaykah Sherzad wearing her Zarif Design photographed by Mashid Mohaderin.

Source: Mohadjerin, 2019.

She presents her collections in the fashion circuit, galleries, and museums from New York, Paris, Milan, New Delhi, and London. Using clever marketing strategies, Sherzad collaborates with key fashion stakeholders and celebrities including Agnes B. Marina Abromovic, TSE Cashmere, Ethical Fashion Initiative, and Deepa Chopra, MOMU in Antwerp. Zarif Design exemplifies how brands could work with artisans as valued partners.

Lies van Assche and Nadia Mohmand – Doek – Belgian social textile art incubator

Doek, which means 'canvas' in Dutch, is a Belgian social textile art incubator, which facilitates meaningful artistic engagement between communities, individuals, and talented newcomers (Flanders Arts Institute, 2012). Doek's mission is to connect people from all cultures to share intangible textile heritage. Nadia Mohmand, a master embroiderer from Afghanistan and Lies van Assche, the founder of Doek met through one of its city programs. Recognizing the need to bring attention to Afghan embroidery, they have since worked together on artistic and art-educational initiatives. For the project, Afghaans Borduren (2019–2020), they reviewed the forgotten Afghan embroidery collections in Museum archive as a creative project, which subsequently led to a masterclass at the AP Arts department in Antwerp in February 2020 titled *Leaving Traces* (DOEK VZW, 2020). In a community art project called *Stadstof*, Van Assche invited people to embroider a place of personal emotional value on a large-scale map of Antwerp made from old tablecloths (DOEK VZW, 2021). The workshop tours the various neighborhoods with the intention to create a hand-embroidered artwork. Mohmand with her knowledge of Afghan embroidery and other embroiderers were hired as valued consultants to guide participants with minimal sewing skills. Doek is an example of a non-profit incubator working with social design and social enterprise principles to empower artists, artisans, refugees, and immigrants through creative concepts to gain employment.

Manizha Wafeq and made by Afghan Women trademark

Made by Afghan Women is a trademark and an e-commerce platform that certifies and promotes authentic Afghan products. Women entrepreneurs are then able to reach the local and global digital market. The trademark gives them visibility and legitimacy as vetted businesses (Made by Afghan Women, 2022). Out of desperation, Afghan women have taken up artisanal crafts in a haphazard way to make money due to the Taliban restrictions. Manizha Wafeq, the founder of Made by Afghan Women, launched the website in November 2022 with the aim to help women navigate e-commerce, secure online payment systems, to handle shipping and distribution from Afghanistan to the world. E-commerce is a lifeline for struggling entrepreneurs, trying to get sales.

Aseel App and Qanawiz Fashion – Kabul-based brand

Qanawiz Fashion, a Kabul-based brand, sells their products on a special shopping app called Aseel. After graduating from Kabul University, Asila Sadaat, launched her brand Qanawiz in 2017 at the age of 22 (Latifi, 2023). Sadaat's mission is to prove women can run a profitable business. Sadaat enlists local tailors and artisans to work in her atelier. The fabric and materials are sourced from Kandahar, Uruwgan, Khost, and Paktia. However, Qanawiz needs to sell outside of an improvised Afghanistan to generate income.

Nasrat Khalid, CEO and founder, created Aseel, a humanitarian crisis donation app and marketplace to support entrepreneurs such as Qanawiz to sell handmade products (Aseel, 2017). The app, which started out serving Afghanistan and Turkey, aims to assist three billion people excluded from the digital economy.

Aseel manages donations raised from people-led campaigns, emergency food package donations, disaster funds, and crowd-funding.

Since female employees are pressured to work from home or face severe punishments from the Islamic Emirate Authorities, entrepreneurs have created segregated areas to keep men and women apart in compliance with Taliban decrees. Furthermore, in Herat and Mazar-e Sharif, entrepreneurs have set-up women-only markets as a countermeasure. In defiance of restrictions, Sadaat makes trendy garments at all price points that appeal to contemporary Afghan shoppers living in other countries (Latifi, 2023). Sadaat employs 30 or so textile workers who design the Pashtun dress and other sorts of garments. The Qanawiz case study points to the benefits of social and purpose-driven entrepreneurs, withstanding the carbon footprint of transportation. The vital role of online marketplaces during times of conflict cannot be dismissed to support suppressed communities.

Embroidery as a sustainable craft

Beyond its source for economic and social justice, Afghan Embroidery as exemplified by the Pashtun dress has aesthetic appeal and the potential to popularize decorative practice, particularly in upcycling and circular fashion as a counter to overproduction.

First, the basic embroidery technique involves freeform stitching or thread count using a needle and thread that is easy for beginners to learn. Afghan embroidery stitches or patterns are referred to as *gul dozee*, *khamak dozee*, *taashamar dozee*, *taarkashee dozee*, *mura dozee*, and *charma dozee*. All of them involve using the most common stitches: the stem stitch, the chain stitch, and the satin stitch (Daly, 2000). Second, slow fashion incorporates, upcycling, repair, and mending as its pillars, particularly visible mending. Embroidery is utilized in visible mending, darning, and applique to upcycle and repair second-hand garments and to repurpose excess stock to extend garment life. In a paper on mending, Anna Konig, Lecturer in Textile History states: "Ultimately, then, mending should not be positioned as a trivial activity at all. It is profoundly important in environmental, social and economic terms, and not just as a metaphor, but as a democratic action that is as materially tangible as it is empowering" (König, 2013, p. 584). Third, new embroidery hubs should be incorporated in the cities to decorate, repair, and recycle torn or second-hand garments to bolster a repair economy. Fourthly, designer ateliers can hire well-paid artisans under the direction of a practitioner or designer to create slow and seasonless fashion with shared revenue streams. Lastly, government subsidies and incentives should support and encourage the repair economy to bolster embroidery centers.

Over the centuries, embroidery, the art of needle and thread, has had various levels of status in clothing history. The etymology of the word embroidery comes from the French word 'broderie' which means embellishment. Embroidery is a form of decoration applied to fabric, an aesthetic practice. What is thought to be one of the oldest known evidences of beaded embroidery[1] was found in graves from the Upper Paleolithic period in a region of what is today Russia (Trinkaus & Buzhilova, 2018). Surviving examples of embroidery from around the 3rd to 5th century BCE were found in China, Egypt, and Sweden (The Textile Research Centre (TRC) Leiden, 2017). It has been given the attributes of luxury and wealth. It has always been recognized for its utility in repairing and mending.

Embroidery mentioned in passing, immediately conjures up a hobbyist sitting in a rocking chair or a housewife doing some needlework. Even today, embroidery is dismissed as trivial. It is a women's craft. It is not considered high art. Some scholars and feminists have demonstrated how women's activities such as embroidery are often less valued. Books have been written on the topic including *Threads of Life: A History of the World Through the Eye of a Needle*, *Stitching resistance: women, creativity, and fiber arts*, *Women's Work: From Feminine Art to Feminist Art*, or *the Subversive Stitch*. The books reveal embroidery and needlework are used to bring attention to social justice work, climate action, and human rights such as stitching names of victims on headscarves in Argentina, stitching slogans to raise awareness, and mending to reduce overconsumption.

Debates on its worth and worthiness continue as it goes in and out of fashion. In the late 2000s, embroidery, knitting, and other crafts have risen in popularity as part of the maker trend, Do-It-Yourself, slow fashion movement, well-being economy, and craftivism movement. Today, the value of embroidery is being recognized as a key technique in repairing, visible mending, and invisible mending. Museums, such as the Wereldmuseum and the V&A, have organized exhibitions and workshops that have highlighted the political and social aspects of embroidery and other textile crafts.

Conclusion

The intersection of sustainable fashion practitioners, conscious consumers and social enterprises, and textile artisans is already breeding innovative solutions. One crossroad of traditional textiles and sustainable fashion reveals embroidery's potential in the practice of upcycling and visible mending. Embroidery can be used to extend a garments' life. Part of the slow fashion movement, the joy of embroidery is beautifying old garments by taking time to mend holes and other traces of use. Embroidery also has shown its potential for regenerative fashion practices.

The study of the Pashtun dress of Afghanistan reveals embroidery is part of the country's intangible cultural heritage, but also a crucial source of employment for women. Social enterprise is a pillar in ethical fashion and should be the standard business model in the fashion industry. Embroidery takes the form of activism within the framework of purpose-driven entrepreneurship. Initiatives like Kandahar Treasure and Aseel are prime case studies of social enterprises that support the community and preserve intangible cultural heritage. The Case studies of Zarif Design, Doek VZW, and Qanawiz prove embroidery is a powerful vehicle for employment, resistance, and community. The project Made by Afghan Women stands out as a testament to the transformative potential of skills like embroidery and craft businesses that contribute to the well-being of people. Countless examples that are not listed here exist of risk-taking entrepreneurs and social enterprises uplifting Afghan women textile artisans and embroiderers. Under the Taliban regime where women are not allowed to work or be seen in public spaces, embroidery becomes more than a craft, it is an economic lifeline for women and their families. Embroidery is often not seen as more than a hobby in the West or in the Global South. Embroidery needs to move beyond being seen as a hobby or as traditional but as an innovative sustainable practice. A strong bridge is needed between the rising wave of slow, conscious, and circular fashion built up on the DIY movement and craftivism and the social enterprise movement for Afghan entrepreneurs to develop a sustainable fashion future.

Note

1 Ivory beads were found arranged in a way to suggest that they would have been sewn onto clothing (Trinkaus & Buzhilova).

References

Ahmed-Ghosh, H. (2003). A History of Women in Afghanistan: Lessons Learnt for the Future or Yesterdays and Tomorrow: Women in Afghanistan. *Journal of International Women's Studies*, *4*(3), Article 1. https://vc.bridgew.edu/jiws/vol4/iss3/1

Aziz, R. (2011). *Hijab – The Islamic Dress Code: Its Historical Development, Evidence from Sacred Sources and Views of Selected Muslim Scholars*. University of South Africa, Pretoria. http://hdl.handle.net/10500/4888

Daly, C. M. (2000). *Afghan After a Fashion: The Fusion of Politics with Religion and Women's Textile Craft Economies*. Textile Society of America Symposium Proceedings. https://digitalcommons.unl.edu/tsaconf/769/

König, A. (2013). A Stitch in Time: Changing Cultural Constructions of Craft and Mending. *Culture Unbound*, *5*, 569–585. https://doi.org/10.3384/cu.2000.1525.135569

Tapper, R. (2008). Who Are the Kuchi? Nomad Self-Identities in Afghanistan. *The Journal of the Royal Anthropological Institute*, *14*(1), 97–116. https://www.jstor.org/stable/20203586
UNT College of Visual Arts + Design. (2014). *Dress – Kutchi Group, Pashtun Peoples, Afghanistan.* University of North Texas Libraries, UNT Digital Library. https://digital.library.unt.edu/ark:/67531/metadc276981/m1/4/
Vogelsang, G., & Vogelsang, W. (2017). Afghan Dress. In *Pashtun Traditional Dress.* TRC Leiden: Leiden.

Sources

Amnesty International. (2022). *Human Rights in Afghanistan Amnesty International.* Amnesty International. Retrieved March 7, 2024, from https://www.amnesty.org/en/location/asia-and-the-pacific/south-asia/afghanistan/report-afghanistan/
Aram, F. (2023, October 2). *Embroidery: A Feminine Art Struggling to Survive in Afghanistan. Zan Times.* Retrieved March 5, 2024, from https://zantimes.com/2023/10/02/embroidery-a-feminine-art-struggling-to-survive-in-afghanistan/
Aseel. (2017, November 9). *Aseel App.* Assel. Retrieved March 8, 2024, from https://aseelapp.com/europe/vendor_shop/qanawiz-fashion.html
Aubrey, A. (2010, December 25). *When Afghanistan Was in Vogue.* The Polyglot. Retrieved March 8, 2024, from https://the-polyglot.blogspot.com/2010/12/when-afghanistan-was-in-vogue.html
Bennett, C. G., Hamilton, R. W., Ruiz, A., & Steinberger, R. M. (2012). *Order and Disorder: Alighiero Boetti by Afghan Women.* Fowler Museum at UCLA: Los Angeles, CA.
Brismar, A. (2014). What is Sustainable Fashion? – Green Strategy. Green Strategy. Retrieved May 19, 2024, from https://greenstrategy.se/sustainable-fashion-definition/
Chalabi, M. (2023, August 15). *Women in Afghanistan: From Almost Everywhere to Almost Nowhere.* UN Women. Retrieved March 7, 2024, from https://www.unwomen.org/en/news-stories/feature-story/2023/08/women-in-afghanistan-from-almost-everywhere-to-almost-nowhere
DOEK VZW. (2020). *Afghaans Borduren.* DOEK VZW. Retrieved March 31, 2024, from https://doek-vzw.com/afghaans-borduren/
DOEK VZW. (2021). *STADSSTOF – EEN Community-Art Project.* DOEK VZW. Retrieved March 31, 2024, from https://doek-vzw.com/sterrenstof-2-0/
Feminist Majority Foundation. (2021). *Taliban Edicts against Afghan Women and Girls.* Feminist Majority Foundation. Retrieved March 7, 2024, from https://feminist.org/our-work/afghan-women-and-girls/taliban-edicts/
Flanders Art Institute: Doek. Residences & Workspaces. Belgium, Antwerp. (2012). https://www.kunsten.be/en/residences-and-workplaces/ent:dkb:org:387584/doek-vzw/
Grall, V. (2019, December 20). *Lost in Time: Groovy Afghanistan.* Messy Nessy Chic. Retrieved March 8, 2024, from https://www.messynessychic.com/2013/06/10/lost-in-time-groovy-afghanistan/
Hamidi, R., & Littrell, M. (2017). *Embroidering within Boundaries: Afghan Women Creating a Future.* Thrums Books.
International Labour Organization. (2015). *Home-based Workers: Decent Work and Social Protection through Organization and Empowerment.* International Labour Organization.
Kandahar Treasure. (2017). *About Us.* Kandahar Treasure. Retrieved March 31, 2024, from https://kandahartreasure.com/about/

Latifi, A. M. (2023, June 8). *For Afghan Women, Fashion and Crafts Offer a Work Lifeline*. The New Humanitarian. Retrieved March 3, 2024, from https://www.thenewhumanitarian.org/news-feature/2023/06/08/afghan-women-fashion-and-crafts-offer-work-lifeline

Made by Afghan Women. (2022, November). *About*. Made by Afghan Women. Retrieved March 7, 2024, from https://madebyafghanwomen.com/about/

Maizland, L., & Robinson, L. (2023, January 19). *The Taliban in Afghanistan*. Council on Foreign Relations. Retrieved March 6, 2024, from https://www.cfr.org/backgrounder/taliban-afghanistan

Marescalchi, A., & Bennett, C. G. (2011). *Boetti by Afghan People: Peshawar, Pakistan, 1990*. RAM Publications, Santa Monica, CA.

Mohadjerin, M. (2019). *Textile as Resistance Exhibition, November 15, 2019 until February 16, 2020*. MoMu ModeMuseum and Texture Kortrijk.

Paine, S. (1994). *The Afghan Amulet: Travels from the Hindu Kush to Razgrad*. Penguin: London et al.

Paine, S. (2006). *Embroidery from Afghanistan*. University of Washington Press: Seattle, WA.

Paine, S. (2010). *Embroidered Textiles: A World Guide to Traditional Patterns*. Thames & Hudson, London.

Pitt Rivers Museum. (2016). *Embroidered Visions: Photographs of Central Asia and the Middle East by Sheila Paine*. Pitt Rivers Museum. Retrieved March 5, 2024, from https://www.prm.ox.ac.uk/event/embroidered-visions

Satenstein, L. (2021, October 5). How One Afghan Woman Is Embracing Her Traditional Dress. Vogue. Retrieved March 6, 2024, from https://www.vogue.com/article/afghan-women-ethnic-dress-lema-afzal

Social Enterprise UK. (2018, June 4). All about Social Enterprise. Social Enterprise UK. Retrieved May 18, 2024, from https://www.socialenterprise.org.uk/all-about-social-enterprise/

The Textile Research Centre (TRC) Leiden. (2017, May 20). Brief History of Hand Embroidery. Retrieved May 19, 2024, from https://trc-leiden.nl/trc-needles/techniques/embroidery/general-embroidery/brief-history-of-hand-embroidery

Time Staff. (2020, March 5). Queen Soraya Tarzi: 100 Women of the Year. Time. https://time.com/5792702/queen-soraya-tarzi-100-women-of-the-year/

Trinkaus, E., & Buzhilova, A. P. (2018). Diversity and Differential Disposal of the Dead at Sunghir. *Antiquity*, 92(361), 7–21. https://doi.org/10.15184/aqy.2017.223

United States Department of State. (1995, January 30). *U.S. Department of State Country Report on Human Rights Practices 1994 - Afghanistan*. Refworld. Retrieved March 8, 2024, from https://www.refworld.org/reference/annualreport/usdos/1995/en/24738

United States Institute of Peace. (2023). *Tracking the Taliban's (Mis)Treatment of Women*. United States Institute of Peace. Retrieved March 7, 2024, from https://www.usip.org/tracking-talibans-mistreatment-women

Vigne, N. (2020). De la minijupe au tchadris: les différentes conceptions de l'identité afghane de 1975 à 1978 au travers du vêtement féminin. Dumas.ccsd.cnrs.fr, 2 vol. (72, 48). https://dumas.ccsd.cnrs.fr/dumas-03203200

7 Discourses of craftsmanship in fashion media

On (in)visibility and (dis)empowerment within the fashion system

Ira Solomatina

Introduction

As the fashion industry is facing a reckoning with its unsustainable ways, one discourse around sustainability is achieving a notable prominence – that of the craft of fashion artisans. In fashion media, in fashion studies, and by sustainability enterprises, artisanal craftsmanship and knowledge are looked at with hope and anticipation – as, indeed, vessels of possible solutions to overproduction, overconsumption, and harmfulness of fast fashion. Traditional fashion crafts are believed to offer an alternative to the ongoing decline in quality and value of fashion items, and the matter of fashion craft is often linked to the concept of slow fashion, arising from tradition and heritage. In such discourses, artisanship tends to be framed as a pure and unchanging source of knowledge, from which the contemporary fashion system is encouraged to learn and borrow. At the same time, the living conditions of artisans are presented as in need of improvement.

These celebrations of craftsmanship intend to honour the skill and craft of fashion artisans. And artisan-focused initiatives, stemming from the industry's interest in craft, oftentimes succeed in improving the living conditions and well-being of individual communities. Numerous examples of this have been widely publicised and highlighted in fashion studies and fashion publications. Notably, initiatives like the International Folk Art Market in the United States (Frater & Hawley 2018) or the Handloom School in Maheshwar have been praised for offering artisans opportunities for monetising their craft through connecting them to the realms of luxury fashion.

In this chapter, however, instead of inquiring into the effectiveness of individual artisan-focused initiatives within the fashion industry or celebrating them uncritically, I would like to focus on the discourses around craftsmanship in fashion and, specifically, in mainstream fashion media. These, as I argue, tend to be laden with ambiguity – while celebrating craftsmanship, they might reiterate Orientalist stereotypes to prioritising certain expressions of artisanship over others. Dominant representations of fashion craft in fashion media seem to conform with the values and demands of the dominant fashion system rather than to disrupt them in order to promote and accommodate

DOI: 10.4324/9781003508076-10

the industry's sustainable turn. Here, I produce a critique of such discourses, questioning their ability to challenge existent imbalances and injustices of the fashion system.

I am adopting a critical approach to fashion media, pointing out such media's shortcomings and inefficiency in approaching complex social issues. In academia, fashion media have been theorised as "cultural intermediaries" (Rocamora 2009), defining and communicating the meanings and value of fashion items, aesthetic standards within the fashion system, and dominant fashion trends and tendencies. Fashion magazines produce what Lazzarato (1996) calls 'the cultural content' of a commodity, doing the labour of imbuing fashion objects with desirability and worth. Promotion of consumption has been a key feature of fashion publications, and their reliance on advertising budgets has made them reluctant critics of the fashion system (Winship 1987; Ballaster 1991; Duffy 2013). Fashion publications' comfortable relationship with consumption has largely defined their outlook on political and social issues with their avoidance of grave, unresolvable, and complex political themes, which are viewed as incompatible with incitements to shopping (Duffy 2013).

Nevertheless, the past two decades have seen an increase in political talk in fashion media, with the traditionally lifestyle-oriented titles turning to discussions of equality, human rights, feminism, sustainability, and other political matters (Banet-Weiser 2018; Keller 2020). Especially, references to climate change have been prominent and frequent in the fashion media, as the fashion press is increasingly confronted with the negative impact of the fashion industry on climate. Mentions of fashion artisans and artisanship, in the contexts pertaining to environmental and social sustainability, abound in traditional fashion titles like Vogue, Glamour, or Teen Vogue. In the publications' coverage, communities of craftspeople emerge as bearers of possible solutions to the climate crisis, but also as problematic sites, affected by poverty, lack of education, and opportunities. Communities of craftspeople and fashion artisans are configured as repositories of traditional knowledge about nature and craft, which can be employed by contemporary fashion industry for more sustainable ways of production. But as troubled sites, on the margins of global North, they also emerge as settings for productivity, awaiting to be worked and improved by an entrepreneurial outsider. These contradictory representations of fashion craftsmanship point to the inherent inconsistency of fashion media's coverage (Ballaster 1991), but also to the struggle of the fashion magazine to redefine and reinvent itself for the era of fluctuating economy, and within the rising influence of social media and exigencies of the visibility economy (Duffy 2013).

Here, I am challenging the dominant discourses on craftsmanship and artisans within fashion media, employing postcolonial and neoliberal critique. First, I will offer an overview of literature that will help me approach the magazines' discourses. I would like to contextualise the article's subject in relation to the history of fashion and craft and within neoliberal discourses of social responsibility. Then, using a discursive analytic approach, I will turn to specific discourses of fashion craft and artisanship in fashion magazines, analysing them in more detail.

Literature review: Productive sustainability

The matter of artisanship and craft in contemporary fashion cannot be separated from the history of fashion, and the space and meaning that fashion craftsmanship has historically held in it. In the fashion system, largely defined and shaped by the Western and Euro-centric notions of taste, class, and race, fashion craft and artisanship have held value as long as they were incorporated in the Western fashion system that accommodated the ideas of appropriateness, prestige, and value shaped during the colonial era (Jansen & Craik 2016). Only in such contexts were crafts considered valuable and aligned with fashion, the latter being, according to the views of nineteenth and early 20th-century theorists, exclusively a Western industry (Simmel 1957). What allegedly made (Western) fashion was specifically its proclivity to change, underpinned by class distinction and capitalist growth. Outside of the dynamic Western domain, clothes were believed to be static, unchanging, and traditional, testifying to the allegedly unchanging and static character of the non-West, as it appeared in the colonial imagination (Said 2003). This distinction between change and tradition underlies a persistent dichotomy between Western fashion and non-Western costume.

Current scholarship in fashion and cultural studies attempts to complicate and challenge this simplistic duality. Numerous studies indicate that the non-Western traditional 'costume' was never as eternally unchanging and constant as colonial anthropologies portrayed it (Jansen & Craik 2016). Traditional garments have always existed in complex relationships with history and culture, and non-Western crafts, similarly, adapted to the economic and cultural demands within colonial and postcolonial contexts. Under such readings, tradition emerges as a dynamic and malleable form susceptible to manipulations, adjustments, and erasures. Thus, as anthropologist Phyllida Jay demonstrates (2017), the Indian design tradition, as it is known across the West and globally, has been a result of complex economic processes and colonial mechanisms that prioritised certain forms of craftsmanship and design over others – to see it as the essence of Indian aesthetics and taste, would not only be incorrect but would also reinforce a further erasure and exoticisation of the Indian design tradition.

Intensified globalisation adds a layer of complication to the history and current status of non-Western crafts, as people, labour, and designs become increasingly implicated in what Arjun Appadurai (1990) terms 'financescapes' and 'imagescapes' of global capitalism, and the notion of tradition becomes an important stake in global anxieties about change and values. What is perceived as 'westernisation' clashes and converges with local traditions, provoking questions about authenticity and loss, in which fashion is oftentimes a key stake. Notably, Simidele Dosekun, in her work on postfeminism in Nigeria (2020) has commented on the general uneasiness with which expressions of fashionable and globalised femininity are met in Lagos. Focusing on the globalised postfeminist sensibility, Dosekun's research suggests that the neoliberal idea of empowerment, based on individual action and entrepreneurialism, cannot foster relevant and collective political change. I'd like to further comment on the limitations within the neoliberal notion of empowerment in the context of the magazine's sustainability talk.

Importantly, at the historical conjuncture when the world's economy, media, and fashion have become inextricably connected, flows of ideas, images, and trends, as well as neoliberal ideas of empowerment gain currency across the globe, too. Depending on the socio-political and cultural contexts, their interpretations and impact vary, but their presence is palpable in global popular culture and within corporate responsibility initiatives that advocate change through individual labour and consumption.

One of the topics that has been readily adopted within corporate responsibility discourses, garnering visibility worldwide has been sustainability. It represents a major theme within the global political and public conversation of the past few decades, and, unsurprisingly, sustainability has also become a buzzword in global marketing and a major cause within corporate responsibility initiatives. The rise of corporate responsibility is often linked to a spate of socio-political developments under neoliberalism, most significantly, with the decline of the welfare state and rise of the consumer citizen, which epitomise the assumption that there exists a direct association between ethical consumption and positive social change. Corporate responsibility is particularly prominent at a time when the affordances of social media grant it increased visibility and impact – and socially conscious practices may be performatively channelled online to garner customers' attention and approval.

Corporate responsibility initiatives have been the subject of many a critique of neoliberalism. As media scholar Sarah Banet-Weiser has pointed out (2013), in such initiatives, corporate interests inevitably have an edge over political change, and the values and ethical commitments of corporate actors tend to be profit-driven. Corporate responsibility initiatives reward individual consumption-based engagement over collective action, encouraging customers to express political beliefs and affiliations through 'shopping for change'.

Neoliberal discourses transform political and social issues into sites of continuous productive engagement without aiming to resolve them. Commenting on the rising popularity of 'green products', cultural sociologist Jo Littler indicates the paradoxical discrepancy between the visibility of environmental issues and the inadequate corporate response to climate change. She writes, "anxieties about climate change are clearly being mobilized through a number of green products, which are marketed as ways to cut down on carbon dioxide production to save or help the planet, from bags for life to eco radios and calculators" (Littler 2012: 79). In Littler's view, 'green consumption' emerges as commodity fetishism, shaped by corporate interests, marketing, corporate competition and consumer choice – a site of ongoing productivity, appearing to generate change but never quite achieving it.

Elsewhere, media scholars Rosalind Gill and Akane Kanai point to a strong association of socio-political marginalisation with positive declarations of change and empowerment in marketing campaigns, noting that systemic inequality becomes "curiously associated with desirable trends and the circulation of normative affective orientations towards capitalism" (Gill & Kanai 2020). Inasmuch as such declarations work to incite an affective response from consumers, their effectiveness lies in their message and visibility, or, reiterating Sarah Banet-Weiser, "to be visible becomes an end in itself, not a means to a different end, such as social change" (Banet-Weiser and Higgins 2022).

A steady feature of neoliberal discourses on political change is their compulsory positivity. In alignment with the promissory nature of neoliberalism (Ong 2017; Gill & Kanai 2020), such discourses focus on happy and positive resolutions of stories about disenfranchisement, discrimination, and struggle, emphasising the effectiveness of suggested approaches. This focus on positivity and happy resolution has been widely criticised in cultural and media studies. Rosalind Gill and Shani Orgad demonstrate how an exigency of positivity is employed to foster individual engagement, self-discipline, and labour on the self, while blocking the ways for critical engagement with the political (Gill & Orgad 2018). The promise of a happy resolution in neoliberal discourses can be viewed through the lens of what philosopher Lauren Berlant defines as 'cruel optimism' or a deceptively optimistic attachment to "compromised conditions of possibility whose realization is discovered either to be *im*possible, sheer fantasy, or *too* possible, and toxic" (Berlant 2011). Feminist scholar Sara Ahmed refers to Berlant's definition of cruel optimism as she expands on her view of happiness – as a regulating and disciplining cultural myth. Looking into 'what happiness does', Ahmed exposes connections between cultural prescriptions for 'right' behaviour and the "promise of happiness", which dictates an optimistic orientation to future happiness (Ahmed 2010).

This brief literature review seeks to roughly outline the context, in which I would like to situate discourses on artisanship and craft in fashion media. This is the context shaped by the exigencies of economy of visibility, facilitated by social media, that accommodates and shapes the expressions of corporate responsibility. It is also, notably, positioned within the neoliberal governmentality that prioritises individual labour and engagement as effective methods for solving grave political and systemic issues. Thus, contextualising the discourses on artisanship will help me to critically interrogate their potential for disturbing the status quo within the fashion industry and suggest new ways for approaching sustainability and corporate responsibility initiatives.

Methodology

The discursive-analytical approach this chapter adopts is inherently political and thus well-suited for a critical assessment of fashion media's discourses. Methods of critical discourse analysis "see discourse – language use in speech and writing – as social practice" (Fairclough & Wodak 1997: 258), which indicates the workings and effects of power. As linguist Ruth Wodak argues, reiterating Foucault's views on power, discursive events are shaped by institutions and social practices but also shape them, helping to "produce and reproduce unequal power relations between, for instance, social classes, women and men, and ethnic/cultural majorities and minorities through the ways in which they represent things and position people" (Wodak 2014: 303). The methods of the critical discourse analysis are quintessentially interpretative and explanatory (Fairclough & Wodak 1997). This work relies on the linguist Norman Fairclough's (1995) method based on description, interpretation, and explanation of discursive practices. Another discursive analytic approach that has been very valuable throughout this research has been elaborated by Jonathan Potter and Margaret Wetherell and relies on the concept of the interpretative repertoire, which constitutes a repository of recurring ideas, motifs, and themes that allow the reader to identify patterns across texts and connect them to wider political, social, and cultural contexts (Potter & Wetherell 1987; Potter et al. 1993).

This chapter is situated within the Anglo-American and Indian contexts and draws on research data obtained from three fashion and lifestyle publications – Vogue US, Vogue UK, and Vogue India. These three titles focus on middle-class and upper-middle-class readers. Vogue US is, probably, the most mainstream publication of the three, with a significant international following, beyond the US. Vogue India, launched in 2007, emerged in the context of post-liberalisation era in India that opened the country to foreign investment, fostering growth of middle classes. It mainly targets upper-middle- and middle-class urban women. Vogue UK has recently emerged as one of the most innovative and original titles in the global family of Vogue magazines. Under the leadership of Edward Enninful, the magazine has been praised for its bold and refreshing fashion editorials as well as its thoughtful approach to socially sensitive issues – such as its coverage of essential workers during the COVID-19 pandemic. Vogue magazines present a particularly interesting case for critical discourse analysis because of the brand's revered and authoritative status in the industry – believed to set up and embody the values of the industry, they encapsulate mainstream and popular discourses on fashion trends and tendencies. The chapter covers the timespan between the autumn of 2020 until the autumn of 2023, and, in total, 39 articles, both in printed magazines and online, have been analysed for this work. I selected the articles that specifically mention craft, fashion artisans, and craftspeople, attempting to embed them in larger socio-cultural contexts. Whereas references to craft in the analysed media are frequent, they tend to pertain to the quality and artfulness of fashion items, in this work, I focused specifically on the pieces that address communities of artisans and craftspeople in fashion, and highlight the relationship between 'traditional crafts' and the fashion system.

Stories of craftsmanship in the fashion industry: Discourses in Vogue magazines

The magazines' discourses on artisans and craftspeople are orientated towards the global fashion industry, and the luxury fashion industry in particular. In Vogue US, Vogue UK, and Vogue India, discussions of artisan communities and craftspeople mainly appear in the contexts that relate to the global and local production of luxury fashion. Artisans and their craft are brought into spotlight when they are associated with already-established fashion brands and designers, most often in the context of collaborations. Thus, in Vogue US, the craftspeople and artisans of India are discussed for example through their recent connection with Dior and the brand's designer Maria Grazia Chiuri:

> Maria Grazia Chiuri's destination Cruise shows for Dior celebrate the craftsmanship of artisans and heritage ateliers around the world, from Seville to Athens. For 2023, fans of Dior and dazzling handiwork alike are in for a treat, as today the Parisian maison staged a pre-fall show in Mumbai, in celebration of India's excellence in embroidery, embellishment and textiles.
>
> (Hawkins 2023)

Similarly, a description of the designer Gabriela Hearst's collaborations with Navajo and Bolivian artisan centres the designer as the driver and initiator of these initiatives, saying: "Gabriela Hearst knows how to give a good collaboration" (Allaire 2022) and further elaborating on the designer's creative decisions and leading role she played in the collaborations with craftspeople she initiated. It is through a contact with established brands and designers that crafts and artisanship are claimed to move forward and modernise: "It was a thoughtful nod to the exquisite craftsmanship that's often found within Indigenous culture. And for Earth Day, Hearst is only continuing this spirit forward" (Allaire 2022).

Even though craftspeople and artisans are sometimes praised for their own merit – it is through the gatekeeping of established designers and collaborations with famous brands that their work and craft garner attention and recognition of fashion media. Such takes on artisanship aptly represent the aspirational status that star designers have in the industry, but also do little to contest the dichotomy between active, entrepreneurial designers, integrated in the Western fashion system and artisans, who appear to be momentarily elevated by such collaborations. Paradoxically, while fashion media routinely claim how important and indispensable artisans and craftspeople are to the industry, this lack of coverage of artisanal communities, testifies to the contrary.

In their foregrounding of the figure of a designer or creative director, fashion media offer limited representations of craft, focusing only on those elements of craftsmanship and artisanal work, which are instrumental and useful for fashion brands. The publications highlight the traditional crafts that are productive and monetisable, by being involved into the production of luxury-fashion products. References to craft and artisanship that are not integrated in the fashion system are erased from fashion media's discourses. This testifies to a broader orientation of fashion media towards capitalist productivity and its embrace of neoliberal entrepreneurial values. Just as entrepreneurship is consistently praised and promoted in neoliberal discourses, fashion craftspeople, and artisans gain ever more validation in fashion media, as they engage in entrepreneurial efforts and are integrated in the global markets of labour and production.

The focus on the involvement of a famous designer may also be viewed as a testimony to the rise of celebrity humanitarianism (Brough 2012), in which a famous person's participation in humanitarian relief emerges as a reputational asset within the economy of visibility. The humanitarian action of helping artisanal communities thus appears to be a resource that ensures a heightened visibility and accrual of social and cultural capital for a designer or a brand. At the same time, the paradigm of celebrity humanitarianism reinforces the contrast between a Western celebrity designer and (non-)Western artisan, the latter always assumed to be in trouble. The issues that are assumed to plague artisans' communities are repeated from article to article – poverty, lack of education, or lack of access to the global fashion market. The socio-political reasons behind them, however, are seldom addressed – in one example Vogue UK includes a brief criticism of India's government's failing COVID-19 response as the reason behind the drastic worsening of conditions for Indian artisans in 2020, but immediately shifts responsibility to support Indian craftspeople's community to Western designers:

> Before this second wave set in, India's textile and apparel industry had already been devastated by the pandemic. Brands cancelled or refused to pay for orders last spring, leaving millions of factory workers and artisans in India, Bangladesh, Cambodia and beyond out of jobs. (The #PayUp petition successfully moved dozens of companies to pay what they owed.) But even as consumer spending rebounds in the West, brands aren't placing orders like they used to; some are scaling back their collections, while others are moving production elsewhere, and that trickles down to the factory workers and artisans. The Worker Rights Consortium found that even the garment workers who have stayed employed are earning far less than in 2019.
>
> (Farra 2021)

Here, the West and India are put in opposition to each other: while the pandemic is less urgent in the West, India is undergoing a disastrous surge of COVID-19 cases. However, instead of looking into the political reasons behind that (designer Rahul Mishra is quoted as calling out inadequate governance, however, his words receive no further commentary), the magazine focuses on Western designers and brands as responsible for fixing the crisis within artisanal communities. In doing so, Vogue foregrounds corporate responsibility as a source of political change, but also urges Western designers to take responsibility for non-Western artisanal communities.

In the majority of the Vogue US and Vogue UK articles, the social issues affecting artisans appear to be constant and inherent, and their association with non-Western spaces is unquestioned and is shown as 'natural'. The unique socio-political challenges that crafts and artisanal communities face and the locally relevant, historical circumstances that have shaped them remain largely overlooked. In accordance with the neoliberal paradigm of the moral consumer citizenship (Littler 2012), an interference of a Western designer is shown in a cruelly optimistic way as a solution to the issues and problems affecting artisanal communities – they modernise the craft, upskill, and employ artisans, providing reformed and improved products of fashion craft to customers. Notably, artisans are referred to as a group or community and remain largely unnamed and unindividualised, in contrast to designers or entrepreneurs, who are referred to by name (Allaire 2022; Farra 2021; Hawkins 2023).

Thus, portrayals of artisans and artisanship in fashion media centre on the established fashion system, while further entrenching Orientalist and neocolonial discourses, as they situate artisans within the neoliberal economy of visibility. The Orientalist, essentialising representations of craftspeople's communities occur through frequent references to tradition, heritage, and century-old craft, which tend to emphasise an ongoing, unchanging nature of the craftspeople's labour, or, as one Vogue article puts it "wonders of the vast breadth of specialisms that have been passed down through centuries" (Mower 2023). In this last quote, referring to the 2023 Dior show in Mumbai, the history of Indian craft is simplified as an uninterrupted, linear, and continuous process that evokes the image of an unchanging, static culture.

Another article from Vogue India employs a yet more striking description of artisan women, who work for the brand Zazi Vintage:

> The latest collaboration with Kullvi Whims and its ancestral craft of knitting honours women who intuitively follow the cyclical rhythm of nature, singing songs of fertility, life and creation in the goddess temple. Up in the Himalayas, the goddess is said to have turned into a spider and woven a temple that is shaped like a web.
>
> (Tewari 2023)

In this quote, it is suggested that women artisans pursue their 'ancestral craft' 'intuitively' in accordance with traditional rituals. Their labour is thus reconfigured as their cultural essence, which is emphasised by allusions to intuition and a legend, which appear to explain the women's motivation for pursuing their artisanal craft. The passage evokes Wendy Brown's critique of (neo)colonial equations between non-Western people and their culture, which suggests that while the (presumably) Westernised subject *has* culture, colonial subjects "*are* culture" (Brown 2006, emphasis added). An invocation of eternal, unchanging crafts suggests that artisans are not only removed from the fashion industry but also from progress. This distance is then framed as problematic and in need of rectifying, which an interference of an internationally known designer or brand is believed to provide.

I'd like to note here that in Vogue India, the viewpoint on crafts and craftsmanship shifts. Similarly, artisanal labour is celebrated when established brands incorporate it into their offering, but fashion crafts are also discussed as an object of national pride. Associations between crafts and the nation occur, as articles mark the occasion of the National Handloom Day, continuously evoke the role of Gandhi in fostering khadi as part of a movement for national independence. The texts on craftsmanship highlight India's cultural diversity – as different parts and communities of India are linked to a variety of traditional crafts. Thus, an online article about India's President Droupadi Murmu's choice of sari for her swearing into the office reads: "The Santhali weave sari was not only a nod to her tribal roots, it also was a huge shout to the handloom heritage of this country. Santhali is a native weave form of East India, and in particular of her own state of Odisha that is worn by tribal people" (Assomull 2022). Here, the assumption is made that the president's choice of a sari elevates tribal people, yet, what remains unexamined is her affiliation with the ruling Bharatiya Janata Party (BJP), infamous for its divisive politics and state-level endorsement of discriminatory practices across India, which have pervasively and ongoingly affected tribal communities, communities of Adivasi and Muslim Indians. While the Indian Vogue focuses on instances that showcase the greatness of Indian crafts and their diversity, it avoids discussing the conditions of production of craft and living conditions of artisans amidst rampant communal tension and violence.

At the same time, Vogue India's pieces on artisanship indicate a tension between tradition and renewal, as they argue that crafts need to be "reformed not sustained" (as states Malika Verma, entrepreneur and founder of Border&Fall, a digital publication and creative agency, in an interview on the occasion of the National Handloom Day (Chou 2022)). Elsewhere, Vogue India wonders: "How do you infuse newness into a sacred, old weave? The textile heiress and CEO Palak Shah at Ekaya Banaras discusses material memory and breaking new ground in one of the country's most long-standing textile traditions" (Raniwala 2022). Another piece comments:

> A textile renaissance has gripped the country. The textile Industry (sic) is India's 2nd largest employment generating sector, but lately it has

> entered, perhaps, for the first time since Independence its popular era. Homegrown textiles and crafts are front and centre of fashion and lifestyle brand's marketing plans and words like thread counts, handspun weaving clusters are part of a new fashion vocabulary. There is a renewed interest in heritage weaves, but as long as they takes *(sic)* us forward.
>
> (Makhija 2022)

The examples above demonstrate the contradiction between a celebration of fashion craft and the need to include it in the fast-paced fashion industry, modernise it, and make it an entrepreneurial cause, which occurs through designers and facilitators, embedded in the industry. Such readings have a lot of similarities with global discourses on fashion designers' modernising grip of crafts, but they also resonate with India's nationalist discourse, which prioritises technical progress and sees modernisation of the tradition as a sign of India's national greatness (Mazzarella 2003). This paradoxical convergence of themes also demonstrates how comfortably fashion magazines accommodate contradictory and seemingly incongruous discourses, but also how easily neoliberal sensibility adapts to local conditions.

Conclusion

This chapter has addressed discourses on fashion crafts and fashion's artisanal communities in three Vogue magazines, published in the USA, UK, and India. The intent of this chapter was not to denounce the many initiatives that focus on helping artisans and work to sustain and elevate their craft, but to cast a critical gaze on fashion media's approaches to fashion craftsmanship and artisanship. Situating contemporary craftsmanship discourses within the economy of visibility and addressing them against the backdrop of postcolonial and neoliberal critique, the chapter has pointed out a number of paradoxes and inconsistencies in mainstream media's discourses on fashion and craftsmanship.

Within mainstream fashion media, represented here by selected Vogue magazines, crafts, and artisanship are placed in the position of a double entanglement – while traditional crafts and artisanal communities are revered for their sustainable ways, predicated precisely on being removed from and located outside of the Western fashion industry, their inclusion in the fashion industry and involvement with fashion industry become conditions for their prominence and visibility in fashion media. Modernisation of fashion crafts is an ongoing trope within fashion media that risks reiterating Orientalist and neocolonial stereotypes about stagnant non-Western craftsmanship, steeped in tradition, and dynamic Western fashion. An involvement of a designer, integrated in the Westernised fashion system, operates as a driver for the modernisation of crafts, but also an instance of brand activism, portraying a Western brand or designer as a benefactor to struggling communities. This contradiction testifies to a limited capacity of mainstream fashion media to meaningfully engage with historical power imbalances or address neocolonial power structures within the fashion industry.

Although this chapter notes the similarities in the approaches to artisans across titles, it also hints to differences in their takes. In one instance, Vogue UK attempts a politically engaged look at the Indian artisans, dispensing with the Orientalist discussion of timeless heritage and tradition and situating them within the political context of the pandemic-time India. In Vogue India, however, the discourse of fashion craftsmanship is built upon the nationalist myth of India's 'unity in diversity' that stands in stark contradiction with the divisive right-wing politics of the state's ruling party BJP. While Vogue India portrays fashion crafts as worthy of national pride and celebration, it also calls on further modernisation of fashion artisanship in line with India's nationalist discourse.

Far from being an exhaustive analysis of craftsmanship discourses in mainstream fashion media, this chapter is an attempt to complicate and challenge our approaches to craftsmanship and to question their embeddedness in harmful and unproductive neoliberal and neocolonial structures of power. In its critique of mainstream fashion media, the chapter calls for a need to see discourses on sustainability as part of a larger historical context.

References

Ahmed S. (2010). *The promise of happiness*. Durham: Duke University Press.

Appadurai, A. (1990). Disjuncture and difference in the global cultural economy. *Theory, Culture & Society*, 7(2–3) 95–310. https://doi.org/10.1177/026327690007002017

Ballaster, R. (1991). *Women's worlds: Ideology, femininity and the women's magazine*. London: Macmillan Education.

Banet-Weiser, S. (2013). *Authentic TM*. New York: New York University Press.

Banet-Weiser, S. (2018). *Empowered: Popular feminism and popular misogyny*. Durham: Duke University Press.

Banet-Weiser, S., & Higgins, K. C. (2022). Television and the 'honest' woman: Mediating the labour of believability. *Television & New Media*, *23*(2), 127–144.

Berlant, L. (2011). *Cruel optimism*. Durham: Duke University Press.

Brough, M. M. (2012). "Fair vanity": The visual culture of humanitarianism in the age of commodity activism. In S. Banet-Weiser & R. Mukherjee (Eds.), *Commodity activism: Cultural resistance in neoliberal times* (pp. 174–194). New York: New York University Press.

Brown, W. (2006). *Regulating aversion: Tolerance in the age of identity and empire*. Princeton: Princeton University Press.

Dosekun, S. (2020). *Fashioning postfeminism: Spectacular femininity and transnational culture. Dissident Feminisms*. University of Illinois Press.

Duffy, B. E. (2013). *Remake, remodel: Women's magazines in the digital age*. Urbana, IL: University of Illinois Press.

Fairclough, N., & Wodak, R. (1997). Critical discourse analysis: An overview. In T. van Dijk (Ed.), *Discourse and interaction* (pp. 67–97). London: Sage.

Fairclough, N. (1995). *Critical discourse analysis: The critical study of language*. London and New York: Longman.

Frater, J., & Hawley, J. (2018). A hand-crafted slow revolution: Co-designing a new genre in the luxury world. *Fashion, Style & Popular Culture*, *5*(3), 299–311.

Gill, R., & Kanai, A. (2020). Woke? Affect, neoliberalism, marginalised identities and consumer culture. *New Formations: A Journal of Culture/Theory/Politics, 102*, 10–27.

Gill, R., & Orgad, S. (2018). The amazing bounce-backable woman: Resilience and the psychological turn in neoliberalism. *European Journal of Cultural Studies, 23*(2), 286–306. https://doi.org/10.1177/1360780418769673

Jansen, M. A., & Craik, J. (2016). Introduction. In M. A. Jansen & J. Craik (Eds.), *Modern fashion traditions: Negotiating tradition and modernity through fashion* (pp. 1–22). New York: Bloomsbury.

Jay, P. (2017). On Indian minimalism. *Vestoj*. Retrieved September 28, 2023, from http://vestoj.com/on-indian-minimalism/

Keller, J. (2020). A politics of snap: Teen Vogue's public feminism. *Signs: Journal of Women in Culture and Society, 45*(4), 817–843. https://doi.org/10.1086/707797

Lazzarato, M. (1996). Immaterial labour. In P. Virno & M. Hardt (Eds.), *Radical thought in Italy: A potential politics* (pp. 133–151). Minneapolis: University of Minnesota Press.

Littler, J. (2012). Good housekeeping: Green products and consumer activism. In S. Banet-Weiser & R. Mukherjee (Eds.), *Commodity activism: Cultural resistance in neoliberal times* (pp. 76–92). New York: New York University Press.

Mazzarella, W. (2003). 'Very Bombay': Contending with the global in an Indian advertising agency. *Cultural Anthropology, 18*(1), 33–71.

Ong, A. (2017). *Neoliberalism as exception: Mutations in citizenship and sovereignty*. Durham: Duke University Press.

Potter, J., Edwards, D., & Wetherell, M. (1993). A model of discourse in action. *The American Behavioral Scientist, 36*(3), 383–401. https://doi.org/10.1177/0002764293036003008

Potter, J., & Wetherell, M. (1987). *Discourse and social psychology: Beyond attitudes and behaviour*. London: Sage.

Rocamora, A. (2009). *Fashioning the city: Paris, fashion and the media*. London: Tauris.

Winship, J. (1987). *Inside women's magazines*. London: Pandora Press.

Said, E. (2003). *Orientalism*. London: Penguin Books.

Simmel, G. (1957). Fashion. *American Journal of Sociology, 62*(6), 541–558. (Reprinted from 1904, *International Quarterly, 10*, 130-155).

Wodak, R. (2014). Critical discourse analysis. In R. Wodak (Ed.), *Critical discourse analysis* (pp. 302–316). London: Sage.

Sources:

Allaire, C. (2022, April 22). Gabriela Hearst partnered with Bolivian artisans on chic, handcrafted bags. *Vogue UK*. Retrieved August 31, 2023, from https://www.vogue.co.uk/fashion/article/gabriela-hearst-bolivian-artisans-collaboration

Assomull, S. (2022, July 27). How the choice of a handloom white sari has made President Droupadi into a style icon. Vogue India. Retrieved August 31, 2023, from https://www.vogue.in/fashion/content/how-the-choice-of-a-handloom-white-sari-has-made-president-droupadi-into-a-style-icon

Chou, C. (2022, August 7). Why handloom needs to be reformed, not 'sustained'. *Vogue India*. Retrieved August 31, 2023, from https://www.vogue.in/fashion/content/why-handloom-needs-to-be-reformed-not-sustained

Farra, E. (2021, May 10). How designers can support India's artisans & factories amid the COVID-19 crisis. *Vogue UK*. Retrieved August 31, 2023, from https://www.vogue.co.uk/fashion/article/india-covid-19-crisis

Hawkins, L. (2023, March 30). 5 things to know about Dior's craft-focused Pre-Fall 2023 show in Mumbai. *Vogue UK*. Retrieved August 31, 2023, from https://www.vogue.co.uk/gallery/dior-pre-fall-2023-mumbai-5-things-to-know

Makhija, V. (2022, August 22). Sutr Santati by Abheraj Baldota Foundation celebrates 75 years of India with a contemporary take on Indian crafts. *Vogue India*. Retrieved August 31, 2023, from https://www.vogue.in/fashion/content/sutr-santati-by-abheraj-baldota-foundation-celebrates-75-years-of-india-with-a-contemporary-take-on-indian-crafts

Mower, S. (2023, March 31). Christian Dior's Mumbai show spotlights the extraordinary craftsmanship of India's artisans. *Vogue US*. Retrieved August 31, 2023, from https://www.vogue.com/article/christian-dior-pre-fall-2023-mumbai-chanakya-foundation

Raniwala, P. (2022, March 22). How the sacred old Banarasi textile is finding 21st century prevalence. *Vogue India*. Retrieved August 31, 2023, from https://www.vogue.in/fashion/content/how-the-sacred-old-banarasi-textile-is-finding-21st-century-prevalence

Tewari, B. (2023, January 2). This vintage label is reviving the crafts and weaves of India with a style-forward appeal. *Vogue India*. Retrieved August 31, 2023, from https://www.vogue.in/fashion/content/this-vintage-label-is-reviving-the-crafts-and-weaves-of-india-with-a-style-forward-appeal

8 An embroidery diary

Ioana Corduneanu

Needle trails on the Silk Roads

If I had been to keep a diary of this trip to Central Asia, rather than making it a written one, I would have embroidered it! It would have been easier for me to work my impressions with needle and thread directly into the fabric. My affinity to this craft goes back to my childhood and my very roots. I was born in Bucharest, Romania, in 1975, and raised by my extended family, three generations living under the same roof. Before I'd even started school, my grandma, who happened to be a teacher, took the opportunity to educate me *outside* of the system that she knew so well. She gave me a pen and paper, watercolours, fabric and sewing needles and she said: "Now you can share your imagination with us. Write, draw, paint, embroider. We'll understand you". So, I've been working with all these tools ever since, and needle has remained one of my best friends throughout. But I can't use it right now in this book to take you along with me, into this world rich in textures and colours, patterns and symbols. I have only the keyboard to convince you that embroidery is a language. It is a visual, universal language, with regional dialects that do not coincide with words in the spoken language.

Embroidery has never been merely ornamental. It has always also fulfilled practical, functional roles as well as being a form of communication: It reveals beliefs and superstitions, aspirations and prayers and addresses the ultimate desire of all – the desire to be seen as special, unique, even powerful! It can be an expression of status. The meanings of embroidered symbols are not often documented, but can usually be 'decoded' using contextual evidence and various 'keys' hidden in spoken folklore. Embroidery and storytelling often go hand in hand with metaphors. The colours of the yarns set the tone of voice, expressing emotions.

Traditional Romanian embroidery is a melting pot which has shown me the connectedness of the craft. Bucharest has never looked like your typical European capital. It functioned as a place of passage, opening doors between east and west, north and south. Even in the instance that written testimony should have vanished, the memory of the commerce that brought the city to life lingers on embroidered artifacts. Saxon smocking techniques mix with

DOI: 10.4324/9781003508076-11

precious metallic accents brought from Jaipur. Due to this internationality in embroidery, I knew I wouldn't need much English, Uzbek or Russian words to communicate with Uzbek artisans. Because my fingers speak a dialect of Uzbek embroidery. One of the many techniques we often use is presented by Therese de Dillmont in her Encyclopaedia of Needlework as the "Roumanian stitch" (de Dillmont 1890, pp. 542–544). It is, in fact, a variation of the famous Bukhara stitch.

In Romania, this embroidery technique is alive and well, even if it was at some point in danger of being replaced by velvet inserts. But it is still practiced, it is acknowledged and spoken for. I was curious to get to see it for myself in Bukhara, Uzbekistan, but didn't want to get my hopes up. Uzbekistan hasn't necessarily had the best context for crafts to thrive in recent and modern history. Its lands were absorbed into the Russian Empire, almost at the same time as Bessarabia. Travelling to this area, as well as to parts of Ukraine, illuminates the lasting effects of the occupation. The Russian language had been imposed on people, the new alphabet – conducted to similar effects. When asked by one of our colleagues, in one of the workshops of the Responsible Fashion Series in Tashkent, the Uzbek artisans spoke with the same longing I once heard from Moldavian artisans: "We want to reconnect to our roots, we need to remember who we are". In some other parts of the world, there are people who had the dubious privilege to break away from their roots, because they chose efficiency, profit and economic power. Some of their artisans kept functioning, appreciated or not, as rare birds performing for very few.

Meeting the artisans from Uzbekistan and Kazakhstan alike was for me like meeting long-lost sisters that were never too far away. I organised one of the workshops in Tashkent as a place of exchange about and with craft. I had brought various embroidery materials to stitch with and also showed some examples of *blouses roumaines* which were either embroidered with traditional patterns or with experimental ornaments and symbols to tell a story around current issues, i.e. sustainability. There were no translation issues in this communication, just using cloth and needle (Figure 8.1).

Embroidery is like a store of information. It isn't static though; it can be transformed and communicated in many different ways. It connects crafters even digitally. As can be seen in Figure 8.2, the smartphone is an important tool in the crafters community.

It's also a joy to engage with those who have never tried embroidery. They are open-minded and so they learn faster than those who have to overcome their familiar barriers. During the last 12 years since I started *Semne Cusute*, I met with so many beginners, so often holding their hand as they make that first step, picking up the embroidery needle. It is impossible to remember all of their names or their faces. But I remember hands. I keep these memories of them taking their first stitch. There is a lot of emotion that goes into it, there is hesitation, hope, some sort of leap of faith. That you will come out on the other side of the fabric in the right spot. The

Figure 8.1 Workshop in Tashkent.

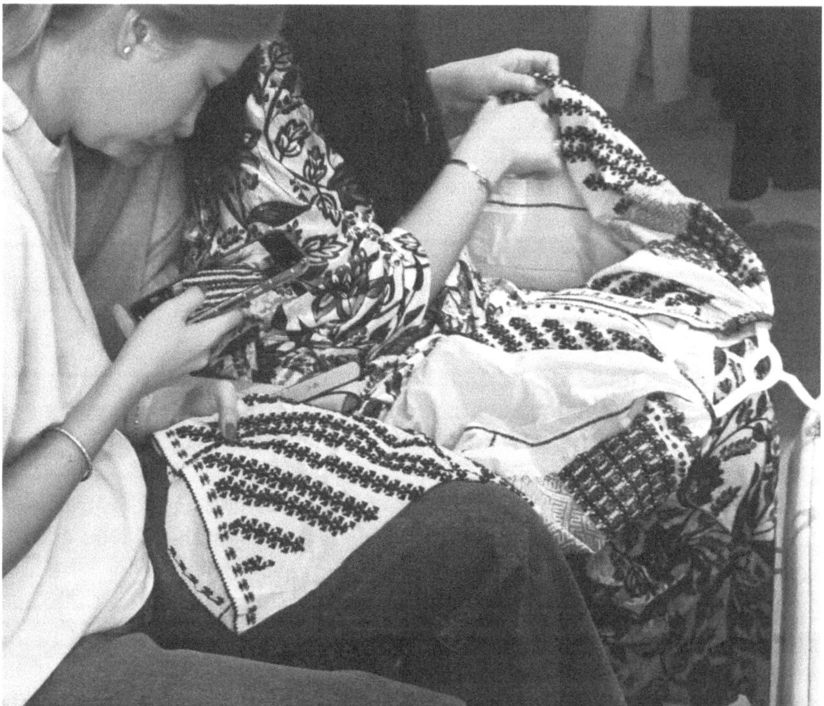

Figure 8.2 Embroidery networks are formed through social media and other digital connections.

sinuous path of the needle on the front and back of the fabric is one of the strongest motifs used for the borders in both Uzbek and Romanian embroidery. Always on the edge, protecting the borders of your whole textile universe, this sinuous path with its rhythm of ups and downs, is the essence and the symbol of a journey. It's a succession of ups and downs, achievements and failures, good times and bad times. For us as people and artisans, and for the crafts themselves. Adorned with suns, stars or with flowers, as a prayer for a meaningful journey through life: "May flowers bloom ahead of you and may you leave flowers behind".

Shared impressions, page by page

One of the important embroideries that have weathered the difficult time of cultural suppression during Soviet reign in the region is *suzani*. This is going to be an important term for our story. The word refers to a Uzbeki embroidery style, but it is derived from the Persian *suzan* (سوزن) and means 'needle', 'the art of the needle', 'needlework' or even simply 'embroidery'. The fame of this craft is also palpable in southern Romanian villages. "Oh, this was made with a Persian Needle", elderly women will say, admiring the rich, fluffy embroideries of the vintage shirts their mothers made during their youth. As of this moment, there are enough vintage *suzani* textiles to be sold off on the internet and in tourist spots across Uzbekistan. But make no mistake, the sellers are not artisans, and the tourists bargain for coats covered in *suzani* motifs that actually belong on home textiles. Unfortunately, being eye-catching is enough for consumer-fashion.

Each *suzani* I admired on this trip would deserve at least a couple of pages to fully appreciate the mark it has left on me. I often find myself wondering what impression other people see in the same piece of embroidery. Sometimes I wonder, if embroidery has the power to reflect, like a mirror, exactly what the viewer needs or wants to see. Upon initial observation, we all tend to focus on the colours and shapes. Perhaps it would be beneficial to consider that embroidery should not only be slow in its creation but also in its 'consumption'. Perhaps it would be more rewarding to meditate on it as if it were a painting. It is also worth noting that each individual's perception of an image is influenced by their cultural background, personal experiences and the tales they have heard.

There are a number of different types of compositions for *suzanis* found in Uzbekistan, and for me, it is impossible to admire them without comparing them with similar narratives found in Romanian textiles, which constitute my 'mother's tongue'. I believe that the same motivations and hopes are expressed in shapes that are different mainly because of the different environments and available resources. It could be said that it is the same world and the same heaven, seen from a slightly different angle.

Some *suzani* designs feature unusual trees that appear to expand across the fabric. They appear to grow and hold, in their sinuous branches, a variety of entities brought together: tulips, pomegranate, almond flowers and even graceful birds. For my eyes, this tree is not as impossible as it may first appear. It would be an incorrect assumption to think that this embroidery is simply a depiction of the real world. It would be futile to compete with nature or create an image that you can already see around you. It is possible that this tree could be considered the tree of life. Its roots connect the underworld with the sky, and it could be argued that everything important in life is included there. I must admit that I am not at all surprised to see tulips growing in a tree. I've often observed the branches of this tree bearing wheat, birds and bees attracted by the buds, and of course, stars.

During Romanian rituals, the tree of life embodies a real tree and provides a comforting presence during significant moments of passage. For us, the tree of life is a fir tree. For a wedding, a young tree is cut and decorated with flowers cut from paper, with ceremonial bread, baked in the shape of birds (hence the wheat). Similarly, for a funeral, a similar tree is prepared by relatives and friends. The tree is there with us, as it is believed to act as a spiritual elevator, connecting the underworld with the sky. It is possible to pray to a tree, and it is also possible to pass secrets or wishes to a tree. No matter how surreal a tree might appear on a *suzani*, I would find it to be familiar and reassuring. I've read so much about this subject, but I just can't see these *suzani* with the tree of life motif in any other way. I feel like the concept is too deeply rooted in my part of the world.

Also, there are *suzani* with gardens, which, at least to my eye, resemble heaven. It is a conceptual image and not a depiction of reality. The climate is not particularly friendly for such vegetation to grow spontaneously: it must be cultivated and tended. In reality, the climate in Central Asia is rather dry.

It could be said that water is a symbol for life. When a new life is welcomed into this world, water is also spilled, not only blood. It's thought that spilling water on the graves of the departed is a kind of metaphorical gesture expressing the hope for their rebirth in the afterlife. The presence of water, depicted as fountains, or vases holding flowers, or gardens full of flowers, is a symbol of the hope for the soul's immortality. And vegetation is a clear sign of the presence of water. It's totally normal not to represent water directly, like in drops, rain, waves or rivers. It would be a pity to be so direct when we can be so poetic using a needle. On traditional Romanian shirts, we embroider vines or meandros full of leaves and flowers and we call them 'rivers'.

And now you might be wondering what the point is of thinking about death and heaven when, in fact, it's about a young girl working on her embroidered dowry. But it was only natural for her, as she prepared for her wedding, to think about all the changes in her life and the new role she would take on in her new home. Her future life should feel like heaven: cultivated and tended. She'll have a new family to look after with lots of wisdom and diplomacy. Each flower might be carrying her thoughts and reminding her of those moments and her initial goals in the future. Just picture her female relatives helping her with her embroidery, chatting to her and sharing their experiences. They all remain connected through the delicate silk threads.

I was taught that heaven is depicted on rugs with strong borders, which are well defined and protected, not by angels, actually, but by the wolf's fangs symbol and also by a river. The Uzbek heaven depicted in *suzani* is also firmly defined by borders. The Romanian heaven depicted on the carpets is often black, reminiscent of fertile earth and populated with wheat, basil flowers, mallows and lily of the valley. These rugs are woven from wool threads, which provide a solid, stable and reassuring presence.

In fact, both Romanian rugs and Uzbek *suzani* heavens are displayed on walls, functioning as thermal proofing. And I like to believe I can comprehend the concept of a tranquil, serene and gracious heaven as depicted in Uzbekistan. Yes, it is important to define your personal idea of harmony before marriage and work for it, no matter your cultural background. Even if the Uzbek heaven is bright and floating, while our heaven is dark and anchored, I believe they are equally wonderful. Could I address the readers and ask how they imagine heaven and how would they depict it only with needle and thread? It would be an interesting exercise.

There are also examples of *suzani* with stars, displayed in a precise order. It might be said that six, eight or nine entities, round in shape with a halo, are sufficient to express the idea of stars. Again, there is no need or point in trying to imitate the night sky. The stars were of great significance to our ancestors who lived in tune with nature. The night sky was their map, before the compass was invented. The night sky was their planner, before the calendar was invented. Observing the night sky was of great importance to our ancestors, as when certain stars align, they serve as a signal for an important event. The farmers would plan their activities around these signals. They would have been awaiting further guidance from the earth, which might have sent subtle indications through certain insects or birds: 'now it's the right time for plowing', 'now it's the right time for mowing' and so on. A well-planned life, a predictable life, was a safer life, leaving you less exposed to the unpredictable. However, at a certain point, the narrative of our cultures, Uzbek and Romanian, undergoes a transformation. Romanian tales don't teach us to resign ourselves to a fate 'written in the stars'. There is no fixed path and each of us has the opportunity to design our own course in life and to make our own choices. As children, we were told that future is shaped by the choices and actions we make, and we are continually presented with challenges; courage, empathy and truth are always rewarded, at least in the stories.

Despite my best efforts, I was unable to identify this concept within the Uzbek *suzani*. None seems to be showing the story of a girl who left into the world to reshape her future, trying to overcome her condition. But there is a future and there is a hope for new ideas and realities to be embroidered.

Embroidery, no matter how intricate, is not the only way to understand a culture. And it's not a shortcut for this. It would seem that there are now many 'dictionaries of symbols' available, which may be of interest to those who wish to gain a quick insight into a foreign culture. Even if based on fragments of truth, they are in the best scenario a window opened to a different set of values and beliefs. While we can see through it, I wonder if we can really find the door to cross over to the other side. And this is why I will never risk 'translating' the Uzbek *suzani* and their symbols. I have only dared to describe the way I perceive them, in my own circumstances, dictated by my background.

Let's turn the page now! In some cases, it might be useful to take a closer look at the reverse side of the embroidery as well. However, I feel it is not the most respectful thing to do, and I try to avoid it if the author is present and I don't really intend to study or buy that piece.

Some embroidery techniques employ an unusual thick thread to enhance the texture and volume of the patterns. It is therefore difficult to distinguish between them, as they tend to merge into one another. In order to reproduce or archive the pattern in a digital, vectorial format, it might be helpful to view the backside of the fabric, where the thread is tensed.

Another reason to view the reverse of the fabric is to ascertain whether the embroidery techniques have been executed correctly. This can also provide some insight into the degree to which cultural influences have been absorbed by a particular region. If I may offer an example, it would be Romanian embroidery using gold thread. It was therefore of great interest to me to see that the technique is still in use in Bukhara. It seems that in the south-west region of Romania, women had the opportunity to study closely the oriental textiles that carried these techniques used for gold thread embroidery. It is only when you study the reverse side of the fabric that you discover that the gold thread is kept only at the visible part of the cloth, being fixed by almost invisible cotton threads. This is the correct way to operate with this type of thread. Similarly, in Jaipur, in India and Buchara, in Uzbekistan. Even if the metallic thread is now less precious, as it is produced from a copper alloy rather than gold, it is still fragile. It is possible that the metallic thread deteriorates from friction in the eye of the needle and also from the fabric.

In contrast, women from the far north-east regions of Romania were less exposed to oriental/Ottoman textiles and trade, which might have meant that they had less opportunity to see and study original pieces on the backside. They tried to achieve a similar effect, using the metallic thread as they would any other embroidery thread. While they look amazing, they do put both the fabric and the metallic threads and flat band at risk. In some cases, it might be advisable to study the reverse side of the fabric in order to avoid having to devise a solution to a problem that may already have a perfect solution elsewhere.

I have observed that some people may look at the reverse side of an embroidery to identify knots or imperfections, in order to determine if the piece was hand-made. However, this can sometimes be a challenging and unreliable method. It is possible to create exquisite pieces, with specific patterns and embroidery techniques that allow double-face embroidery to be used on see-through fabrics. However, there are also plenty of ways to hide both ends of the yarns within the intricate embroidery, which serves to safeguard them. Sometimes, when the back side of the embroidery looks too close to perfection, we might be forgiven for assuming it was created for sale in the first place, by a person who practiced the craft by strict method. If the embroidery was not planned in all its details from the beginning, we may be able to trace the spontaneous changes by unexpected and apparently illogical jumps on the back, from one pattern to another.

Embroidery as sustainable practice?

Is Embroidery a sustainable practice? Embroidery is much more than a beautiful story; it is also a valuable practice in textile crafts. It could be said that embroidery was born as a sustainable practice in the first place, way before this word even existed. I must mention that Uzbekistan happens to be one of the best places in the world to support this statement.

Exploring in more detail, we find the answers contained in the fabric and in what we hope to achieve. Embroidery adds meaning to our textiles. However, that is not the main reason embroidery has been conceived of and practiced for so long. This form of visual communication can be seen only as an added value. In order to understand the true role of embroidery, we will take the wonderful textile crafts of Uzbekistan, one by one.

Perhaps we could consider whether we would like to communicate through vivid colours and hypnotic patterns. Ikat could offer the solution. The remarkable colour combinations that can be achieved through such a creative process are endless.

Perhaps we could consider adding graphics, shapes and symbols, through a method that is easy, and precise. A very good option is block-printing, which is a quick and effective way to add images to the entire surface of the fabric.

Perhaps we might consider expressing our social status through glamour. We can add gold and silver thread embroidery, which would undoubtedly make our message stand out.

Compared with the crafts mentioned above, perhaps embroidery doesn't look like an efficient way to achieve the desired results.

Perhaps it would be helpful to try to envision the fine, plain-woven fabric as a structure. When using fine, silky threads, this structure may not be as stable as it could be. So it would be important to reinforce it. Embroidery could be considered a solution, functioning for the fabric in a similar way to steel reinforcement for concrete. If we consider the garments of the aristocrats, people from the upper classes, we might find that this theory does not always stand up to scrutiny.

It is important to remember that the most valuable lessons regarding sustainable practices often come from people who are determined by circumstances to manage their modest resources with great care. It would be advisable for them to learn to plan in advance and to respect the advice offered by those with a lot of experience. That is why I consider that the everyday clothes created and worn by ordinary people are of most interest to this study. For instance, traditional Romanian clothes often feature specific embroidery, which is often found in the same areas, well defined and not randomly. Embroidery patterns are placed where they are needed, for instance along the hems and in areas where the fabric is tensed. It is important to note that respecting this placement for the embroidery goes beyond mere tradition. It is simply a wise way to make your own clothes. It might be the case that you simply need to embroider your shirts in certain places in order to ensure they will last longer, perhaps for more than a lifetime.

It seems reasonable to suggest that taking care of your clothes is a sustainable practice in itself. It would be advisable to wear them with care, wash them with care and keep them with care. And in the event that they tear, it would be advisable to repair and mend them properly. When we mend something, we try to do it in a way that is both long-lasting and aesthetically pleasing. If we consider the topic of care and planning, it might be said that embroidery is, in fact, a form of pre-mending. It should be in our understanding that the additional threads added to the fine fabric, intricately included into the structure, are there in fact to add strength and resistance. And since we understand that embroidery responds to a need, once we ensure that, we can afford to add extra value. It is an opportunity that we should not miss.

It might be said that traditional embroidery could be the answer to sustainable embroidery. It's practical, first and foremost, and that is the secret that has kept it alive. It's not something that is done just for fun or to pass the time.

Yes, it is important to note that not all types of embroidery can be considered sustainable. Embroidery is a slow process, which can sometimes be considered slow fashion. However, speed alone is not sufficient to make a craft sustainable. To earn this definition, it should bring real, solid and relevant benefits. It could be said that traditional embroidery is an expression of collective wisdom, observations passed and validated by generations. In my humble opinion, it is the most complex of all textile crafts. In order to do it right, it would be important to understand the properties of the natural fibres grown into a specific region, as well as the way they are processed through spinning and weaving. It would be beneficial to consider the climate and the comfort that the clothes must bring. It would be beneficial to gain an understanding of the main activities and occupations of the people for whom the garments are intended, in order to ascertain how the cutting patterns can be designed to ensure freedom of movement, while also providing thermal protection. It would be important to have an understanding of how a specific cutting pattern will use the fabric, and how it will resist all sorts of forces that may appear in its structure. It would be beneficial to gain an understanding of the properties of the embroidery yarns and select those that are compatible with the fabric. It would be crucial to gain an understanding of how these embroidery yarns perform at their best and which stitches and techniques complement them. In light of these considerations, it would be beneficial to identify those embroidery patterns that are most suitable for execution and representation, while ensuring compliance with the aforementioned technical requirements. Finally, it is important to be aware of the grammar of the symbols, which means using the selected patterns to reflect the narrative in a way that can be recognised and valued by the other members of the community. While abiding by these guidelines, it is also important to consider how to create an original composition that allows for the expression of creativity and personality.

It is indeed the case that embroidery can be carried on by strong fabrics as a beautiful ornament, a display of status and celebration of glamour. However, as the world changes and the powerful seek more impressive methods to display their wealth, they may choose to move away from embroidery, eventually replacing it with digital printed images. And of course, they should not be blamed or shamed.

However, there are instances where the roles are reversed, and embroidery can be used in a more strategic manner. It can be incorporated to reshape the silhouette, add resistance and even defy gravity. It is possible that this type of embroidery may have more chances of survival if people are aware of its role.

The delicate depiction of heaven seen on Uzbek *suzani* cannot simply levitate. It might bend under its own weight, considering also its large size. However, the fine silk cotton fabric is empowered by the rich silk threads embroidered on it, making it more compact. Our spiritual beliefs and traditions might change from a generation to another, but we must obey the laws of our planet, gravity included. Geometry, physics, chemistry, logic and new technologies are our allies and they will never go out of fashion. Embroidery embodies them in the most beautiful way.

I wish I could say this trip was a chance for me to discover the embroidery of Eurasia and Central Asia and get charmed by it. But that would be a platitude. Rather, this trip gave me the chance to take the pulse of this craft today, and also to form an impression of what lies ahead for it in its future. We will never know what could have been, for the crafts and artisans of Central Asia, without occupation. I am looking forward to returning to Uzbekistan in 20 years from now and already anticipate the changes. My wish for all artisans in Central Asia is that they can seize the bloom of opportunities awaiting them and contribute to their collective cultural dowry, leaving a legacy of stars, pomegranate and almond flowers behind.

And, I would also like to invite all readers to take this beautiful path that embroidery is offering and this can start anywhere: by getting on a flight to Tashkent or by opening a new browser window, for semnecusute.com.

References

de Dillmont, T. (1890). *Encyclopedia of needlework*. Mulhouse. Retrieved from https://archive.org/details/encyclopediaofne00dill/page/n7/mode/2up

UNESCO. (n.d.). *Caravanserais: Cross-roads of commerce and culture along the Silk Roads*. UNESCO Silk Roads Programme. Retrieved June 12, 2024, from https://en.unesco.org/silkroad/content/caravanserais-cross-roads-commerce-and-culture-along-silk-roads

9 Building inclusive culture through tradition, craft and emerging technologies

Elisabeth Lloyd Pfahl

Global trends and present shifts

Craft reminds *us* of where *we* came from and how *we* as community are evolving generationally. Examining the dynamics wherein craftspeople work today reveals the relevance of the decentering attributes afforded by tradition, creativity and hand-work within our global landscape. Fuelled by population shifts to urban centres, increasing job turnover, remote work, desires for convenience, environmental concerns and technology, there is a growing trend for individuals to reduce their material consumption footprint in favour of smaller or more temporary homes, personal mobility, flexible life-styles and renewable-repurposed products. The United Nations (UN) estimates that more than half of the world's population was residing in cities by 2007. To better understand consumers, it is important to consider that high-income countries throughout the world sustain 81% of their population in urban areas, while city dwellers comprise 58% of middle-income countries and 34% of low-income countries. Framing Silk Road regions within Ritchie et al.'s 2021 statistics, 58% of the Kazakhstan population and 50% of the Uzbekistan population lived in cities while 35% of the Indian population and 63% of the Chinese population were urban dwellers (Ritchie et al., 2018/2024). Global demand for metropolitan residences continues to increase, cost per urban square meter tends to be higher than that of rural property, and typically, financial realities dictate smaller homes with less space for material objects. Hence, the vast majority of the global consumer market needs to purchase less volume than two decades ago.

Remote work, new visa opportunities and Airbnb style property rentals drive global nomadism and afford a sense of home while never owning a bed or spoon. In 2022 with rising Western trends to seek hybrid work, voluntary U.S. employee turnover was estimated to increase nearly 20% from pre-pandemic averages (Gartner, 2022). There are now at least 61 countries that offer remote work visas (Mussari, 2024), and in large cities throughout the world, it is common to find visually-similar cafés teeming with a vast range of foreigners working on laptops. This influx provides local artisans with a more diversified consumer market. Urban bicycle/car rental and multi-drop

DOI: 10.4324/9781003508076-12

stations reduce the need for transportation ownership. One can pack a carry-on bag, land in a new country and step seamlessly into a fully functional everyday life with no need for acquisition.

Global desire for easy-access/least-friction consumption drives the development of digital subscription products and spearheads the *Convenience Revolution* (Hyken, 2018). Near-instant gratification is becoming an increasingly common consumer expectation. Subscription services enable consumers to use objects, content streaming and programs almost immediately and without physical ownership or long-term commitment to a particular product. Near paperless lives are enabled by small tablets containing thousands of books. Virtual digital mailboxes receive physical mail, scan envelopes, enable one to select items to be opened and receive emailed scans of desired documents. There is no need to be tied to a physical address in order to read physical mail (O'Reilly, 2024). Regional periodicals are accessible digitally from anywhere, and nearly all fiscal transactions can be accomplished without physical currency. Zoomed virtual business meetings, medical appointments and seminars are becoming the efficient normative expectation. Every month, new technological products further eliminate the needs for object ownership and provide new, endlessly changing landscapes of upgraded solutions. We exist in a state of constant flux as Kelly describes: "In the intangible digital realm, nothing is static or fixed. Everything is becoming" (2016).

Weekly shopping has become an increasingly digital activity delivered conveniently to doorstep or the curbside rather than involving routine human engagement (Charm et al., 2020). In 2022, 20% of all global sales were made online by 2.14 billion online shoppers who spent an estimated $5.5 trillion online. Global online sales are expected to reach $7.3 trillion in 2025 (Orzol & Szopik-Depczynska, 2023). Steady global online growth from 2015 to 2025 will continue to cause a reduction in physical retail spaces and in-person retail engagement (Reuter, 2023). Browsing for gifts has become an increasingly solitary afternoon at a desk rather than walking into fragrant, privately owned boutiques and chatting about product stories with shopkeepers.

Environmental concerns also have begun to reduce desires for new stuff (Moss & Bapna, 2020). *Reduce, reuse, recycle and up-cycle* has become today's environmental mantra (World Economic Forum, 2022). As an increasingly predominant part of consumer psychology (Coppola et al., 2021, this mindset encourages circular business models that reduce waste/lessen environmental impact (Jensen, 2022). Yet today all human-made *anthropogenic mass* outweighs global living bio-mass. And on average, there is more anthropogenic mass produced every week than the weight of each person on the planet (Elhacham et al., 2020). Our global stuff weighs more than all life on earth. The UN estimates that in 2022 a record 62 million tons (Mt) of e-waste was produced, an increase of 82% from 2010 and projected to rise another 32%, to 82 million tons, in 2030. The study concluded that only

1% of rare earth element needs are met by recycling (ITU, 2024). Companies address renewability challenges directly while continuing to sell new products. Apple offers recycling of all outdated Apple products and encourages customers to trade-in phones of all brands, iPads, laptops and Apple watches for credit on a new device (Apple, 2024).

Fortunately, increasing preferences for secondhand clothing are beginning to reduce consumer desire for new, more disposable fashion (Yang et al., 2024). Additionally, the use of recycled materials has begun to drive corporate identity and lure environmentally concerned consumption. In spring 2024, 98% of Patagonia's new collection used recycled materials that allowed them to avoid 8,500 metric tons of CO2e emission. According to the Environmental Protection Agency (EPA), this reduction is enough to power more than 1,070 homes for one year in the United States (Patagonia Inc., 2024a). Patagonia's "*Worn Wear*" program promotes reuse/longevity of garments by selling used Patagonia products (Patagonia Inc., 2024b). In Uzbekistan where 30% of the workforce is involved in cotton-related industries, there is a focus on sustainable cultivation methods (GIZ, 2020) and a resurgence of traditional, high-end, slow-production processes including handloomed Ikat (Gibson, 2015). From many angles, less is becoming more in our post-pandemic materialistic world.

Parallel to this observed reduction in object engagement, possession and amassing over the last few decades, Goldhaber (1997) built upon Simon's (1971) attention theory and concluded that the global economy is shifting from a physical object-based economy to one based on the capacity for human attention.[1] Goldhaber argued that the economic shift from material-based production/distribution to information-based production/management will be inherently backed by our most desirable and scarcest resource, attention. The rarity of our attention is due to time limitations. We each have only 1440 minutes/day to accomplish goals, identify ourselves within community and engage others (Kelly, 2016; Warzel, 2021). Goldhaber (1997) predicted in *Wired* that "As the net becomes an increasingly strong presence in the overall economy, the flow of attention will not only anticipate the flow of money, but eventually replace it altogether". Underlying the attention economy is the profitability of the data economy (Baeza-Yates & Fayyad, 2022). Our attention has become the product (Orlowski-Yang, 2020). This cyclical process of translating a private experience into a fungible commodity is known as Surveillance Capitalism (Zuboff, 2019). Today technology platforms profit from the monetization of our engagement/attention and then lure us back in as consumers of *like-interests*.

Not only has an attention/data-valued economy become common within Western societies, but so too has social isolation and loneliness (Kannan & Veazie, 2023; Thompson, 2024; Perfas, 2024). In America, the *Loneliness Epidemic* has become so wide spread that the U.S. Surgeon General released a 2023 report comparing the risk of premature death due to loneliness to that of smoking. Among six guidelines of the recently established *National*

Strategy to Advance Social Connection are recommendations to 1) maintain a relationship with technology that does not detract from *meaningful and healing connection* with others and 2) cultivate a *culture of connection* in the practices of everyday life (Murthy, 2023, May 3). Restated, to flourish within our rapidly shifting material/technological realities, we need to 1) be ever mindful of information philosopher Floridi's (2014) exploration of human connection with the *infosphere*[2] and his conclusion that the infosphere is becoming an inseparable part of individual understanding of self/culture, thereby reshaping human reality and 2) build and engage humanizing culture that fosters everyday social connection; meaningful human engagement; and healing contact. If, as Floridi explains, the infosphere exists as an integral part *within* the individual, then the individual can avoid loneliness by choosing to engage only those portions of the infosphere that enhance authentic human connection in everyday life/culture. As Harari (2022) reiterates: "Technology is never deterministic...it depends on the choices we make".

Theoretically social media could serve to connect differing groups, bridge social capital and expand understanding of others; however, social media is dividing us further. Algorithmic *like-us* filtering and a reduction in physical neighbourhood activities lessen the opportunity to engage and empathize with "other" (Vinnakota, 2017). Within social media communities, we are not tending to expand our frame of reference beyond self. While Millennials are more likely to identify as multiracial and adopt non-conventional gender identities than previous generations, they are not outpacing previous generations in their rejection of race/gender stereotypes (Johfre & Saperstein, 2019). Personal identification is being specified more openly, but racism, sexism and us-them are not reducing at the same pace. Boundaries, polarization and isolated group identification are being reinforced by choices in attention regardless of desires for individual identification, self-expression and self-acceptance.

Driven by the shift from object-based to attention-based monetization, search results derive increasingly from content with the greatest number of *hits* and the micromanagement of users' online activity. Designed to amass user data and rapidly grow big business, this approach breeds uniformity rather than providing an opportunity for the user to explore alternative or regional content (Born et al., 2021). In turn, this greatest user-response/personal-similarities-echo-chamber spurs an algorithmic homogenization of culture (Hynes, 2021). Ranging from TikTok to Spotify to Google, non-transparent, algorithmic curations channel a user's exposure to normative, predominantly mainstream, Western-influenced content and thereby, obstruct diverse human exchanges and creative potential throughout the world. This process reduces the visibility of both marginalized and cutting-edge genius that may require prolonged consideration before it resonates and is valued. In *Filterworld,* Chayka (2023, p. 9) explains: "By *flatness* I mean homogenization but also a reduction into simplicity: the least ambiguous, least disruptive, and perhaps least meaningful pieces of culture are promoted the most. Flatness is the lowest common denominator, an averageness that has never been the marker of humanity's proudest cultural creations". Content is being culled to show us *average* positioned at the top of the bell curve while innovative cutting-edge lies on the tails of the curve.

Algorithmic streaming platforms such as Netflix and Spotify not only influence user content feeds, and thereby the ability for users to select their own culture freely (Murindanyi et al., 2024), but also prompted the impactful Hollywood strike addressing inequitable changes in traditional distribution channels, copyright protection, salaries and artist's royalty structures (Zhuang, 2023). New product dissemination models that combine streaming, gaming and social platforms will afford increasingly interactive consumer experiences and allow profitable corporate mergers of artistic, influencer and content assets (Deloitte, 2024).

Today all creatives stand on shifting ground where machine learning can appropriate existing human works and extrapolate new output indefinitely and with efficiency greater than much of human capacity. In other words, hand-makers and laborers are not alone; millions of additional professionals face transformational shifts in their *crafts* within upcoming years. Rapidly evolving AI imaging, writing and analytics programs are aiding a vast creative and intellectual workforce engaged in activities including architectural rendering, graphic design, content writing, coding, accounting, investments, diagnostic medicine and legal counsel. A February 2024 Pew Research Poll suggests that 20% of American adults working for pay used ChatGPT to aid tasks at work, whereas in March 2023, the same group polled at 8% (Pew, 2024). In one year, the professional American employment of ChatGPT has more than doubled. Rather than causing human obsolescence, AI platforms appear to be serving, at least in part, as new tools for individuals to increase productivity and, potentially, spark new layers of meaningful culture.

Not only is human culture being impacted algorithmically, but now GenAI machines are generating independent machined culture. Today we begin to observe novel, dual-cultural interaction between human culture and machine culture (GenAI/Intelligent machine output) in the process of meaning making (Natale & Guzman, 2022). Increasingly, since the 2000s, algorithms have impacted means by which cultural content *transmits* and consequently what one can *select*. Now for the first time in history, GenAI is generating new cultural *variation*. As seen analogously within physical Darwinian evolution (Darwin, 1872), significant changes in input to cultural traits (*variation)*, cultural replication (*transmission*) and cultural success (*selection*) alter cultural evolution (Max Planck Institute, 2024). In "Machine Culture", Brinkmann et al. (2023) propose the following roadmap and structure for identifying and understanding these moments of massive cultural evolutionary flux: "**a**, Novel cultural artefacts are generated through machines. **b**, Machines transmit and potentially mutate cultural artefacts. **c**, Machines select between different cultural artefacts. **d**, Humans select among diverse machines". Can this four-part exchange between human and machined cultures yield cultural artifacts that encourage regional inclusivity, exceptional fringe creativity and human flourishing or will it become a greater homogenizing blender?

Parekh (2002) suggested that "No culture embodies all that is valuable in human life and develops the full range of human possibilities. Different cultures thus...complement each other, [and] expand each other's horizon of thought". If so, machine culture holds the potential to further expand human experience, communication, connection and, perhaps, to create an entirely new human–machine discourse. Brinkmann et al.'s (2023) model suggests a significant, inextricable, increasing engagement between human and machined cultural artifacts over time and, potentially, a reciprocal relationship between human and machine. Accessing this human-machine *transmission* is an essential and ongoing task to ensure a collectively positive, inclusive human-machine co-evolution of the greatest benefit to humanity. Change, a constant "becoming", (Kelly, 2016) is inevitable, and the more awareness and imagination we invest into human culture–machine culture engagement, the richer and more productive the potential outcomes.

Present challenges for handmade production

For centuries throughout the world, craftspeople (and farmers) have been society's backbone, creating products deemed necessary for daily personal life and reflective of community and culture. Continuing today, the hand-making sector is the second largest global employer after agriculture and is comprised primarily of women, youth and rural populations. Hand-making often incorporates frequently evolving, smaller-batch productions grounded in circular economic principles, regional traditions, local materials and broad-ranging appeal to global markets (Phillips, 2021).

Craft traditions always have involved replication and new iterations as society and technology evolve. As Western aid programs accelerated in the 1970s and 1980s, governmental/international public-private initiatives successfully developed market-savvy handmade products and distribution channels, but many programs failed to cultivate local design-thinking skills or sustainable global sales platforms necessary to stimulate further significant independent product evolution and fiscal growth. These observations are evident within multiple cases in Pakistan, India, Indonesia, Cambodia, Laos, Bangladesh and Sri Lanka (Bembatoum-Young et al., 2000; Majeed et al., 2023).

All the following discussions on hand-making draw directly upon my participant observations, training, collaboration and living with artisans of China, Myanmar, Thailand, Nepal, Tibet, India and Pakistan during the past 19 years (2005–2024). Artisan educational training and fiscal support platforms can make significant impact. Most artisans work independently or in isolated village clusters where there is an immense need for public-private-corporate global support. More direct artisan-consumer sales platforms and expansion of micro-loans are necessary to float material costs and unpredictable distribution issues, such as those experienced dramatically during COVID-19 (Jaitly et al., 2023). The Silk Road tourism project is one example of an ongoing initiative that has addressed educational, fiscal and job creation for 31 years (UNESCO, 2024). It was introduced at the UN Tourism's General Assembly in Indonesia in 1993 with missions of promoting: (1) Cooperation/regional prosperity/stability, (2) a high-quality tourism brand and (3) natural/cultural richness of Silk Road regions (UN Tourism, 2018).

In considering challenges of craft production and creative outputs since the 2010s, it is essential to analyze the impact of artisan *inspiration* drawn so heavily from the Internet/apps. Mobile phone access and inexpensive data enable artisans to *surf* endlessly for images of perceived market demand and to replicate. Just as Chayka observes in *Filterworld* "The culture that thrives in filterworld tends to be accessible, replicable, participatory, and ambient. It can be shared across wide audiences and retain its meaning across different groups, who tweak it slightly to their own ends" (Chayka, 2023, p. 5). Increasingly, we see much global craft becoming a homogenized consumable or reproduced by lower quality, less costly techniques. Resulting outputs range from misunderstood consumer desires to average to the rare, irregularly glistening gem. As Helen Lewis explained humorously in the Atlantic "sharing the Internet with America is like sharing your living room with a rhinoceros. It's huge, it's right there, and whatever it's doing now, you sure as hell know about it". The world is trapped in America's culture war (Lewis, 2020). Artisan traditions refined within particular regions for centuries are being influenced by American algorithms directing what culture is produced.

The onslaught of slick images and shifting market demands prompted craft to begin competing *against-the-machine* rather than to *outshine-the-machine*. Much craft began to dilute into quantity-over-quality output, mimicking Western tastes with only a fraction of the work flourishing as economic powerhouses or refined collector pieces of religious or cultural significance. Consequently, many master craftspeople no longer receive local community admiration for their work, and often their children abandon family crafts in search of urban dream jobs seldom obtained (Ellis & Lo, 2019).

Corporate Business-to-Business (B2B) sales have furthered quantity-over-quality and disposable product trends by feeding upon high-volume, low-cost products. Larger private factories are the primary hand-making units that have bank leverage necessary to sustain large material overheads and payment delays common in high-volume, low-cost productions. In most of these factory scenarios, crafts people receive negligible profit while factory owners reap rewards and Western buyers garner the majority of return.

Although today vast numbers of previously thriving craft-centric communities struggle to engage new audiences and revenue channels (Krishnamoorthy et al., 2024), it is indicated that creative manufacturing and handmade (CMH) sector reached sales of US$830.4 billion in 2023 and projects that the market will reach US$1,864.1 billion by 2032, a growth rate (CAGR) of 9.4% during 2023–2032 (Research and Markets, 2023). Clearly, there is ripe opportunity for these hand-makers to flourish, enrich and strengthen the ethnic/creative fabric of their nations.

Tools: Unique attributes of handwork, creativity and tradition

How can handwork, creativity and tradition respond to this confluence of present shifts and challenges: urbanization, digital nomadism, the Convenience Revolution, environmental concerns, less "stuff", the Attention Economy, Surveillance Capitalism, loneliness, algorithmic homogenization, GenAI, Machine Culture and Silk Road artisan/cultural growth? Individuals yearn to identify, connect, participate, *do good* and enhance their human connections. The era of empty social media platforms, *faceless stuff* and dulling cultural feeds rings hollow. The dawn of fewer, more meaningful interactions and materialities is ripe to shine. If 21st-century hand-made production is to advance on significant and equitable commercial scales, makers must consciously cultivate human connection, yearning and identification lacking in mass productions and algorithmic culture. Based upon my hand-production experience, I believe materiality with *guts and soul* holds the potential to become as profitable and far more meaningful than global, disposable-mass-production and pop-influencer culture.

Our greatest human asset is the unpredictability of the mind: to imagine, to experiment and to incorporate unique individual experience into the making. The counterpoint to *disposable* corporate materiality, desires for meaningful identity narratives and the dullness of algorithmic culture is to cultivate valuable human skillsets and reassess integration/engagement of hand assets. It is time to re-conceptualize *product*, reassess cultural values, rethink craftsmanship, reorganize output methods and cultivate spirals of interdisciplinary collaboration.

There is sex appeal in a product's narrating its influences: its cultural origin, the maker, developmental processes, clear and sustainable material sources and a meaningful connection to the end user. Increasingly, it is not the product itself that sells, but rather consumer identification and engagement with product content. Visual variants are advantageous product features. Irregularities can humanize an object, evoke a sense of human touch and emotionally connect product owner to maker. The deliberate transformation from irregular error to celebrated asset appeals to our instinctive identification with the organic and stirs a visceral response. Consumers want to engage products that reinforce their personal beliefs and social-cultural allegiance. Artisanal products encapsulate and empower these growing consumer desires.

Plato used the Greek term *tékhnē* to mean manual craftwork that he considered lesser than knowledge, yet stoics developed the idea that virtue is *tékhnē* or craft of life (Parry, 2020). Successful identity-building narratives, *the craft of life*, involve human engagement and touch-of-a-hand, and these are not digitized easily (Hynes, 2021). Amid today's sea of content, refined artisan know-how is rarified knowledge that becomes a winning powerhouse when integrated innovatively with emerging technologies. Traditionally, master artisanship[3] demands creative autonomy, *conception-to-finish* knowledge, skill, judgement and integrity; however, single-person autonomy can limit and be counter-productive amid complexities of today. It is no longer possible to be master-of-all. Artisans' improvisation and intimate material awareness combined with an emerging *technology tool box* can push all creative boundaries.

While some craft skills have been replaced by better technological output, there are many crafts that retain unique characteristics and material capabilities unmatched by technology. As example, large, one-of-a-kind objects fabricated by repousse techniques would otherwise require huge diecast moulds costing over $100,000 to mass produce the same object. Consumer desire for mass individualization (Jiang et al., 2016) can be readily satisfied by hand-making's intrinsic one-of-a-kind nature. Reintegrating artisanship into industry need not be a charitable cause grappling with extinction, but rather a viable path to enrich product with robust narrative, cultural signifiers, marketing authenticity and unique value that contributes to product impact/longevity. Twenty-first-century industrial, inter-relational creativity demands letting go of autonomy from all sides and joining larger analytical, cyclical, inspirational and nurturing systems. Our material future will be shaped by reformulations of globalized cost arbitrage, emerging technologies, new materials and the messy, human-centric creative process of make-shred-remake into *meaningful materiality* (Pfahl, 2020).

The repetition of craft skills is a form of meditation that is healing and grounding to the practitioner. Rather than being antiquated, hand-making practices cultivate focus at a time when attention is everyone's greatest commodity. There is a direct correlation between the inherent Attention Economy question, "Where do I choose to invest my attention?" and craft practice. Much popularity of Do-It-Yourself (DIY) craft can be correlated to fundamental human needs for focus and the physicality of making that increasingly are lacking in life today (Warraich, 2024).

Obsolescence does not imply irrelevance. Obsolete objects and skillsets are physical markers of a community's multi-generational energy investment into objects as well as records of social/technological evolutions. In contrast to machined objects, human energy is encapsulated in a hand-made object and thereby inherently engages one of today's pressing questions: "What is the value of my energy in the face of GenAI and emerging technologies?" Handcrafts afford an opportunity to identify with our roots; consider present needs, habits and desires; and select values that we wish to flourish within our present and future moments.

The *contemporary* moment is comprised of the newest cutting edge, the present main-stream and the deep roots of yesteryears. Each *Now* is an amalgamation of future, present and past. Today is an opportunity for artisanship to further its key role of outshining-the-ordinary, challenging assumptions and embodying multigenerational understandings of self, collective and other.

Future identity and inclusivity building in a post-pandemic world

If an individual is to change their practice effectively, they must believe in the change. Strategies and dreams without foresight can: (1) disappoint/disempower, (2) be expensive and (3) reduce future belief in confronting risks, engagement and growth. Hence, this paper approaches the strengthening of identity and inclusive culture through tradition/craft/emerging technologies from a pragmatic/wholistic approach developed through my work in Silk Road regions: (1) the reality, (2) the tools, (3) defined value sets, and (4) obtainable, realistic future outcomes.

Today tradition is key to cultivating human connection and inclusive societies. Viewing the present through the lenses of traditions facilitates the questioning of our societal and personal assumptions; it is a touch-test for who we are, who we wish to become and where we will choose to go. Tradition is the taproot of collective identity and holds the power to maintain both upright strength and grounding in storms. As Henrich (2016) suggests, the secret of human success lies not in our individual intelligence, but on the ability of humans to come together collectively to socially interconnect and learn from one another over generations. Revisiting the past through today's filters reveals both collective progress and loss, growth and repeated mistakes. Traditions hold great power as solid footings upon which to venture into new, prosperous, purposeful, creative territories. Tradition enables inclusive present and future growth.

Humans need to feel a sense of belonging, to feel safe, seen and heard. The loneliness epidemic indicates that these fundamental feelings are lacking in many individuals and communities today. Social isolation can begin to spur fundamental questions of personal identification and value. "What differentiates me from other? How do I identify myself within society?" Crafts and culture reinforce a sense of belonging: tradition, identity, culture, participation and familiar place. Increasingly, global consumers seek products that offer unique narratives, cultural value and emotional connection (Research and Markets, 2023). Today there is opportunity to merge traditional craft motives, contemporary regional imagery and GenAI to explore more inclusive social spaces, sense of belonging and meaningful human connection.

Globalization and the resulting multicultural societies have made it less likely for a community to live within one belief system. Most nations and communities today exist within a layering of diverse religious and political and moral belief systems, reflected in multiplicities of rituals, celebrations and customs within shared space. Engaging dynamic, multi-traditional identities within community are key to ensuring the harmonious, productive, prosperous co-existence of all members. Both human and machined cultural output can be vital tools for ensuring meaningful human connection and inclusivity today.

Future economic, environmental and cultural opportunities

As I understand, having lived and worked with artisans for years, cultivating a flourishing, technologically supported artisan ecosystem can expand opportunities for a significant global labour force; increase local fiscal returns; strengthen circular economic practices; foster more inclusive, community-strengthening environments; and cultivate meaningful contemporary creative outputs.

Equitable management and distribution platforms can afford enormous fiscal support for hand makers and creatives. Given hand-makers prevalent access to mobile phones, new apps are a logical means by which to develop innovative distribution channels and transparent platforms that calculate production cost; track orders, production progress and distribution of product; minimize back-stock; and monitor direct fair profit practices. A successful app could distil the handmade supply chain to direct artisan-consumer or artisan-retailer (B2B) sales. Isolated rural workers could choose to unite under one collective and thereby, sell higher volume, quality and/or achieve greater visibility productions sold directly to global consumers or B2B. This type of app model holds potential to host thousands of hand-makers/craft clusters worldwide and free them from the loss of earnings in typical factory and isolated rural contexts.

Public and Private E-commerce platforms continue to hold huge future growth and marketing potential for the handmaking and creative community (PBP, 2024).

Global System for Mobile Association (GSMA) estimates that "By the end of 2030, there will be around 1.4 billion 5G connections in Asia Pacific, equivalent to 41% of total mobile connections. 5G is expected to benefit every sector of the Asia Pacific economy, especially services and manufacturing" (GSMA, 2023). There has been some software development such as Powered by People (PBP) that is designed to aid hand-makers in production management, market access and financing challenges. PBP claims to enable artisans to retain a note-worthy 25-35% of final revenue (PBP, 2024).

Generative AI diffusion platforms can spawn new inspiration that responds to both traditional and contemporary culture. Development of customized, isolated AI databases holds potential to optimize craft productivity, sales and distribution; enhance awareness of tradition; enrich inclusivity/community cohesion; and grow contemporary regional content grounded in *local* rather than homogenized algorithmic influence (Mann, 2024). English language *prompts* and internet data feed most GenAI programs. This bias poses setbacks for communities grounded in other languages but can be addressed by mobile phone translational programs. Incorporating non-digitized regional data into a customized GenAI database will be essential to generate content truly reflective of a specific society's past/present and potentially inspire meaningful future culture. Given GenAI's new terrain, it will be increasingly important to engage questions and explore potential outcomes: "How can merging GenAI and hand-making aid in building thriving communities, inclusive social spaces, belonging and meaningful human connection? How will GenAI tools influence artisanship and begin to inform aesthetics, desires, behaviors and object distribution?" There are no singular answers as yet, but rather an umbrella of questions that will/must expand to create outcomes of global human flourishing.

Who determines relevant content is a sticky wicket and legitimate concern in GenAI database development. There is risk of accelerating isolation if regional diversity focus does not also encourage broader meaningful connection to global collectives. How to ensure constructive co-creation of human and machine artefacts is a pressing question (Brinkmann et al., 2023). Experimentation with an isolated GenAI craft/culture database is required to understand how these tools can influence artisanship productively and play roles in informing community histories, aesthetics, values and desires.

Documentation of living crafts is essential for future generations to appreciate cultural traditions, hand skills, ingenuity, human energy and individual expression that are encapsulated in handmade objects. Regional databases of hand-making skillsets, cultural tradition and intangible cultural heritage are essential to the success of customized GenAI projects. Additionally, recording craft skills will aid in re-envisioning future applications of traditional techniques. As Kelly has observed "The collective is found in the confluence of varying community traditions and ever evolving individual identities" (Kelly, 2023). Traditions must be recorded, understood and valued beyond surface appearance if contemporary identities are to engage tradition in new, impactful ways.

Fashion, luxury goods and art world collaborations with artisans can increase diverse cultural exposure and re-elevate craft relevance. People throughout the world are craving products that reinforce meaningful unique identities, emotional engagement and cultural meaning. It is essential for private business and artistic sectors to value/harness the future fiscal potential of producing quality, handmade works reflective of culture.

Intrinsic environmental advantages of craft will accrue. Rural community-grounded production is a highly sustainable platform and comprises the majority of craftspeople worldwide. Successful rural productions tend to use locally accessible materials, reduce flight to urban centres, enable women to work from/near home and minimize energy consumption.

Collaborative educational initiatives of experts, industry, artisans and community can be strong facilitative models with capacities to uplift local, underrepresented participants and lead to sustained economic growth. From 30 March to 8 April 2024 in Margilan, Uzbekistan, 60 trainees, experts and master artisans explored traditional craftsmanship, local historical contexts, contemporary culture, design and entrepreneurship. Project goals were multiple to 1) create sustainable income/job opportunities for local communities, particularly women and youth; 2) Safeguard/promote awareness of common intangible cultural Silk Road heritage; 3) Strengthen design, craft quality and contemporary relevance via master artisans and designers; and 4) Create cultural platforms to support sustainable heritage-based tourism. This shared endeavour is organized by UNESCO (2024) and funded by the European Union and multiple local initiatives. Used as example, this and many other projects hold potential for concrete outcomes provided that training is reinforced through practice/continued feedback; disseminated to non-attendee, community participants; and supported by local/national marketing, distribution, exhibition and micro-loans.

Conclusion

Tradition both incubates and challenges new creative domains. Craft reminds *us* of where *we* came from and how *we* as community have evolved generationally. Artisanship is living documentation of past generations' resilience, needs, values and traditions. Contemporary environments that reflect tradition and strengthen multi-generational engagement are vital as populations support increasing numbers of elderly people. Craft evolved to satisfy a community's primary needs, religious beliefs, social customs and desires for luxury and beauty. Regardless of homogenizing global trends, today's artisan skills are living identities of community's past/present foothold. Surviving craft skills of yesterday are powerful tools that can cultivate collective reflection and understanding-of-self tomorrow.

Today is an opportunity to recognize the transformative power of incorporating traditional artisanship into contemporary arts, luxury goods, and both human and machine cultures of tomorrow. All Silk Road nations possess both unique and shared cultural influences that can be harnessed responsibly by emerging technologies to strengthen sustainable local ecosystems, cultural development, inclusive social spaces and flourishing human connection.

Notes

1 In addition, Simon (1971, pp. 40–41) described his belief that we live in an attention economy where "What information consumes is rather obvious: it consumes the attention of its recipients. Hence, a wealth of information creates a poverty of attention and a need to allocate that attention efficiently among the overabundance of information sources that might consume it".

2 *Infosphere,* as understood for purposes of this paper, includes all data, information, communication and knowledge generated via all information and communication technologies (ICTs) that are capable of not only recording and transmitting, but also processing information.

3 For purposes of this paper, a*rtisan*, *craftsperson* and *hand-maker are* used interchangeably as a non-automated, hand-skilled producer of objects.

References

Apple (2024). *Apple trade in*. Apple. Retrieved May 2, 2024, from https://www.apple.com/shop/trade-in

Baeza-Yates, R., & Fayyad, U. M. (2022). The attention economy and the impact of artificial intelligence. In H. Werthner, E. Prem, E. A. Lee, & C. Ghezzi (Eds.), *Perspectives on digital humanism*. Springer. Retrieved January 6, 2023, from https://link.springer.com/chapter/10.1007/978-3-030-86144-5_18

Bembatoum-Young, M., Bouchart, D., Duque-Duque, C., Dhamija, J., Ford, T., & Maarouf, N. (2000). *Evaluation of UNESCO's programme for crafts promotion 1990-1998: Final evaluation report*. UNESCO. Retrieved September 29, 2006, from https://unesdoc.unesco.org/ark:/48223/pf0000119101

Born, G., Morris, J., Diaz, F., & Anderson, A. (2021). *Artificial intelligence, music recommendation, and the curation of culture*. Toronto: University of Toronto.

Brinkmann, L., Baumann, F., Bonnefon, J. F., Derex, M., Muller, T. F., Nussberger, A-M., & Rahwan, I. (2023, November 20). Machine culture. *Nature Human Behaviour*, 7, 1855–1868. Retrieved December 4, 2023, from https://doi.org/10.1038/s41562-023-01742-2

Charm, T., Coggins, B., Robinson, K., & Wilki, J. (2020). The great consumer shift. McKinsey & Company. Retrieved February 13, 2021, from https://www.mckinsey.com/~/media/McKinsey/Business%20Functions/Marketing%20and%20Sales/Our%20Insights/The%20great%20consumer%20shift/ten-charts-show-how-us-shopping-behavior-is-changing.pdf

Chayka, K. (2023). *Filterworld*. New York: Random House.

Coleman, S., & O'Reilly, D. (2024, July 31). Best virtual mailbox services of 2024. *U.S. News & World Report*. Retrieved April 29, 2024, from https://www.usnews.com/360-reviews/business/best-virtual-mailbox-services

Coppola, C., Vollero, A., & Siano, A. (2021). *Consumer upcycling as emancipated self-production: Understanding motivations and identifying upcycler types*. Amsterdam: Elsevier.

Darwin, C. (1872). *On the Origin of Species* (6th ed.). Project Gutenberg. Retrieved May 12, 2024, from https://www.gutenberg.org/files/2009/2009-h/2009-h.htm

Deloitte. (2024, March 20). *2024 Digital Media Trends*. Deloitte. Retrieved May 10, 2024, from https://www2.deloitte.com/us/en/insights/industry/technology/digital-media-trends-consumption-habits-survey.html#introduction

Elhacham, E., Ben-Uri, L., Grozovski, J., Bar-On, Y. M., & Milo, R. (2020, September 12). Global human-made mass exceeds all living biomass. *Nature*, *588*, 442–444. Retrieved February 13, 2021, from https://doi.org/10.1038/s41586-020-3010-5

Ellis, S., & Lo, J. (2019). An economic assessment of Asian crafts. In A. Mignosa & P. Kotipalli (Eds.), *A cultural economic analysis of craft*. Palgrave Macmillan. Retrieved February 10, 2023, from https://doi.org/10.1007/978-3-030-02164-1_14

Floridi, L. (2014). *The fourth revolution: How the infosphere is reshaping human reality*. Oxford: Oxford University Press.

Gartner. (2022, April 28). Gartner says U.S. total annual employee turnover will likely jump by nearly 20% from the prepandemic annual average. *Gartner.com*. Retrieved June 12, 2024, from https://www.gartner.com/en/newsroom/04-28-2022-gartner-says-us-total-annual-employee-turnover-will-likely-jump-by-nearly-twenty-percent-from-the-prepandemic-annual-average

Gibson, R. (2015, September 25). The new Silk Road. *New East Archive*. Retrieved July 14, 2022, from https://www.new-east-archive.org/articles/show/4731/new-silk-road-uzbekistan-suzani-ikat-embroidery-fergana

GIZ. (2020, December). Uzbekistan: Sustainability and value added in the cotton economy. Retrieved July 14, 2022, from https://www.giz.de/en/downloads/giz2021_en_Factsheet_Cotton_Uzbekistan.pdf

Goldhaber, M. W. (1997). Attention shoppers! *Wired*. Retrieved December 20, 1997, from https://www.wired.com/1997/12/es-attention/

GSMA. (2023). *The Mobile Economy Asia Pacific 2023*. GSMA. Retrieved April 12, 2024, from https://www.gsma.com/solutions-and-impact/connectivity-for-good/mobile-economy/wp-content/

Harari, Y. N. (2022). *FAQs*. Ynharari.com. Retrieved May 8, 2024, from https://www.ynharari.com/faqs/

Henrich, J. (2016). *The secret of our success*. Princeton: Princeton University Press.

Hyken, S. (2018). *The convenience revolution*. Shippensburg: Sound Wisdom.

Hynes, M. (2021). *The social, cultural and environmental costs of hyper-connectivity*. Leeds: Emerald Publishing Limited.

ITU. (2024, March 20). *The Global E-waste Monitor 2024*. E-Waste Monitor. Retrieved May 2, 2024, from https://ewastemonitor.info/the-global-e-waste-monitor-2024/

Jaitly, J., Ram, G., Somany, A., & Tyabji, L. (2023, September 26). *Thinking through policy development initiatives for Indian crafts*. Asia Society. Retrieved September 26, 2023, from https://asiasociety.org/india/events/thinking-through-policy-development-initiatives-indian-crafts

Jensen, H. H. (2022, January 27). 5 circular economy business models that offer a competitive advantage. *World Economic Forum*. Retrieved August 16, 2023, from https://www.weforum.org/agenda/2022/01/5-circular-economy-business-models-competitive-advantage/

Jiang, P., Leng, J., Ding, K., Gu, P., & Koren, Y. (2016). *Social manufacturing as a sustainable paradigm for mass individualization*. Thousand Oaks, CA: Sage Publications.

Johfre, S. S., & Saperstein, A. (2019). State of the union: Racial and gender identities. *Pathways: The Poverty and Inequality Report 2019*. Stanford Center on Poverty and Inequality. Retrieved June 6, 2023, from https://inequality.stanford.edu/sites/default/files/Pathways_SOTU_2019_RaceGender.pdf

Kannan, V. D., & Veazie, P. J. (2023). US trends in social isolation, social engagement, and companionship. Amsterdam: Elsevier.

Kelly, K. (2016). *The inevitable*. New York: Penguin Books.

Kelly, K. (2023). Over the long term, the future is decided by optimists. Retrieved February 15, 2023, from https://kk.org

Krishnamoorthy, P., Saksena, M., Dhillon, M., & Dhanwani, R. (2024, March 5). Craft and capital. *Asia Society*. Retrieved March 5, 2024, from https://asiasociety.org/india/events/craft-and-capital-investing-indias-handmade-economy

Lewis, H. (2020, October 27). The world is trapped in America's culture war. *The Atlantic*. Retrieved January 11, 2021, from https://www.theatlantic.com/international/archive/2020/10/internet-world-trapped-americas-culture-war/616799/

Majeed, I., Bhat, A. H., & Azam, R. (2023). The role of government in promoting handicraft industry. *Shodhkosh: Journal of Visual and Performing Arts*, *4*(1), 429–442.

Mann, H. (2024, March 3). AI homogenization is shaping the world. *Forbes*. Retrieved March 3, 2024, from https://www.forbes.com/sites/hamiltonmann/2024/03/05/the-ai-homogenization-is-shaping-the-world/?sh=188e1dca6704

Max Planck Institute. (2024). AI-driven cultural evolution. *MPIB*. Retrieved April 2, 2024, from https://www.mpib-berlin.mpg.de/1682202/05-ai-driven-cultural-evolution

Moss, K., & Bapna, M. (2020). 4-indicators that the reuse and resale market is on the rise. *WRI*. Retrieved May 6, 2021, from https://www.wri.org/insights/4-indicators-reuse-and-resale-market-rise

Murindanyi, S., Nakate, A., Kyebambe, M. N., & Nakibuule, R. (2024). Responsible artificial intelligence for music recommendation. *ResearchGate*. Retrieved May 21,

2024, from https://www.researchgate.net/publication/378249770_Responsible_Artificial_Intelligence_for_Music_Recommendation

Murthy, V. (2023, May 3). *Surgeon general's advisory on our epidemic of loneliness and isolation*. U. S. Department of Health and Human Services. Retrieved November 7, 2023, from https://www.hhs.gov/about/news/2023/05/03/new-surgeon-general-advisory-raises-alarm-about-devastating-impact-epidemic-loneliness-isolation-united-states.html

Mussari, L. (2024, April 17). The 61 countries with digital nomad visas and remote work permits. *Freaking Nomads*. Retrieved April 20, 2024, from https://freakingnomads.com/digital-nomad-visa-countries/

Natale, S., & Guzman, A. L. (2022). Reclaiming the human in machine cultures. *Media, Culture & Society*, *44*(4), 627–637. Retrieved September 23, 2022, from https://doi.org/10.1177/01634437221099614

Orlowski-Yang, J. (2020, January 26). The social dilemma. *Exposure Labs*. Retrieved June 6, 2021, from https://www.thesocialdilemma.com/faqs/

Orzol, M. & Szopik-Depczynska (2023). Development trends in e-commerce sector. *ScienceDirect*. Retrieved December 16, 2023, from https://www.sciencedirect.com/science/article/pii/S1877050923015703

Parekh, B. (2002). *Rethinking multiculturalism: Cultural diversity and political theory*. Cambridge, MA: Harvard University Press.

Parry, R. (2020). Episteme and techne. *Stanford Encyclopedia of Philosophy*. Retrieved September 30, 2022, from https://plato.stanford.edu/entries/episteme-techne/#Stoi

Patagonia, Inc. (2024a). How clean are your clothes? Patagonia. Retrieved May 1, 2024, from https://www.patagonia.com/hidden-cost-of-clothes/.

Patagonia, Inc. (2024b). Retrieved May 1, 2024, from https://wornwear.patagonia.com

PBP (Powered by People). (2024). About us. Powered by People. Retrieved March 26, 2024, from https://www.poweredbypeople.com/pages/about-pbp

Perfas, S. L. (2024, February 14). What do we do with our loneliness? *The Harvard Gazette*. Retrieved March 1, 2024, from https://news.harvard.edu/gazette/story/2024/02/harvard-thinking-podcast-explores-loneliness-epidemic/

Pew American Trends Panel (2024, July 7-November 2). Pew Research Center. Retrieved April 8, 2024, from https://www.pewresearch.org/wp-content/uploads/2024/03/SR_24.03.26_chat-bot_topline.pdf

Pfahl, E. L. (2020). Making materiality meaningful for artists and artisans in the 21st century. *LinkedIn*. Retrieved June 12, 2024, from https://www.linkedin.com/pulse/making-materiality-meaningful-artists-artisans-21st-century-pfahl-1d/?trackingId=tZ5p862NM7WXgNRHzyiYcA==

Phillips, A. (2021, June 15). How the creative manufacturing and handmade sector can craft a post-COVID-19 future. *World Economic Forum*. Retrieved September 30, 2021, from https://www.weforum.org/agenda/2021/06/creative-manufacturing-handmade-sector-growth/

Research and Markets (2023). *Handicrafts market report by product type, distribution channel, end-use, and region 2024-2032* (ID: 5936035). Retrieved February 5, 2024, from https://www.researchandmarkets.com/report/handicraft

Reuter, D. (2023, April 11). 50,000 US retail stores to disappear by 2028 as shopping completely transforms, study finds. *Business Insider*. Retrieved February 13, 2024, from https://www.businessinsider.com/us-retailers-close-50k-stores-over-next-five-years-ubs-2023-4?op=1

Ritchie, H., Samborska, V., & Roser, M. (2018, September & 2024, February). Urbanization. *Our World in Data*. Retrieved March 8, 2024, from https://ourworldindata.org/urbanization

Simon, H. A. (1971). Designing organizations for an information-rich world, 40-41. In M. Greenberger (Ed.), *Computers, communications, and the public interest*. Baltimore, MD: Johns Hopkins Press.

Thompson, D. (2024, February 14). Why Americans suddenly stopped hanging out. *The Atlantic*. Retrieved February 5, 2024, from https://www.theatlantic.com/ideas/archive/2024/02/america-decline-hanging-out/677451/

UN Tourism (2018). Silk Road. *UNWTO*. Retrieved June 2021, from https://www.unwto.org/silk-road

UNESCO (2024). National training in traditional craftsmanship, design and entrepreneurship. *UNESCO*. Retrieved April 20, 2024, from https://www.unesco.org/en/articles/national-training-traditional-craftsmanship-design-and-entrepreneurships-safeguarding-intangible

Vinnakota, R. (2017). Retrieved May 14, 2024, from https://www.aspeninstitute.org/blog-posts/social-media-divides-us/

Warraich, J. (2024, March 7). The rise of DIY culture. *Medium*. Retrieved April 4, 2024, from https://medium.com/@jasmeet.warraich/the-rise-of-diy-culture-empowering-creatives-in-the-digital-age-d4687d0bee04

Warzel, C. (2021, February 2). I talked to the Cassandra of the Internet age. *The New York Times*. Retrieved February 5, 2021, from https://www.nytimes.com/2021/02/04/opinion/michael-goldhaber-internet.html

World Economic Forum (2022, May 22-26). History at a turning point. *World Economic Forum Annual Meeting*. Retrieved March 5, 2022, from https://www.weforum.org/agenda/2022/01/5-circular-economy-business-models-competitive-advantage/

Yang, J., Mamun, A. A., Reza, M. N. H., Yang, M., & Aziz, N. A. (2024, February 7). Predicting the significance of consumer environmental values, beliefs, and norms for sustainable fashion behaviors. *Asia Pacific Management Review*. Retrieved March 3, 2024, from https://www.sciencedirect.com/science/article/pii/S1029313224000010

Zhuang, Y. (2023, September 25). Writers' strike ends with tentative deal. *The New York Times*. Retrieved September 29, 2023, from https://www.nytimes.com/2023/09/25/business/wga-writers-strike-deal-explained.html

Zuboff, S. (2019). Surveillance capitalism and the challenge of collective action. *New Labor Forum*, *28*(1), 10–29. Retrieved November 8, 2023, from https://journals.sagepub.com/doi/full/10.1177/1095796018819461

Part III

Collaborating and diversifying to decentre fashion

10 The power of diversity

The interaction between craftspeople and designers as a resource for a diverse fashion system

Jure Purgaj and Sabine Albert

Introduction

For years, the fashion industry has faced immense challenges, such as having to deal with a lack of sustainability, a lack of transparency, overproduction, and little to no consideration of the cultural as well as physical diversity of customers – and all this embedded in a Western-oriented closed fashion system (Kawamura, 2005). The consequences of not overcoming these difficulties include piles of waste both from worn and new clothing and contributing to climate change due to overproduction and associated high consumption of resources (Morgan, 2015). Craftspeople and fashion designers are both part of this problematic industry. They design clothing through creative processes and generate innovation-driven products. When looking for a solution to the challenges of the fashion system, it could be productive to study how their roles could be adjusted to bring about positive change. These two professions are both situated at the beginning of the production lines. They have influenced the development of design and technology. By working together and leveraging the skills of both professions as equal, they have pushed the boundaries of what we can create and also what we can imagine.

Regarding creativity and innovation, the close connection between design and craftsmanship is significant in bringing new ideas to life. But while being bound by this connection the two professions pursue different goals and face different challenges. Designers see their task as proposing solutions to problems they have identified. While craftsmen generally focus on materials, implementation, and production processes in their field of activity. Their erstwhile cooperation has become more and more divided with the progressive specialization of the individual professions due to the separation of art from science tracing – something that originated in the Renaissance, when a new understanding of the individual fields of activity and the associated tasks as distinct. Until the Renaissance, artist and craftsperson used to be united in one and the same individual since there was not, at that point in time, a separation of the two professions in the sense in which it exists today. Apprentices, who did not, then, see themselves as artists but as craftspeople, were trained

DOI: 10.4324/9781003508076-14

by masters in workshops. In the second half of the 16th century, the first fine arts academies were formed to pursue two goals. First, the academies were to open learning and teaching opportunities that the workshops had little or no opportunity to provide such as studying and drawing the nude body, and second, to raise the artist's social status (Bell, 1963). The specialization of art and science and their division in the 19th century (Zhu & Goyal, 2019) also served to separate art and craft. The by-product of this separation fitted in with the later processes of the industrialization of Europe and the desire for new products: the designer. The Industrial Revolution demanded and favored a separation of skills, resulting in specializations in the different affiliations (Mareis, 2011) of the artist, the craftsperson, and the designer.

Mindful of the limiting effect of this historical development, the program of the international conference by the Responsible Fashion Series 2023 in Uzbekistan and Kazakhstan focused on the idea of the interactions that occur when knowledge is exchanged between local and international artisans, craftspeople and designers. Following on from that, this chapter investigates which resources can emerge from closer collaboration between craftspeople and designers to foster a responsible and diverse fashion system. Because, while advances in sustainability and transparency in the fashion system are being made (Anguelov, 2021) – such as the use of renewable energy sources and natural organic materials in the production processes, listings of producers and suppliers or alternative business models such as trading and second-hand clothing – the issue of diversity still needs to be addressed. This means diversity in the sense of designing for all and also diversity in the sense of sharing diverse knowledges between craft and design. It is assumed that the first will automatically be resolved if the latter is assured.

Because both craftspeople and designers are located right at the beginning of the production processes and are thus in the position to channel all further actions along the production line, such as the handling of products and resources, thus bringing the issue of heterogeneity to the forefront through the way how and what they design and build. In line with diversity management approaches from business and education science, for example, fashion can be adapted to customers and markets through an optimal degree of consideration of plurality. Furthermore, long-term learning can be achieved from diversity by using differences of producers in a targeted and integrative way (Vedder, 2006). Design can be more inclusive through collaboration and mutual learning between craftspeople and designers, which means that all participants' positive resources are used responsibly in a shared process. However, this is only possible if both understand how the other learns, thinks, and works and which challenges they must overcome. Resources, in this context, are understood to mean, for example, differences in knowledge, experience, approaches, and cultures of the people involved. These various perspectives are considered to develop better solutions to the challenges in the fashion industry, leading to new ideas and innovations. The following research question arises in this context: "What resources emerge from the interaction between craftspeople and designers?"

This research project is based around a workshop conducted with members of distinct professional groups including academics, artisans, artists, craftspeople, designers, lecturers, and writers at the Responsible Fashion Series event in Tashkent. The aim was to work on creating a diverse fashion system that understands heterogeneity, openness, and global cooperation of various people and cultures as a potential for a more sustainable future. Along with this research-guiding question, the central concepts of difference, diversity, attitudes, and learning will be addressed first, followed by the description of the research design and the presentation and discussion of the research results. The aim is to make the resources that can be created through cooperation, considering diversity and appreciation of both professions with the proposed research method visible to promote necessary changes in the fashion system.

Theoretical perspectives on diversity and mutual learning

In this chapter, the project is situated in the current state of research. The focus is on the central concepts of diversity and shared learning as well as the respectful attitude that is a prerequisite for bringing designers and craftspeople closer together. First, the terms that are used are introduced via the intersectional approach.

Differences – An intersectional analysis approach

Modern societies encompass differences in identities, social affiliations, and group characteristics. This chapter focuses on appreciating and understanding these differences as resources and using them to benefit the fashion industry by making it more sustainable. On the one hand, the issue of how the positive resources of craftspeople and designers can be used to consider the diversity of the people for whom fashion is produced is significant for the research question. On the other hand, the differences between craftspeople and designers are considered as well with a view to enabling new ideas and innovations in the design and production process to meet the current challenges in the fashion industry adequately. With professional specialization, such as becoming *either* a craftsperson *or* a designer, and the lack of opportunity to meet and exchange ideas in person, other separating processes inevitably occur – such as adoption of remote workflows and networking. This situation involves differentiating between 'us and them,' which symbolizes the distinction of an unspoken norm from its deviation (Riegel, 2016). Such assessments and classifications into 'normal' and deviating groups of people are counterproductive if one wants to recognize diversity and use its positive resources. For this, diversity competencies are productive, such as the ability to engage in non-judgmental dialogue, to change perspectives, to be flexible, and to tolerate ambiguity (Walgenbach, 2017). The individual differences between people are essential, but this article focuses on the collective differences of groups (Mecheril & Plößer, 2022) due to their central importance in diversity approaches. Accordingly, socio-structural orders of difference must be conceptualized in terms of their overlaps and interactions via the intersectional approach (Walgenbach, 2017). Such structural categories include gender, ethnicity, social milieu, and/or bodies through which people identify themselves (Winkler & Degele, 2010). In social interaction and practices, people are often distinguished from each other using categories, and demarcations between them cause either inclusion or exclusion, valorization or devaluation (Riegel, 2016). In order to describe forms of social practices and their causes, Sabine Albert (2022) has developed a model working with the premise that people, depending on the context in which they live and have been socialized in, hold specific descriptive and normative images of people. These concepts of human beings include beliefs and subjective theories oriented to specific values and closely related to emotions. It is an inner attitude of mind, the essential positioning toward persons, situations, things, and their evaluation. When it comes to a purposeful attitude toward concrete people in certain situations, the attitude becomes visible to outsiders through interaction, language, posture, and movement. This perspective eventually results in the forms of practice, such as communication, actions, or even decisions that are made. The forms of practice, in turn, induce, reinforce, or dampen the image of the person (Albert, 2022). Common patterns of perception, orientation, and interpretation in societies determine relations of power and inequality. According to Pierre Bourdieu (1992, 1993), people's position in the social field depends on the types of capital available to them. While designers usually have a high degree of cultural, social, and economic capital, craftspeople are often associated with low cultural capital (Jurt, 2012). This social status is also very evident in the fashion industry. While the most prominent fashion designers are predominantly male-read individuals, predominantly women and female-read individuals construct and execute the designs in workshops. When changing the perspective on the addressees of the fashion design process, social differences, gender, individual body shapes, and cultures become the focus of interest. Fashion is primarily designed and produced with a person in mind, who conforms to a particular norm or notion of the designer. Structural and constructed differences become significant primarily in social interaction and affect both the participants in fashion's design and production processes and the addressers of fashion. The next chapter explains how these differences can be used constructively for the design process and what the term diversity has to do with it.

Diversity – Conceptual considerations

Differences between people are also referred to as heterogeneity, diversity, and/or variety. Heterogeneity comes from ancient Greek and is composed of héteros (other/different) and génos (class/species) (Kluge, 2011). It means otherness or difference concerning individuals, groups, or societies. A norm is presumed, necessitating a point of comparison to which characteristics or bundles of characteristics are related. This establishes individual or societal expectations of normality and identifies deviations (Wenning, 1999). At this point, it becomes clear that reducing complexity in the form of structural-level categories makes sense, leading to simplified analysis and better understanding. Reducing categories cannot do justice to this diversity. Therefore, there are expandable categories or further characteristics (Winkler & Degele, 2010). Thus, when speaking of heterogeneity, what is meant is a *prevailing* diversity. In contrast to this, the use of the term 'diversity' aims to signify the appreciation of social group characteristics which are thus perceived as a valuable resource. The goal is the mutual recognition of 'otherness.' The focus is not on deficits but on people's abilities, needs, and interests. Applying categories in this context can complicate understanding the complex reality of the individuals involved. Therefore, structural categories and design are inseparable. From this, it can be deduced that categories can also be deconstructed through design. The principle of participation is significant in this context. The experiential knowledge of people enriches the design processes since their reality of life is in focus. The pooling of knowledge about group-relevant facts and their contexts is significant for the sustainability of design processes. Thus, the approach to inclusion is through design and the question of how to design. The design researcher Tom Bieling (2019) calls this approach the cross-functional design approach. He promotes the view of disability as an expertise and not as a disadvantage. This leads to an expansion of the possible areas of application, for example to other diversity dimensions such as gender or language. Accordingly, those affected are directly and actively involved in the design and production process, and inclusion is understood as a two-way process. Especially for design, the approach to the individual life worlds of the persons concerned is essential. In addition to including the addressees of fashion, a joint learning process of craftspeople and designers can enrich fashion production and make it more responsible. Each person becomes part of the process, whether in production or in consumption.

Therefore, it is advocated that such an association of craftspeople and designers, which enables cooperation and joint learning processes, should be always implemented. In order to utilize the resources and potential of all those involved, the distinction between oneself and others must be deconstructed. This concept of cooperation also fosters a humanistic and democratic attitude, enabling individuals to engage on equal footing with equal rights.

The importance of respectful attitude and its expression

According to Albert's above-mentioned model, the inner attitude of mind, for example, to respect people in principle, becomes visible to others via the interface of the goal-directed attitude. The attitude expresses itself through actions and communication through which respect, recognition, appreciation, acceptance, and tolerance toward other people become perceptible. These terms are often used synonymously. However, on closer examination, they have different meanings and can, therefore, be distinguished. Respect (lat. respicere) means to look back. Following this, Robin S. Dillon (2003) understands respect as paying attention to, perceiving, and understanding a person, thus recognizing their importance and individual value. Concerning social inequality, sociologist Richard Sennett outlined respect 20 years ago as "the idea of a limit to the untouchability" (2004, p. 3) of people. This idea protects people in their dignity, autonomy, and distinctiveness. The respect researchers Meyer et al. (2009) refer to this kind of respect as horizontal respect, which is fundamentally due to every human being. From this, they distinguish vertical respect, which is characterized by respecting people based on positive differences, such as unique talents or abilities that a person possesses. Given the heterogeneity of society, Sennett vehemently calls for respecting others and dealing with differences in society in an appreciative manner. Like the concept of respect, recognition is determined by the particular value systems of a given society. Suppose the concept of respect is measured against general humanistic values, dignity, autonomy, freedom, and the basic needs that all people have in common. In that case, recognition finds its expression in concrete contexts and situations and takes into account the individuality of persons (Schmetkamp, 2012). In contrast, through individual evaluations, appreciation is shown to a person or object and is influenced by the context. If acceptance is a process in which persons are accepted, Susanne Schmetkamp (2012) understands the term tolerance to mean that persons are accepted and rejected simultaneously. According to Kant's moral philosophy, a person is respected in his or her dignity and autonomy on the one hand, but what deviates from the norm or contradicts one's convictions is rejected on the other. Basically, it is about a mutually respectful attitude and the appreciation and recognition of contact with each other to understand and use diversity as a resource for standard learning processes, ultimately leading to common creative design processes.

Learning from each other and with one another

The diverse experiences of people and the exchange of individual pieces of knowledge enrich learning. Due to variations in perceptions, interpretation patterns, evaluation criteria, and orientations, it is essential to consider the needs and requirements of the addressees, for whom fashion is produced. Furthermore, it is necessary to bring together all those involved participants with their lifeworlds, experiences, and knowledge to produce fashion (Albert & Purgaj, 2022).

This approach to diversity can be well explained from a phenomenological perspective. Alfred Schütz and Thomas Luckmann (2003) describe people's experiences and knowledge as a pool. The pool of knowledge is surrounded by the horizon, which symbolizes no knowledge. Learning is, therefore, the expansion of knowledge and relearning, whereby the horizon is shifted further away. Relationships between people are essential here, which is why it is necessary to understand others (Husserl & Held, 2007). Openness and empathy are prerequisites for explicating and utilizing people's prior knowledge. Jürgen Habermas (1997) uses the concept of horizon in a different way, not as emanating from the person, but as an area of the lifeworld in which an intersubjective understanding occurs. People can come to an agreement through co-operative interpretations. According to Malte Brinkmann (2022), learning from this perspective is an experiential process that can initiate confusions of things normally familiar and the routine and lead to astonishment. These moments are accompanied by negative experiences that occur when inconsistencies arise that cannot be dealt with using previous knowledge. Klaus Holzkamp (1995) sees such situations as learning occasions that lead to learning motivation. However, only then openness and further experiences are made possible. Learning and experiencing occur with the whole body through social practices that are subject to social norms and structures and through a directedness toward other people and the world (Brinkmann, 2022). The interplay of mental and physical learning underscores the close relationship between design and craft.

Learning as experience is also constantly learning with and from others, thus social and interactive, but also culturally dimensioned. It is about the transmission of cultural techniques and norms. Understanding learning as an experiential process can lead to formative experiences and, consequently, to something new and unfamiliar (Brinkmann). When craftspeople and designers meet respectfully, they try to understand each other and learn from each other in exchange, which serves progress and leads to a responsible fashion industry.

Methodical framework: Design thinking and qualitative content analysis

To answer the research question, a qualitatively oriented category-guided text analysis (Mayring & Fenzl, 2014; Mayring, 2015) is conducted. To collect data for the survey, a design thinking workshop was conducted on 10 March 2023 with participants at the international event organized by the Responsible Fashion Series in Tashkent. Design thinking (Cross, 2011) is a method used in the design field as a tool for developing people-oriented products, situations, and solutions. Although it is not a traditional method of empirical research, the approach was used because it provides accurate insights into people's thinking and behavior through the five phases (empathize, define, ideate, prototype, and test).

Fourteen participants participated in the workshop, and twelve agreed to have their answers used in the evaluation. Questionnaires featured questions both in English and Russian. Of the twelve participants, ten wrote the answers in English and two in Russian. Answers given in Russian were subsequently translated into English. The duration of the workshop was 90 minutes, and the four phases, empathize (1E), define (2E), ideate (3E), and prototype (4E) were conducted and used for the evaluation. Each phase was marked numerically from 1 to 4 and completed with the letter E (example). The further numerals mark the line where the example is in the coding document.

The text data were analyzed using qualitative content analysis following Philipp Mayring's method (2015), and the image data according to Erwin Panofsky interpretive model (2023). The text and image material from the survey were first screened for content that contributed to answering the research question. Then, an explicative qualitative content analysis was conducted by explaining the text via additional material or theoretical reference, leading to the appropriate category via the steps of paraphrasing, generalization, and reduction (Mayring, 2015; Döring, 2023). The categories formed are presented in Table 10.1, which shows the category system.

For the analysis of the images, Erwin Panofsky's model (2023) was used, which has a three-stage interpretation scheme. First, the sense of the phenomenon was worked out by describing what the images depicted. This was followed by an analysis of the meaning by comparing the content with other texts and images. Finally, the interpretation of what the depicted image refers to was carried out, whereby a high level of abstraction was already achieved (Wiesner & Flicke, 2023). The following exemplifications (see Table 10.2) are used for a better understanding:

The consequent category formation from the data was inductive and carried out by two researchers independently. The categories had to have been mentioned in all four phases and have the following frequency (Figure 10.3). On the one hand, the design-scientific and, on the other hand, the educational-scientific perspective was used according to the respective expertise of the researchers in the sense of an interdisciplinary approach. Subsequently, the interrater reliability of the content analytic category system was tested using Cohen's Kappa coefficient (Döring, 2023). The calculated Cohen's Kappa value is 0.76, corresponding to a high agreement.

In the following chapter, the results, which show the resources resulting from the interaction between craftspeople and designers to promote a responsible fashion design system, are being presented and discussed.

Table 10.1 Category system

Category	*Coding rules*	*Anchor examples*
Different people	Coded are passages that describe the differences between people.	"Always have in mind the people I am working with. Never have the same." 1E0013 "I must include more men in my work." 2E0057 "Empowering women + more freedom." 3E0023 "Female read person cannot speak – no mouth. Cannot sense – no sensory organs and does not correspond to the norm." 4E0001
Attitudes	Coded are passages in which terms express an attitude toward others, such as respect, appreciation, esteem, acceptance, tolerance, and understanding the other person	"Tolerance: acceptance, understanding." 1E0105 "Be a voice for others." 2E0007 "To appreciate national designs." 2E0025 "Create Equality to protect diversity." 3E0006 "A space is created where sharing or exchange is possible through attitude." 4E0009
Exchange	Coded are jobs that focus on sharing knowledge, experience, resources, and collaborative work.	"Possibility to explore more for the world. Wearable technology, open-source sharing." 1E0003 "Exchange of experience." 2E0045 "Joint work between writers and academics." 3E0013 "Object in which there are many resources that are exchanged on as gifts." 4E0007
Learning	Coded are places where actions generate knowledge.	"the experience is important." 1E0053 "Diversity leads to education." 1E0037 "How can we teach people to re-evaluate their clothes to keep them in the loop?" 3E0003 "Mix & match." 2E0009 "Get to know the culture to develop something new." 3E0016 "Learning is achieved through engagement with designing and creating." 4E0002

(Continued)

Table 10.1 (Continued)

Category	*Coding rules*	*Anchor examples*
Opportunities	Coded are places where diversity opens opportunities.	"1+1=11" 1E0010 "Variety of styles and fabrics I use, variety of colors and figures." 2E0023 "Diversity means possibilities for future." 3E0019 "New possibilities arise through weaving and combining different materials." 4E0005
Development	Coded are places where progress is the primary concern.	"Diversity is important because you don't stand still, you move and evolve." 1E0032 "The development of the project is important." 2E0053 "Without diversity we have a dead end." 3E0020 "Expresses a constant evolution." 4E0008

Table 10.2 Exemplifications of image evaluation

Example	*Phenomenal sense*	*Sense of meaning*	*Document sense*	*Category*
 *Figure 10.1* Nature *Source*: 2E0039	Three different trees are seen in the illustration. The trees are in different stages of development.	The representation that it corresponds to the natural growth process when there are different stages of development.	After reviewing the participant's text material, it becomes clear that the image indicates that further development and growth are essential in life.	Development
 *Figure 10.2* Face *Source*: 2E0052	The drawing shows large eyes with striking eyelashes. The eyes are directed at something. Below is drawn a mouth, which is open.	The representation means that the attention is focused on something that causes amazement in the person, expressed by the open mouth.	The representation refers to the fact that people are astonished. According to reference to theory (Brinkmann, 2022), amazement triggers confusion and sets learning processes in motion.	Learning

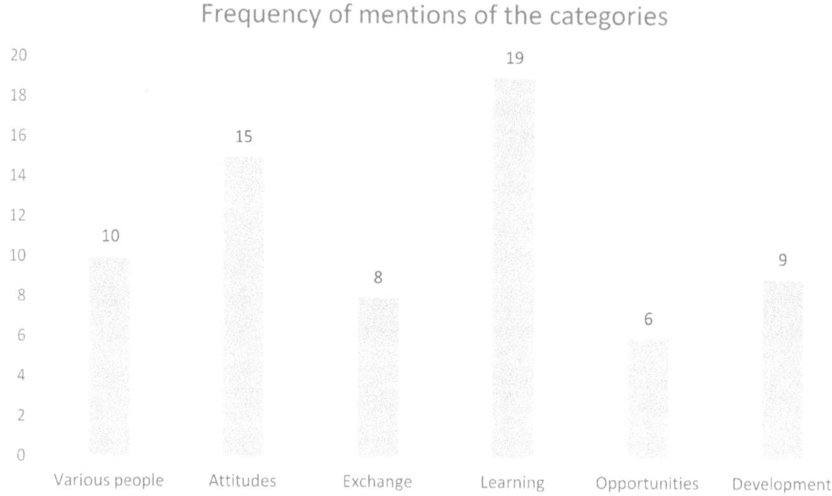

Figure 10.3 Frequency distribution of the categories.

Results and discussion

The participants' responses to the questions about what they understand by diversity, their experiences with diversity in their work, and why diversity is important and beneficial to them resulted in the categories of various people, attitudes, exchange, learning, opportunities, and development. On closer examination, these categories are important resources for the work of designers and craftspeople and are released through their interaction with each other. The fact that craftspeople and designers are characterized by their diversity plays a notable role in the answers. The participants pointed out that everyone has differences, such as work habits or social habits, especially those with whom they work (1E0018). These would have different physical and cognitive abilities (1E0001). However, not only the human being but also the context around the human being would be characterized by diversity (1E00068). Therefore, it would be necessary to consider the person with whom one is working regarding his or her characteristics and background (1E0013) and to include all the different people in the work process to fully appreciate and pick up their contributions and ideas (1E0029; 1E0036). Another aspect that manifests itself in the answers is that people would often express their differences through their dress style (1E0103). According to one participant, in fashion production, the design should consider different age groups and groupings (1E0021). Bodies are also different, the person added. For example, there are people with physical or sensory disabilities (4E0001) which should also play a role in the design process. It becomes clear that, on the one hand, the differences between craftspeople and designers can be used constructively for the design process. On the other hand, the differences between people for whom fashion is made should be considered more. These distinctions can be well implemented by involving people more in the design processes, according to the cross-functional design approach of Bieling (2019).

According to the participants, the diversity of people should be understood as normality (1E0005) and part of life, even part of 'good' people (1E0067), as one participant puts it. Without these parts of life and of people, such creative work would not even be possible (1E0061). The point is that the difference between people is normality, and that people should not have to conform to a particular norm. Accordingly, socially constructed identities must be deconstructed (Winkler & Degele, 2010).This idea requires an attitude that understands diversity as a vital resource and demands respect. Participants repeatedly emphasized that diversity requires an attitude characterized by respect, tolerance, acceptance, and understanding (1E076; 1E0105, 2E0035). Nothing should be taken for granted, and everything deserves appreciation (2E0003). However, this requires being mindful of people to grasp all the differences and understand others (2E0006). This mindfulness is consistent with Robin S. Dillon's (2003) definition of respect to notice, perceive, and understand persons and Sennett's (2004) call to deal with diversity in society appreciatively. In order to avoid some characteristics of people who are not visible and might be overlooked (2E0005), it is important to talk to them (2E0041), especially to listen to them (2E0042). This approach is prevalent in Habermas' (1997) concept of intersubjective or communicative understanding. Similarly, Husserl speaks of understanding the other (Husserl & Held, 2007). The respondents specify that because the more people understand each other, the better they would harmonize with each other (1E0031) and prior knowledge can be explicated to be used constructively (Albert, 2022; Albert & Purgaj, 2022). To facilitate conversations and understanding, a greater number of languages should be learned (2E0059), this clearly points to an appreciation of the respondents of multilingualism. Above all, it is argued that a voice should be given to those who cannot raise theirs (1E0073). It is pointed out that people should travel and live in many countries to adopt an attitude that shows openness (1E0079), tolerance, and curiosity about people and their ideas (1E0101). Appreciating experiences and interest in the world and its different aspects would extend to other countries, cultures, and ways of life (2E0037; 4E0010). A greater variety of ethnicities, people, and cultures would make systems resilient (1E0006) and lead to acceptance (1E0007). However, traditional handicrafts like national embroidery should also be valued (2E0025). This is also pointed out by Brinkmann (2022) when he suggests that learning is always social and interactive, but also culturally dimensioned. At the same time, it involves transmitting cultural techniques and norms, and through the experiential process, it can lead to the development of something new. Therefore, a balance between tradition and progress is essential. This balance means that, on the one hand, the traditional is preserved and passed on to the next generation, and, on the other hand, an opening to the new takes place. Furthermore, an exchange at the national and international level is essential, to see the bigger picture and achieve mutual enrichment (Albert, 2022). According to participants, for teachers, it is essential to challenge dominant paradigms, integrate different world views (1E0019), and to be a role model by respecting different people (1E0077).

In summary, according to participants, exchange is essential in order to understand each other. There needs to be much talking to each other (1E0069) sharing experiences (2E0045). Sharing open sources (2E0017) and linking cultures (2E0055) would promote decentralization of knowledge generation and knowledge sharing (1E0022), leading to more "discoveries for the world" (1E0003). Furthermore, there is a need for sufficient financial support (1E0064; 1E0066). In the context of exchange, it is necessary to be able to express thoughts so that others can listen with interest (1E0008) and ideas should be expressed to make them visible to others (2E0021). As one participant put it, sharing offers the opportunity to "gift others with resources" (4E0007). To do this, it is necessary to leave power imbalances behind and meet on an equal footing. Horizontal respect is required, as is vertical respect, where people admire each other for their experiences, competencies, and knowledge (Albert, 2022).

Exchange leads to joint learning. For the joint learning process, learning from and with each other, the attitude of a learner is essential (Albert, 2022). According to the participants, this requires a shared safe space to try things out and test them (3E0001; 3E0011). More can be learned through diversity (1E0041; 1E0048), as commonality strengthens people and enables acceptance and tolerance (1E0043). Together, people can explore and research (1E0039), solve problems (2E0019; 3E0022), and develop new ideas (3E0017). Commonality increases versatility and flexibility (2E0013), brings freedom (2E0031; 2E0033; 3E0008), and leads to resilience (2E0031) because much energy is released (1E0049). According to a psychological study by Stijovic et al. (2023), social isolation affects people's energy levels negatively. This result suggests that social interaction and problem-solving together have a positive effect on energy levels and thus strengthen resilience. When craftspeople and designers encounter problematic issues, which Holzkamp (1995) identifies as learning occasions, collaborative learning can produce more sustainable solutions, and negative experiences (Brinkmann, 2022) are more easily overcome. Through collaboration, new learning ideas can be found (1E0028), and creative activities can occur in different forms (1E0009). Collaborative learning processes need tools for collaboration, which would need to be developed (3E0002). One participant even states that diversity had been part of their education (1E0065) and was natural (1E0072). A learning process could be stimulated by using a wider variety of patterns, possibilities, and combinations (1E0002), but also varied materials, shapes, colors, and figurines someone designs on (1E0020) that could be mixed up and combined (2E0009) and reassembled (2E0011). Exciting and fun design would allow challenges to be solved (1E0038). As a basis, the handcrafting technique should be learned first (3E0015), and familiarity with the culture should be established to develop something new (3E0016). This familiarity points to the balance between tradition and progress. Consequently, even a sense of wonder (2E0052) could trigger irritations (Brinkmann, 2022) and stimulate learning. Including diversity and shared learning are important and necessary for the creation processes of objects and generally for design (4E0002).

Three participants stated that they thought diversity and learning would bring opportunities for the future (1E0010; 2E0047; 3E0019) and adequate possibilities for situations (1E0016; 4E0005). Thus, one of them adds, that even one plus one could be eleven (1E0042). With this, the participant presumably wants to express that possibilities are also considered that seem unrealizable at first glance and that ultimately make creative solutions possible. Diversity enables accessibility (1E0017; 2E0001) and selecting the best for the many (1E0044). Without diversity, humanity would come to a standstill (3E0020) and would "reach the end" (1E0027; 2E0049), as two participants put it very drastically. Another participant further explains that diversity is necessary for development (1E0025). However, diversity is vital for development (1E0040), not to stand still, to move (1E0032). People should always work on their growth, further development, and progress (1E0045). Because further development and progress are essential for people (2E0039), further development and growth are generally important for life (2E0040), which is "the rule of survival" (1E0046). For moving forward (1E0063), one participant explained, experience is essential (1E0053). This understanding is consistent with Brinkmann's (2022) thesis that learning equates to experience. According to the participants, designing clothes is the focus, and diversity is part of this process (1E0050). Fashion should be in tune with people so that their history can be connected (2E0027) which can be achieved by incorporating local design languages. Craftspeople should be taught how to reuse clothes, for example, by closing holes with small embroideries (3E0005), as this could increase the sustainability of clothes (3E0010). The infinity symbol is used repeatedly by participants (2E0056; 4E0006; 4E0008; 4E0009). This drawing could be understood as an example for continuous development, progress, and growth by including diversity. In summary, this means that embracing diversity – in people, situations, contexts, or even objects – reveals a wealth of experience. This exchange of knowledge opens doors for further development, ultimately leading to a responsible fashion system.

Limitations

Before drawing the necessary conclusions to answer the research question, the methodological limitations of the present study are presented and reflected upon. The results of this study cannot be generalized because the sample size (12 participants) is not representative. In addition, it should be noted that only the responses (108 lines in the coding document), drawings (27), and designed objects (10) of the participants were used for the analysis. Another point that needs to be noted is the composition of the respondents' group. Participants identified themselves as academics, artisans, artists, craftspeople, designers lecturers, millers, and writers. However, these limitations do not affect the accuracy and relevance of the results, as the findings are supported by a careful analysis of the literature, the data, the research method used, and the high Cohen's Kappa value of 0.76 mentioned above.

Conclusion

As the fashion industry faces significant challenges, exploring and questioning established practices and processes is essential. One of these practices that needs to be rethought is the specialization of individual professions within design and the previously neglected handling of cultural and physical diversity. A rapprochement between craftspeople and designers is necessary to enable joint learning processes. The competencies of all participants in the design process should be utilized, and their skills harmonized. At the same time, it is necessary to adopt a humanistic (Schmetkamp, 2012) and democratic attitude and act as equals. This chapter has shown that a community between craftspeople and designers, considering and recognizing all participants, can positively impact diversity in the fashion system. This is unmistakably shown in the results of this study, where resources such as various people, attitudes, exchange, learning, opportunity, and development are to be understood as prerequisites for responsible collaboration. This requirement makes it clear that diversity is a resource that is considered valuable and must be respected to empower the fashion industry to develop responsible and diverse operations. An open, respectful, and appreciative exchange between participants with various skills and backgrounds is essential. This exchange makes it possible to collectively gain new valuable experiences for future decisions and enable lateral collaborations. This means forming a new collaboration that no longer operates only on a vertical, hierarchical level but also allows for horizontal (Meyer et al. 2009) democratic approaches and practices.

While the Industrial Revolution fostered a separation between the professional groups of craft and design (Marcis, 2011), bringing these two professions back together can create valuable opportunities for a distinctive exchange of knowledge. As this research project highlights, the opportunity lies in the fact that a great power of diversity is released through the many resources brought by the participants in the joint process. This power equips the current generation of craftspeople and designers to meet the challenges of modern times and promote a positive change regarding the fashion industry. It is only through the collaboration of various people that creative accountable solutions can be found. While this research project has examined the resources released when craftspeople and designers collaborate, it would be necessary for future research to examine the effects of this collaboration.

These effects could further demonstrate that the power of diversity is a prerequisite for a fashion system that can function responsibly. Another topic that should receive attention in future research projects regarding the structure of fashion is the impact of the separation of professional groups in education, training, and continuing education concerning different diversity dimensions to ensure barrier-free education and togetherness in the design field as well.

References

Albert, S. (2022). *Wie das Menschenbild die Unterrichtspraxis beeinflusst. Empirisch-rekonstruktive Studie zu Respekt aus Schülersicht.* Bielefeld: wbv Publikation. https://elibrary.utb.de/doi/book/10.3278/9783763971312

Albert, S., & Purgaj, J. (2022). *Împreună II.* Chişinău: OeAD-GmbH.

Anguelov, N. (2021). *The Sustainable fashion quest: Innovations in business and policy.* Routledge. https://doi.org/10.4324/9781003153344

Bell, Q. (1963). *The schools of design.* London: Routledge.

Bieling, T. (2019). *Inklusion als Entwurf. Teilhabeorientierte Forschung über, für und durch Design.* Birkhäuser. https://doi.org/10.1515/9783035620214

Bourdieu, P. (1992). *Rede und Antwort.* Frankfurt/Main: Suhrkamp.

Bourdieu, P. (1993). *Soziologische Fragen.* Frankfurt/Main: Suhrkamp.

Brinkmann, M. (2022). Lernen. In M. Feldmann, M. Rieger-Ladich, C. Voß, & K. Wortmann (Eds.), *Schlüsselbegriffe der Allgemeinen Erziehungswissenschaft. Pädagogisches Vokabular in Bewegung* (pp. 277–286). Weinheim Basel: Beltz.

Cross, N. (2011). *Design thinking: Understanding how designers think and work.* London: Bloomsbury. https://doi.org/10.5040/9781474293884

Dillon, R. S. (2003). Respect. *Stanford encyclopedia of philosophy.* Retrieved September 24, 2021 from https://plato.stanford.edu/archives/fall2003/entries/respect/

Döring, N. (2023). *Forschungsmethoden und Evaluation in den Sozial- und Humanwissenschaften.* Berlin: Springer-Verlag GmbH. https://doi.org/10.1007/978-3-662-64762-2

Habermas, J. (1997). *Theorie des kommunikativen Handelns. Band 2. Zur Kritik der funktionalistischen Vernunft.* Frankfurt/Main: Suhrkamp Verlag.

Holzkamp, K. (1995). *Lernen. Subjektwissenschaftliche Grundlegung.* Frankfurt/Main and New York: Campus Verlag.

Husserl, E., & Held, K. (Eds.) (2007). *Phänomenologie der Lebenswelt. Universal-Bibliothek. Band 8085.* Bibliograph. rev. Ausg. Nachdruck. Stuttgart: Reclam.

Jurt, J. (2012). Bourdieus Kapital-Theorie. In M. M. Bergman (Ed.), *Bildung, Arbeit, Erwachsenwerden: Ein interdisziplinärer Blick auf die Transition im Jugend- und jungen Erwachsenenalter* (pp. 21–41). Wiesbaden: Springer VS.

Kawamura, J. (2005). *Fashion-ology: An Introduction to fashion studies (dress, body, culture).* New York: Berg Publisher; First Edition. https://doi.org/10.2752/9781847888730

Kluge, F. (2011). *Etymologisches Wörterbuch der deutschen Sprache.* Berlin: De Gruyter.

Mareis, C. (2011). *Design als Wissenskultur. Interferenzen zwischen Design und Wissensdiskursen seit 1960.* Bielefeld: transcript Verlag. https://doi.org/10.1515/transcript.9783839415887

Mayring, P. (2015). *Qualitative Inhaltsanalyse. Grundlagen und Techniken.* Weinheim. https://doi.org/10.1007/978-3-531-18939-0_38

Mayring, P., & Fenzl, T. (2014). Qualitative Inhaltsanalyse. In N. Baur & J. Blasius (Eds.), *Handbuch Methoden der empirischen Sozialforschung* (pp. 543–556). Wiesbaden: Springer VS. https://doi.org/10.1007/978-3-531-18939-0_38

Mecheril, P., & Plößer, M. (2022). Differenz. In M. Feldmann, M. Rieger-Ladich, C. Voß, & K. Wortmann (Eds.), *Schlüsselbegriffe der Allgemeinen Erziehungswissenschaft. Pädagogisches Vokabular in Bewegung* (pp. 95–102). Weinheim, Basel: Beltz Juventa.

Meyer, M., Eckloff, T., & Van Quaquebeke, N. (2009). Was Schüler sagen, wie Lehrer Respekt verdienen oder verlieren. *RespectResearchGroup*. http://www.respectresearchgroup.org/respect/literatur-s/

Morgan, A. (Producer). (2015). *The true cost* [Film]. United States: Untold Creative.

Riegel, C. (2016). *Bildung. Intersektionalität. Othering. Pädagogisches Handeln in Widersprüchlichen Verhältnissen*. Bielefeld: transcript Verlag. https://doi.org/10.1515/9783839434581

Schmetkamp, S. (2012). *Respekt und Anerkennung*. Paderborn: mentis Verlag GmbH. https://doi.org/10.30965/9783957439420

Schütz, A., & Luckmann, T. (2003). *Strukturen der Lebenswelt*. Konstanz: UVK.

Sennett, R. (2004). *Respekt im Zeitalter der Ungleichheit*. Berlin: Berlin Verlag.

Stijovic, A., Forbes, P. A. G., Tomova, L., Skoluda, N., Feneberg, A. C., Piperno, G., Pronizius, E., Nater, U. M., Lamm, C., & Silani, G. (2023). Homeostatic regulation of energetic arousal during acute social isolation: Evidence from the lab and the field. *Psychological Science*, *34*(5), 537–551. https://doi.org/10.1177/09567976231156413

Vedder, G. (2006). Die historische Entwicklung von Diversity Management in den USA und in Deutschland. In G. Krell & H. Wächter (Eds.), *Diversity management. Impulse aus der Personalforschung* (pp. 1–23). München: Rainer Hampp Verlag.

Walgenbach, K. (2017). *Heterogenität - Intersektionalität - Diversity in der Erziehungswissenschaft*. Opland and Toronto: Verlag Barbara Budrich. https://doi.org/10.36198/9783838586700

Wenning, N. (1999). *Vereinheitlichung und Differenzierung. Zu den ‚wirklichen' gesellschaftlichen Funktionen des Bildungswesens im Umgang mit Gleichheit und Verschiedenheit*. Opladen: Leske + Budrich Verlag.

Wiesner, M., & Flicke, C. (2023). Erwin Panofsky's Interpretationsmodell. Otto-von-Guericke-Universität, Fakultät für Humanwissenschaften. https://bildinterpretation.weebly.com/erwin-panofskys-interpretationsmodell.html

Winkler, G., & Degele, N. (2010). *Intersektionalität. Zur Analyse sozialer Ungleichheiten*. Bielefeld: transcript Verlag. https://doi.org/10.1515/9783839411490

Zhu, L., & Goyal, Y. (2019). Art and Science: Intersections of art and science through time and paths forward. *EMBO Reports*, *20*(1). https://doi.org/10.15252/embr.201847061

11 Courtyard as classrooms

Empowering learners through design research in rural India

Saumya Pande and Richa Sood

Preface

Kheta is a reversible, hand embroidered, repurposed quilted textile. It is traditionally made by women of the remote Shershadadi community in Bihar, in Eastern India (Pande, 2021). This reversible quilting technique only uses needle and thread, no other tool. It demonstrates the mathematical genius of women who are mostly illiterate yet remarkably sensitive to their lived experiences, landscape and built environment. They have migrated along the rivers and remained marginalised as a community for 400 years. This remarkable textile, community identity for Shershabadis, was undocumented till 2017. Here are the key points that led to the due recognition of the textile and writing of this chapter:

> Saumya Pande, fashion design course leader at Indian Institute of Art & Design (IIAD), began independent research on Kheta embroidery in 2017. Over six years, twelve field trips were conducted across Kishanganj and Purnea districts in Bihar. The researcher resided with artisans in villages, documenting variously their practices, processes, and the living tradition of the craft. Nearly 25 villages were covered, with visits to 7-10 households in each village. Several academic papers were written and presentations delivered at national and international levels within five years (De & Pande, 2018). Experts were consulted to confirm Kheta's lack of prior documentation with the specific details of the community. The initiative received government and NGO support. In the course of the work, the Ministry of Textiles (n.d.) started focusing on Kheta's preservation and government schemes were implemented to train women artisans, enhance their skills and help them develop new products. In 2021, the Ministry of Textiles acknowledged Kheta embroidery as an endangered craft, promoting its preservation.
>
> The National Crafts Museum & Hastkala Academy (n.d.) in New Delhi organised a month-long exhibition of Kheta textiles titled *Kheta. The Embroidered Expressions of Shershabadis* in 2022 in academic partnership with the design institute. For this, the women quilters

DOI: 10.4324/9781003508076-15

were invited to demonstrate the documented patterns of Kheta and sell Kheta blankets, throws, runners and notebook-sleeves on the premises. The women left their villages and stepped into an urban space for the first time, accompanied by the menfolk.

The consistent efforts helped Kheta get enlisted as a part of UNESCO's representative list of the Intangible Cultural Heritage of Humanity (UNESCO, 2022), in which 50 textile crafts from India were nominated. This paved the way for Kheta to be also recognised for Geographical Indication status in due course.

The following paper traces the introduction of students to the project with Project-Based-Learning (PBL). This method aims at providing a robust educational ecosystem by creating a large circle of stakeholders and aligned learning objectives.

(Almulla, 2020)

The Indian Institute of Art and Design teaches students about rural craft practices

In 2022, the Indian Institute of Art and Design in New Delhi (IIAD) conducted a classroom project based on traditional craft practices which involved students travelling to meet Kheta women quilters in a rural region of Bihar. The students went to the region to learn from the embroiderers and to receive the opportunity to immerse themselves in the context and effects of this particular craft and its cultural and environmental significance. The project was devised in an interdisciplinary way to provide multifaceted insights and learning opportunities.

The IIAD is uniquely positioned to conceptualise and carry out student research projects that are backed by grass root research by the teaching team. It was set up in 2016 as a private design institute in India. The accreditation from Kingston University (KU), a university steeped in the dynamic and thriving history of design education, provided the opportunity for design academicians to explore radical approaches to subject definition, associated learning cultures and alternative methodology.

The curriculum adheres to national design and educational policy guidelines, which encourage the innovative, explorative and transdisciplinary exploration of new fields of study. One of them is the National Design Policy (2011) paper. This acknowledges the strategic role of design for national and industrial competitiveness and realises the increasing importance of design in economic, industrial and societal development in the 21st century. It envisages the "preparation of a platform for creative design development, design promotion and partnerships across many sectors, states and regions for integrating design with traditional and technological resources" (National Design Policy). This involves focusing on strengthening quality design education at different levels, encouraging the use of designs produced by small scale and cottage industries and crafts, facilitating active involvement of industry and designers in the development of the design profession and more. Design promotion comprises training for craftspeople and artisans, which plays a vital role both in India's economic landscape as well as in establishing the complex socio-cultural context. Craftsmen and artisans are, thereby, equipped to enhance the traditional knowledge, skills and capabilities while being sensitive to global heritage.

Another guideline for the curriculum is the National Education Policy (Ministry of Human Resource Development, 2020). This sets out to ensure that higher education furthers an enlightened, socially conscious, knowledgeable and skilled nation that can find and implement robust solutions to its own problems. National Education Policy identifies as the problems higher education faces as (1) rigid separation of disciplines with early specialisation and streaming of students in narrow areas of study and (2) lesser emphasis on research and research funding across disciplines resulting in low standards of undergraduate studies.

In the backdrop of the guiding principles the design institute upheld its vision of the adherence to sustainability, ethics, respect for and promotion of indigenous practices and cultural identity as part of the contemporary concerns in design education. This vision also includes that *education has to be conducted in an open ended, multidisciplinary, learner-centric environment which allows students to chart their own trajectories as critical thinkers and self-reflexive design practitioners* (Programme Specifications, IIAD, confidential document).

This was particularly suitable for this endeavour as IIAD identified *project-based learning, circular progression between the levels, studio-based learning and common module system* (across levels) as four pillars of the pedagogical ethos. The course leadership was entrusted with the translation of the program specifications in the classroom.

From classroom to courtyard – Planning the project

Real life experiential learning is not an alternative approach, but the most fundamental method of human learning. – Usha Patel, Dean, IIAD

As we negotiated different approaches to project-based learning, especially at the intermediate level which formed the interface with the industry, the space of design pedagogy became a fertile ground for conversations on regionality, diversity and inclusivity in Indian textile traditions for mainly urban students. It was acknowledged that to make young learners' industry-ready, it is critical to embed values of ethicality, problem solving and adaptability within the teaching framework. This was a vital part of the project and was aimed at countering virtual environments and the temporality of trends and flattening of fashion imagery they produce. It was agreed upon that future designers would need to carve their niche in an over-saturated and volatile environment with the values mentioned above. For teaching about community-based crafts, the classroom should be a space where learning, retention and engagement are enhanced and students get to generate their own view point about subject knowledge irrespective of the enclosure, emphasising diversity of experience to be central to a creative curriculum.

One of the ways of achieving this was by bringing indigenous knowledge for immersive learning into fashion studies. The aim of the Craft Project was to explore the classroom beyond the usual institutional boundaries, to ensure authentic experiences of craft as a living practice and understand its context, which includes acknowledging the impact of socio, cultural, economic and environmental aspects that surround craft practices in India. The driving conversations for teaching and addressing the learning for the project were anchored in building student consciousness around craft as a way of living; witnessing a slower process of making so that they explore minimal waste as an approach towards product development. Conversations were focussed on exploring design going beyond 'factory made'.

The project was envisioned as an undertaking in which students enter the space of craft traditions with the aim of learning from the ecosystem by embracing it, by breaking hierarchies and dichotomies, the divide of urban and rural, by nurturing relationships and by acknowledging cultural dialogues before witnessing the making. The project was to be an exemplar for bringing in live grassroot research, as a ground for learning the design process and building a design brief through sustained interaction with the women artisans in the craft cluster. The questions we asked were: Who will learn from whom in a meaningful dialogue? How can tasks and assignments be co-created? How can practice and theory be seen as inherently connected by the design students?

The challenge was to change the spatial dynamics of learning and take the cohort out of the class and away from the campus. Because the premise was that for a typical urban student of design in North India, craft is seen as expensive products in craft bazaars and the disconnect between craft, the context and the consumer is apparent. The aim was to give insights into craft being an expression of the land and the people, a part of everyday utility, not as a curated technique. This goes hand in hand with the acknowledgement of non-western creative practices being firmly rooted in, growing out of and shaping specific social and cultural contexts. Providing this as a first-hand experience is part of the aim of shifting students' perspective towards cultural inclusivity and meeting the increasing demand of diversity in design.

Who came together

For the Kheta embroidery project, teaching was devised to happen in overlapped spaces of multi- and transdisciplinary environments (see Figure 11.1), to co-create through active collaboration of tutors with learners from different design disciplines. While IIAD focussed on design processes and pedagogical framework, Azad India Foundation and Zameen Astar Foundation (www.azadindia.org, n.d.) brought complex contexts and connections with

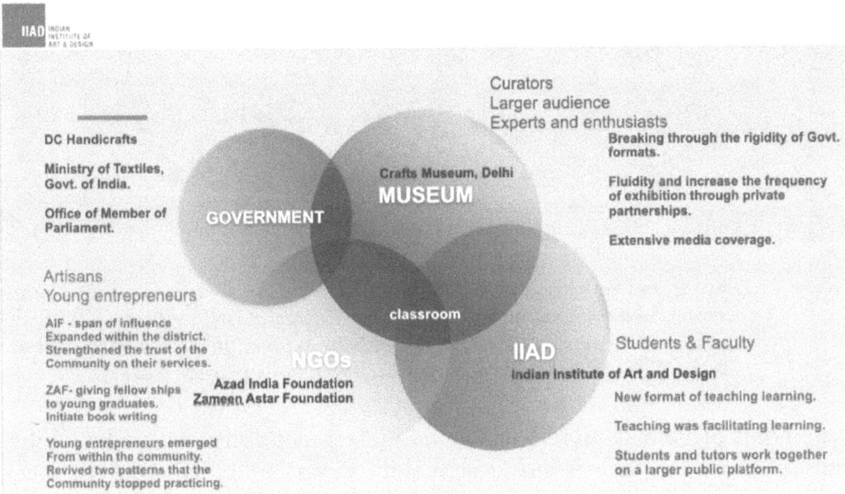

Figure 11.1 A multidisciplinary overlap of teaching, learning, research, curation and craft communities, to create dynamic classrooms. Copyright: Pvt. collection, IIAD, craft project 2021.

craftsmanship. This collaboration facilitated the planning and execution of the study tour to the region of Bihar, which ultimately made the meeting of students with craftswomen of the Shahabadi community possible. This is where the project provided first-hand insights and experience of crafters, crafting and craft in the communities and environments it arose from.

The second phase of collaboration was an exhibition of the quilting technique, the embroidery and embroidered textile objects in the National Craft Museum. This has created a platform for a national presence and conversations for *Kheta,* the quilted textiles of Shershabadis, pursuing the goal of combining research, documentation and curation. This approach brought in design education, practice and curation on the same platform creating fertile intersections for learning and co-creating for learners along with experts and professionals where everybody learns from each other and in turn, benefit the design student and educators alike. An informed study tour was organised to enable an interdisciplinary approach by bringing together students at the various stages of their studies.

The teaching plan

At the core the teaching was the encouragement of students to decode the intangible narratives hidden in the craft form. They learned to understand and read the translation of the intangible to tangible. In the process of decoding, numerous details were unveiled to reveal the narratives and the form. The plan was structured in a way to organically push students to generate

Figure 11.2 Students begin the day by stepping into the courtyards that are vibrant with conversations about these quilted textiles, its connection with the land and its people, emerging as resilient expressions of the Shershahbadi women. Copyright: Pvt. collection, IIAD, craft project 2021.

their point of view as a responsible designer practitioner with adaptability and collaboration as a future design skill. It was unfolded week by week with carefully aligned inputs to scaffold the learning and support the aim of the study tour to sensitively enhance experiential learning within the tactile environment of the craft cluster.

The teaching was embedded in the study tour with the aim of getting students to appreciate craft as a living embodiment of its environment and people and as a way of living (see Figure 11.2) – by living with the people of the community to experience craft as a daily practice.

This format of experiencing craft was planned in the teaching approach, building a multi-sensorial perspective towards the context of the craft. This also involved creating opportunities for a dynamic learning environment (see Figure 11.3) with high tactile elements that juxtapose each other informing the manifestation of Kheta.

Figure 11.3 Students work and learn within the dynamic space of the craft, as a living practice, and take back its essence to unpack an individual design process/language informed by zero waste, reversibility and reuse. Copyright: Pvt. collection, IIAD, craft project 2021.

Masterclasses and expert talks were organised on related topics like – local and rural economy, agrarian economy, Gandhian philosophy and repurposing, deliberating a non-fashion route towards understanding craft. Conversations, activities and tasks related to project deliverables were positioned in order to equip students with relevant thinking and iterating tools. The tasks and assignments were designed for an active engagement with documentation of the craft cluster, where they documented the craft in its larger context – land, river, build spaces and the people. Within the category of crafts, students documented *Kheta and Pankha* (fan), the granaries and basketry.

Specific tutorials were incorporated for zero waste pattern making, quilting and reversible seam finishing techniques, for students to iterate and apply the same for the final garment deliverables. These parameters were made explicit so that students also study the embroidered quilt from the perspective of re-use, reversibility and zero waste. Development of individual design narrative and explorations were made constructive and interactive through curated peer reviews and feedback along with regulated tutor guidance.

From classroom to courtyard – *The Scenario*

When the doors of the courtyards of the craftswomen were opened for the cohort, the boundaries of the classroom became pervasive. Learning took place when the lines that defined inside and the outside became seamless, when the outside very much became the inside:

> It's 7 am in Kishanganj, Bihar (eastern India). Students start walking from the hostel, through the fields, surrounded by the sound water being drawn by the hand pump. They enter the courtyard under the rising sun, bare feet, on a surprisingly chilled clay laden floor. Senior women quilters are waiting for the students for the planned interactions. Tajkhera, the master quilter, puts out the grass mat in her courtyard for students to sit on the mud floor while she ensures that cooking for the next meal is done and out of her way. While she gets the roosters back in their coop, she keeps the old worn-out sarees stacked in a corner ready to be layered for quilting. Her 16- and 12-year-old daughters, Nazrana and Kareema, help students settle down.
>
> They scatter themselves forming clusters, observing, learning stitches, counting and separating threads, attempting the techniques, communicating through sign language and witnessing the multiple dimensions that are informing the Kheta embroidery in the courtyard. The courtyard is an expanse where women are multitasking along with embroidering as a daily chore. In the next half an hour, women from extended family and neighboring houses slowly pour in to help Tajkhera initiate the process of quilting. Each one of the students is closely monitored to

ensure that they achieve the Kheta patterns. All women, mostly illiterate, facilitate the process of learning. With slow practice, the students graduate from simple running stitches to some complex Kheta patterns. The students appreciate the genius of the Shershabadi women as they understand the visual mathematical calculation. With just needle and thread, no other tool, they make the most complex patterns! Students relate to the names of the patterns and observe how the women have related to their surroundings.

What shifted when the courtyard became a classroom?

A courtyard is central to the Indian tradition of living in a humid tropical climate. The modest homes of Shershabadis have only one *aangan* (courtyard), the centralised open space, surrounded by semi-enclosed verandah and built rooms on the outside. Open to sky, these ensure air circulation and ventilation, access to sunlight and privacy to women and children. Most of the time, it is the extension of the kitchen as another *chulha* (mud stove) is added in the courtyard to cook during winter months. As a female domain, the wealth of the household, the granaries, cattle, rosters, etc. are visible at a glance from the courtyard. When required the courtyard becomes space for the *charpai* (woven bed) to be put out for guests to be gathered and entertained or for the menfolk to sleep in the hot summer months. The women of the extended families are able to take care of their newly born, stir the vegetables on the fire stove, feed the cattle, wash clothes, dry them and also work on their quilt in the afternoons. It remains always alive and dynamic, not rigidly fixed, but adapted to daily chores, seasons and human interactions, small and big. Many times, it is used for marriages too.

In the Craft Project, the courtyards of the Shershabadi (see Figure 11.4) became a space where women came together to start off a Kheta, work on it

Figure 11.4 Students sat alongside women, to learn embroidery stitches, embracing their environment blurring the hierarchy of urban and rural. Communication was both emotive and informative. In absence of common spoken language, both communicated through signs, expressions and actions. Copyright: Pvt. collection, IIAD, craft project 2021.

for next several months, bringing together the common collective practices, based on community connectedness and collaboration. It led to:

1 A wider angle of understanding the complex interrelationship of physical and human expression: The students familiarised themselves with the unknown context of the craft and the community and build capacity to work with the unfamiliar. They gained extensive experience of practice of making and doing by observing, negotiating and simultaneously reflecting on the process. Students understood the correlation of motifs and patterns from observing the river, the land, the built spaces and the agricultural practices.
2 Learning collaboratively in a supportive environment: The courtyard became a space for everybody present to become a curious learner. It created a capacity and a supporting environment for each stakeholder to learn a higher or a different skill within and without the discipline. The space was so dynamic that responsiveness became the utmost important element in such a learning. In the days spent by students in the courtyard of various Shershabadi homes or time spent walking up to the river, instruction was not provided or given by the teacher; rather, it was negotiated between students, the local women, the teenaged daughters and accompanying teachers collaboratively, developing as ideas of students emerged and grew. The informal mentoring fostered students' creative pursuit and that of others in a reciprocal and simultaneous way.
3 Open ended, inclusive participation: It generated confidence to take risks and learn from mistakes without fear of censure. Courtyard allowed heterogeneous cohorts with diverse backgrounds to evolve into more fluid and less linear structure in which teaching teams, student groups and the artisans formed and reformed in ways that genuinely recognised and responded to the transience, agility and unpredictability. Most of the students came from urban and semi-urban backgrounds and the exposure to the deepest rural areas of the country helped them understand that as design learners, it was crucial to represent historically marginalised, disadvantaged and underrepresented groups, irrespective of their place of residence. It also became a lesson in design, given the situation of less facilities and privileges.
4 Deep learning in the expansive courtyard: The expansive view of the courtyard wasn't just a backdrop – it was a catalyst for deep learning. This open environment empowered students to confidently voice their opinions, fostering a space for open dialogue and critical thinking. But the learning extended beyond the students. Teachers, too, embraced the role of learners, driven by a passion for and real connection with their disciplines. This journey required a high degree of self-awareness. Teachers had to recognise the impact of their decisions on students and the broader learning environment. This awareness fostered a willingness to take responsibility for their own actions and guide students in navigating theirs.

> It became about the ability to dissect complex topics, draw connections across disciplines and contexts and weave them into a tapestry of learning relevant to the students' lives, their communities and the broader world.

Tasks and assignments were among the most important aspects of student learning as these were designed as thinking frameworks for reflecting, exploring and risk taking in terms of skills of making and challenging their own skill sets. Tasks included creating an experiential personal narrative, which becomes the anchor point for product development, using the lens of sustainable approach to garment making. One of the key learnings for students was to apply the 'approach' of Kheta. Specifically, this comprised of reuse of textiles, quilting, layering and zero waste, to create a garment – and an introduction to reversibility, because Kheta is constructed with both sides of the textile being of equal significance. The assignments required the student to assess the layering and shrinkage in advance and create a quilted yardage, instead of using a ready quilt (see Figure 11.5). The second layer of challenge unfolded during the zero-waste pattern ideation process. Tutors engaged for multiple hours with students (during the third wave of the pandemic, this was done online) to guide on the pattern ideation and scaling up as students experimented through paper folding. Final ideas were discussed through sketches and semi-stitched versions online.

The third level of challenge was to stitch the quilt weight material, which was a major learning, pinned at the skill of material understanding and construction. Students grappled with challenges of seam finishes and garment finishing and fittings, while catering to the parameter of reversibility. These tasks were an opportunity to observe, analyse, explore, apply, reflect and witness their own journey of building a narrative from the intangible to a tangible finished product. Though teaching inputs and tasks were constructed across the four modules with curated emphasis, the main learning was intended to be reflected in the design process module – the process was the main element for assessment and feedback as reflexivity and individual

Figure 11.5 Students create quilts, re-using old sarees and textiles thus engaging with the nuances of challenges of making a textile and planning its form honouring handwork, time, minimal wastage and wearability for a contemporary/niche market. This approach to learning is essentially embedded in IIAD's ethos of learning by doing. Copyright: Pvt. collection, IIAD, craft project 2021.

point of view of the students gets most evident in the journey of reaching the outcome. This was one of the key learnings embedded throughout the project across all deliverables.

The eight-week project culminated in an on-campus exhibition at IIAD, where the students came together to recreate their lived experiences and memories of Kishanganj. Students were encouraged to propose ideas for the display that best communicated what they had experienced, through their documentation of the land, the river, the built spaces and the people. The exhibition was positioned as a teaching strategy making it student led to strengthen teamwork skills, time management, presentation and curation, space planning, material understanding – to enable recalling, revisiting, retention and reconnecting all aspects of study and experience.

The students were provided with holistic and significant learning experiences. The following quotes show that this also provided quite unexpected insights:

> I still remember, the sun was scorching hot and I wondered how we would ever work and learn in this heat? Is the whole day going to be this way? The moment we reached the courtyard, I was shocked to put my bare feet on the mud laden floor. It was so comforting and I knew this was going to be a different experience.
>
> (Sana Saxena, F.D level 5, cohort 2021)

> It completely shifted our concept of a re-do. While learning from one of the women, they would teach a stitch and go do some household chores. On coming back, when she saw what I embroidered was wrong, she simply unravelled it. Seeing how frustrated I was, she smiled and said 'Just do it again'. I learnt to be ok with re-doing something if it had gone wrong.
>
> (Anushka Aggarwal, F.D level 5, cohort 2021)

> We were called to her courtyard at 8am. It was such a different experience going for a class, through the lanes and fields. I realised there is so much for us to learn from them instead. We came in like outsiders, yet they all were so welcoming and open to share their space and stories with us.
>
> (Kartik Mahalwal, F.D level 5, cohort 2021)

> Looking at the chaos in the courtyard, I thought I won't remember anything. But surprisingly I remember every stitch that they taught me. I even remember my mistakes.
>
> (Sana Saxena, F.D level 5, cohort 2021)

> I was inspired by how it brings the community together, sharing stories and working with the needle and thread to express yourselves and

> embracing individuality. It was so inspiring that I took that learning forward in my MDP and researched more about what craftsmanship is and how working with hands is so important for every individual, it led to me the understanding of how it makes one person resilient and provides strength from inside.
>
> (Sanjana Grover, F.D level 5, cohort 2021)

> I learned that design can actually come from anywhere, and suddenly everything started connecting, and that there are multiple ways of generating a design process.
>
> (Jasleen Kaur, F.D level 5, cohort 2021)

The project briefly outlined that the main aim was to understand the social and cultural context that surrounds the craft. But evidencing the craft by living with the community gave the real perspective as that connection came alive for the students. Engaging with the crafters, living with them and spending the days the same way they do, and learning to understand *Kheta* through the lens of their environment, created a sense of openness and comprehension that craft practice is open to interpretation, yet anchored in its context. One of the interesting aspects students shared was seeing mending as a design approach. Mending is not to be perceived as rectifying a mistake, rather as an act of 'keeping together'. As an embodiment of their spirit, resilience and expressions, mending the quilt was a sense of healing, restoring the texture of the community. Understanding that there are multiple ways to generate a design process – was an experiential process. Witnessing a rudimentary approach to a design process away from the urban viewpoint helped the students to identify their own learning barriers and take ownership of their work.

Interdisciplinarity and participation

The campus exhibition of the project results at IIAD was a rehearsal to prepare, plan and step up for the national-level exhibition at the National Crafts Museum. This was a larger platform where expertise across departments was deployed to plan and execute the exhibition. For the first time in India, an education institute across design departments, several NGOs, the crafts community and several government bodies came together to showcase a common cause, on one platform (The Indian Express, 2022).

The intradisciplinary project was initiated within the department faculty, researchers and students across levels collaborating as co-workers. This included procuring, organising Kheta quilts, planning the contents, content writing, creating graphic panels, printing and preparing the quilts and textiles for display. Fashion Design (FD) and Interior Architecture Design (IAD) faculties working together along with students on space planning, dimensions, layouts, lighting, material and props. FD and Communication Design

(CD) collaborated for branding of Kheta for the exhibition, sale and display at Crafts Museum.

While fashion students explored aspects of techniques, quilting, reversibility and zero waste (for garment design), IAD and CD students collaborated on their own academic learnings and mandate embedded in their participation. Another final level CD student took up branding strategy for *Kheta* as her graduate project. Rest of the final level CD students, as part of their study tour, created a documentary film capturing the spirit and resilience of the Shershabadi community from Kishanganj which was showcased at the National Craft Museum, New Delhi during the month-long exhibition in March 2022 (IIAD, 2024).

Conclusion

In India, traditional crafts embody a vibrant interplay between individual expression and community. This is especially true for marginalised groups, where the craft and craftspeople are sustained by the community's collective strength. Women from extended families join forces. They gather used sarees to begin a Kheta, meticulously ensuring the quilt's sides are creased, folded and layered. When they start off a Kheta, securing the layers with stay stitches, they work in unison, each embroidered line precisely parallel to the last. This collaborative spirit fosters solace and resilience. Together, they celebrate even slow progress, each woman creating a unique, signature quilt on her own.

The documentation and curation necessitated the craftswomen to travel from the comfort zone of homes to urban spaces. But it ensured a safe environment and gave them a platform to reach out to a niche audience in the national capital. For the first time this brought them to newer markets, textile enthusiasts, researchers and buyers, realising the value of their skills beyond the boundaries of their land, both in terms of appreciating the precision, its unique visual appeal, cultural context and monetary value. An uninterrupted space was created where the artisan could directly interact with visitors and potential customers, unpacking the unexplored potential of the craft technique in terms of product development. This encouraged young entrepreneurs (see Figure 11.6) who emerged from within the Shershahbadi community, to take initiative to bring the textile quilt to urban platforms.

The project was a whirlwind of collaboration, demanding seamless coordination across different disciplines. Field experts from various backgrounds were brought together to tackle tasks like acquiring materials and merchandise, arranging travel for local craftswomen and liaising with museum officials and the workforce to set up the exhibition space. But the responsibilities didn't stop there. Ensuring everything ran smoothly also involved proofreading materials, overseeing the printing of catalogues and binding of books, designing invitations (both physical and digital) and even installing temporary structures at the exhibition site. This project truly demanded a unique skillset: the ability to work across disciplines (transdisciplinary), adapt to different

Figure 11.6 Ashraful Haque. 25-year-old Shershabadi, now running Kheta Women Collective. Copyright: Pvt. collection, Prof. Saumya Pande, Crafts Museum, Delhi. March 2022.

tasks creatively (creatively mobile), handle unexpected situations with agility and maintain a focus on all aspects of the project (multi-oriented).

Newer potential and possibilities for the various stakeholders

The interdisciplinary work on the project encouraged young minds to participate in research and explore new mediums for documentation, while formulating their individual point of view. Students viewed research as a medium of active learning to broaden their perspectives on the subject, adding more dimensions as future design practitioners. Student immersion was heightened as they worked alongside tutors blurring the power dynamic, creating a community of learners.

Taking the conversations for curation forward this was a unique opportunity for Crafts Museum, New Delhi to come together in a joint venture with academic institutes and NGOs for a common cause. It took away the rigid government regulations, making the museum an aggregator for larger community building, threading together craft communities, textile researchers, design educators, practitioners, urban customers, corporates and students.

The project yielded significant benefits for the Government of India across various departments in terms of support for handicraft traditions, enhancement of artisan livelihoods, celebration of cultural heritage and gain of international recognition for unique Indian crafts.

For DC Handicrafts, it potentially identified a new set of artisans practicing the unique 'endangered' Kheta embroidery, bolstering government efforts to support handicraft production. This collaboration led to skill development and product innovation workshops for these artisans, aligning with DC Handicrafts' mission to enhance their marketability. The Ministry of Textiles benefitted immensely from the project's comprehensive documentation of Kheta embroidery, previously undocumented. This paved the way for its potential listing with UNESCO's Intangible Cultural Heritage of Humanity, elevating Kheta's profile and attracting increased support for its preservation. The project's focus also contributed to the Office of Member of Parliament identifying Kheta embroidery as endangered during Mrs. Smriti Irani's ministership.

This recognition now leads to specific programs aimed at safeguarding this precious tradition, held together by the community itself.

References

Almulla, M. A. (2020). The effectiveness of the project-based learning (PBL) approach as a way to engage students in learning. *Sage Open*, *10*(2). https://doi.org/10.1177/2158244020938702

Sources

Azad India Foundation. (n.d.). [online] https://www.azadindia.org/; accessed 14.05.24

Indian Institute of Art and Design. (n.d.). About us. https://www.iiad.edu.in/

Indian Institute of Art and Design (IIAD). (n.d.). Design courses: Best design college in Delhi, India. [online] Available at: https://www.iiad.edu.in/.

Ministry of Human Resource Development. (2020). National Education Policy 2020 Ministry of Human Resource Development Government of India. [online] https://www.education.gov.in/sites/upload_files/mhrd/files/NEP_Final_English_0.pdf; accessed 14.05.24

Ministry of Textiles. (n.d.). *Quality control orders*. Home Ministry of Textiles. Government of India. Retrieved May 17, 2024, from https://texmin.gov.in/quality-control-orders-qco

National Crafts Museum. (n.d.). *Vision and mission*. Ministry of Textiles, Government of India. Retrieved May 17, 2024, from https://nationalcraftsmuseum.nic.in/

National Design Policy. (2011). Approved by the Government of India 2007. Retrieved May 17, 2024, from https://indiadesigncouncil.org/pdf/National_Design_Policy.pdf

The Indian Express. (2022). *Women of the Shershabadi community sew tales of tradition to keep a lesser-known craft form alive*. https://indianexpress.com/article/lifestyle/life-style/womens-day-the-women-of-the-shershabadi-community-and-their-reversible-quilts-kheta-7804910/

UNESCO. (2022). *Handmade for the 21st century*: Safeguarding traditional textiles. https://unesdoc.unesco.org/ark:/48223/pf0000382921

Videos

Indian Institute of Art and Design (IIAD). (2024, February 27). *KHETA: Embroidered Expressions of the Shershabadis*. Craft and Filmmaking Project.| IIAD. https://www.youtube.com/watch?v=EJYBKdSh5NM

Conference Proceedings

De, I. & Pande, S. (2018). The anonymous descendants of Sher Shah Suri. In Collina, L. (Ed.), *Proceedings of the Cumulus International Conference Paris: Together to get there*. Cumulus: Aalto, Finland, pp. 960–985.

De, I. & Pande, S. (2021). The river and the revered: Tracing the impermanence of the land, the people and the embroidered. In Amatullo, M. (Ed.), *Cumulus Roma Proceedings*. Cumulus: Aalto, Finland, pp. 1351–1363.

Media Coverage of the Project Work

Hindustan Times – Sewing tales of Bihar's lesser known Kheta embroidery. https://www.hindustantimes.com/lifestyle/art-culture/sewing-tales-of-bihar-s-lesser-known-kheta-embroidery-101646568059255.html

Indian Express – Women of the Shershabadi community sew tales of tradition to keep a lesser-known craft form alive. https://indianexpress.com/article/lifestyle/life-style/womens-day-the-women-of-the-shershabadi-community-and-their-reversible-quilts-kheta-7804910/

Press reader – Sewing tales of Bihar's Kheta embroidery. https://www.pressreader.com/india/ht-city/20220305/281956021250193

The Hindu – When vertical thread movements make for diagonal patterns. https://www.thehindu.com/news/cities/Delhi/when-vertical-thread-movements-make-for-diagonal-patterns/article65285487.ece

The Voice of Fashion – Quilting Hands, Layered Stories. https://www.thevoiceoffashion.com/fabric-of-india/features/Quilting-Hands-Layered-Stories-4989

12 Fashion and disability. From diversity to equality?

Analyzing practices in the fashion industry

Sara Kaufman, Carlos Gago Rodriguez, and Anna Zinola

Introduction

Fashion ignores disability. This might sound provocative, but, in fact, it is simply the truth. Many people cannot purchase fashion products because they're just not designed for them. These people cannot relate to the fashion images they see in magazines, and, often enough, cannot even access the stores because of architectural barriers.

While some brands, for instance, Tommy Hilfiger, have adaptive clothing lines, and others, such as Collina Strada, make a point of designing for everyone, they remain a drop in the ocean of fashion design.

As far as communication is concerned, diversity has recently proven to be an excellent marketing tool, hence, the sudden appearance of disabled models in the campaigns of brands such as Gucci and Moschino. But can we really talk of inclusive representation, with a 'diversity-issue' appearing once in a blue moon on the newsstand while the same, able-bodied, models grace magazine covers every month? How many of the self-proclaimed inclusive brands have an adaptive clothing line? How many of their stores are wheelchair-friendly?

Disability is, in fact, ignored by the vast majority of society, with disabled people still struggling to receive basic social assistance. While there are some laws guaranteeing disabled people access to the workplace, they are often relegated to generic and low-paid positions. The fashion industry makes no exception; as a matter of fact, disabled people in fashion companies are quite invisible, especially those with a major body disability. No need to say, in fashion education, design for diversity is hardly ever a part of the curriculum.

However, things are changing. There is a growing demand for representation, recognition and awareness and disabled people are claiming their right to be seen, integrated and respected in all fields. The fashion industry has two options: either stick to its old rules, trying to pass tokenism as inclusivity, or adapt to the change and invest in what needs to be done in order to create, communicate and distribute a product that truly speaks to everyone.

DOI: 10.4324/9781003508076-16

This chapter was written for, and presented during, the Responsible Fashion Series Central Asia edition, which took the participants on a journey along the ancient Silk Road in Uzbekistan and Kazakhstan. In order to better connect to the outstanding local tradition in textiles and to how it can/could be used to implement the local economy while at the same time preventing the loss of cultural identity often brought on by globalization, most of the research presented during the conference was centered on design, artisanal practices, sustainability and identity. We, on the other hand, chose to focus on disability as a matter that connects the entire world and which is – still – globally stigmatized. We focused on the Western fashion industry's response to disability, which is the one we as authors know, and which is very much insufficient, in order to give some examples of what could be done and, mostly, of what could be done better, with no other hope than the one to inspire participants from all over the world to simply look at things from a different, more responsible, perspective, which has ultimately always been the goal of the conference.

Incidentally, disability in both Uzbekistan and Kazakhstan is a very uncomfortable topic, and the genuine concern and sympathy that was voiced from the local audience when we presented this paper in Turkestan are perhaps an indicator of the compassion that it tends to inspire. As former Soviet countries, both Uzbekistan and Kazakhstan have largely been influenced by the Soviet Union's approach to disability, which mostly centered on whether or not an individual could work. In this sense, being disabled was simply regarded as not being able to work and earn a living, hence, not being able to contribute to society. This is also the reason why, specifically in Kazakhstan, all disabilities were grouped in three different clusters, indicating whether individuals had limited possibilities to work (cluster 3) or no possibilities to work at all (clusters 1 and 2) (Seitenova & Becker, 2008). While all people with disability had the right to a pension, this was relatively low and, most of all, it hardly compensated for the psychological impact that feeling literally 'of no use' had on an individual and on their family.

Since the fall of the Soviet Union, things have changed for the better. The enactment of a law in 2005 (amended in 2023) "protecting the rights of disabled persons" accompanied by a series of programs between 2002 and 2007, reflected the goals of the Government of Kazakhstan to reintegrate disabled individuals in society (Seitenova & Becker, 2008). However, due to the country's Soviet heritage and its lack of resources, the process to integration is still very long. Disabled people are continued to be marginalized by society, with children excluded from mainstream education (Stewart & Rittman, 2019) and grown-ups having little to none autonomy.

In Uzbekistan disability appears to be an even more complicated matter, indeed, it is hard to find any literature and data on the subject, at least in English. The officially reported number of persons with disabilities is likely underestimated at 2.1% of the population, with a 2019 World Bank study revealing that in fact about 13.5% of Uzbekistan's population aged 3 and above might have some form of disability, and 3.5% might have severe forms of disability (Data: World Bank) (Akipress, 2022). The lack of an adequate healthcare system, paired with the largely rural area of the country, makes it extremely hard and costly to access resources such as diagnosis and rehabilitation centers (which are only available in the capital city, Tashkent), and children with special needs are mostly segregated in the so-called special schools or simply kept at home (White et al., 2022).

Considering these, rather unsettling, facts and data, using fashion – a subject that everyone is always happy to talk about – to discuss disability in a geographical area where it is still regarded almost as a taboo, was perhaps a fortunate idea; hopefully, it helped to shed a different light, highlighting the potentials of a disabled body instead of just focusing on its limitations.

Framework

Inclusivity and diversity have recently become hot topics in fashion, with brands striving to prove how inclusive they are. Since diversity has proved to be an excellent marketing tool, most of the efforts are put into sending a somehow 'diverse' model on the catwalk, featuring disabled models in seasonal campaigns, or taking part in manifestations such as Pride. In some cases, there is also the development of one or more products dedicated to individuals with disabilities.

But is it enough? Is a campaign, or a self-proclaimed adaptive collection, enough to call oneself inclusive? What concept of inclusion do these practices convey? And how does it differ from that of specifically adaptive clothing brands?

To find some answers, this chapter analyzes the practice of four brands offering clothes for people with disabilities, heterogeneous in terms of heritage, product, price positioning and communication:

- Tommy Hilfiger, an American brand specializing in denim, which also has an adaptive clothing line;
- Kiabi, a French, low-price tag brand dedicated to children and newborns, which has recently launched items marketed at children with disabilities;
- Anna Bonny, a Spanish brand that designs undergarments for women who have had a mastectomy;
- IZ Adaptive, a Canadian brand whose offer is focused on wheelchair-bound people.

The analysis develops around three areas:

1. Product – understanding, if and how the items respond to the needs of people with disabilities;
2. Retail (online, offline) – understanding, if and how the distribution channels facilitate the purchase process;

3 Marketing and communication – understanding, how adaptivity is approached, conceptualized and communicated.

The paper also looks at fashion education – with a focus on the Edinburgh College of Arts, in order to understand how fashion schools could respond to the increasing market demand for adaptive garments, while also promoting inclusivity in a practical manner.

The conclusions aim to delineate the state of affairs and the possible evolution of adaptive fashion, while also defining the opportunities that it opens in terms of business.

Adaptive clothing

Adaptive clothes are specially designed for people with one or more disabilities, with the purpose of facilitating their autonomy when it comes to getting dressed. The key to effective adaptive clothing is catering to the vast array of needs different consumers have, while maintaining style and 'fashionability'. No disability is the same, just like no body is the same; therefore, standardizing adaptive clothing is rather tricky. Most commonly, adaptive clothes feature magnetic or Velcro closures, adjustable waistbands, large zippers that are easier to handle, wide collars, stretchy fabrics and loose fits.

There are currently several brands offering adaptive clothing as a side-line or as a main product. This paper focuses on Tommy Hilfiger, IZ Adaptive, Kiabi and Anna Bonny. Their products are examined both in terms of adaptive features and general aesthetic.

IZ Adaptive

Brand history

The founder of IZ Adaptive, Izzy Camilleri, is a celebrated fashion designer who built a reputation designing high fashion for almost 40 years (IZ Adaptive, n.d.: online).

When, in 2005, a customer approached Camilleri directly about custom clothing that would work with her power wheelchair, she realized the challenges that people with disability face every day in order to get dressed and the lack of options available. Camilleri launched the first IZ Adaptive collection, designed specifically for wheelchair users, in 2009.

Adaptive features

While the features of IZ Adaptive clothes ultimately make them suitable for dressing a diverse range of disabilities (as well as non-disabled people), they were originally conceived for wheelchair users and, therefore, developed in order to maximize the comfort of this specific target. The 'Game changer trousers', featuring IZ Seamless Technology™, "take your comfort to another level by removing all of the seams you would normally be sitting on", as well as having flexible waistbands, choice of button or hook and bar closure, and a silhouette that follows the line of the seated body.

The 'Seated Peacoat', "designed specifically to be comfortable while seated", features an "adjusted hemline for a smooth, clean look, flattering to the seated frame" and a double-breasted magnetic closure.

The 'Camilleri blazer' is designed to work for "both the seated and standing body" and it has side zips that "make for easier access and dressing, along with magnetic closures".

More along this line, the 'Boucle Cape' is easy to toss on and works well both indoors and outdoors, and 'Billy Footwear' has a wrap-around zipper that makes it very easy to put on. All clothes are designed according to what the brand refers to as 'Ease-of-Dress' philosophy. Most of the garments are made of blends which include cotton or wool combined with polyester, spandex or acetate.

Product design

In terms of adaptivity, IZ Adaptive is generally well designed although it offers a limited range of options. In terms of aesthetics, the options are even fewer. The brand ideally tweaks existing clothing making them more inclusive, but ultimately the results are very basic, with a color palette of black and neutrals. The menswear includes a couple of fashionable garments, such as a bomber jacket and jeans in recycled denim, but the womenswear is mostly lacking in both style and femininity.

Tommy Hilfiger

Brand history

Tommy Hilfiger first designed an adaptive fashion line in 2016, when the market was still dominated by hyper-functional, medical garments catered to the elderly. Seeing how his daughter with autism struggled with buttons, shoelaces and with certain fabrics, opened Hilfiger's eyes to the need for a more inclusive fashion industry (Tommy Hilfiger, n.d.: online).

Adaptive features

Tommy Adaptive includes various solutions which are divided in three main categories: ease of movement, fits for prosthetics and seated wear. The range of facilitating options allows it to cater to several different kinds of disabilities, though many are only suitable for people with exclusively fine motoric issues. These include magnetic buttons, easy-open necklines, low front – high back (suited for wheelchair users), wide-leg zipper openings (suitable for prosthetic legs) and sensory-style (flat seams and no tags, to soothe bodies with significant sensibilities such as people with Asperger or who have just undergone radiotherapy). Two particularly distinctive features are the internal pull-ups inside trousers and skirts (a simple solution which, nonetheless, is very difficult to find), and a magnetic zip closure with an extended zip pull, which allows the wearer to zip with one hand only. Fabrics include cotton and wool as well as fully synthetic blends.

Product design

Tommy Hilfiger Adaptive collection is "designed for ease of dressing in classic Tommy style", which basically means translating Tommy Hilfiger's style into adaptive clothing. To a certain extent, it manages to do so because the adaptive garments tend to mirror the ones of the main collection. However, the more fashionable pieces from the main line are entirely absent from the adaptive one, which mostly offers sportswear and athleisure. Moreover, most Velcro and magnetic closures are purposely disguised as 'normal' zipper or button-down closures, which naturally leads to the question: Why disguise it instead of just making it beautiful? And also, what exactly is there to disguise?

On the other hand, the adaptive childrenswear line manages to incorporate adaptive features into a playful style, incorporating Tommy Hilfiger's signature best-sellers into functional and fun items suitable for all children.

Kiabi

Brand history

In 2017, French fast-fashion brand Kiabi, known for selling fashionable and fun children clothes at low prices, collaborated with Les Loup Bleus, a clothing brand for disabled children and adults, to create a 17-item collection for children with reduced mobility. Today, Kiabi's 'Easy To Put On' clothing line is available on the brand's French e-commerce platform (Kiabi, n.d.: online).

Adaptive features

The collection includes shirts with snaps along the shoulders that make putting them on easier, easy-zip sweaters with large zippers (easier to handle), jackets with zippers on the sides and on the sleeves, jeans with elasticated waist and cord closure (legs slightly wider, longer back rise), and reversible shirts that "promote the autonomy of the child who does not have to worry about having put on his t-shirt the wrong way round!" – Most garments are made 100% cotton, with the occasional spandex addition.

Product design

Like all Kiabi products, Kiabi 'Easy To Put On' clothes are pretty, playful and designed to allow freedom of movement to a small body that does not have the anatomy of an adult one (broad shoulders, hips, waistline, breasts). However, unlike the previous brands which are focused on offering solutions, Kiabi seems to be mostly focused on the design as the adaptive features are somewhat questionable. Snap buttons, especially on the shoulders, are still very hard to manage if you have limited motricity, and the zippers could have been replaced by Velcro. The trousers are adaptive only up to a point (they have a cord closure, which is something that all children tend to struggle with, whether or not they have motoric disabilities), and the reversible shirts, while altogether cute, kind of miss the point of adaptability in clothing.

The 'Easy To Put On' collection was originally created for children with disabilities, but currently it seems to cater more to children who are simply learning to dress themselves. This could explain why it presents itself as an *easy to put on* collection instead of as an adaptive one.

Anna Bonny

At age 42, Noelia Morales was diagnosed with invasive ductal carcinoma. She had her right breast removed as a part of her treatment. She decided against getting breast reconstruction, however, she quickly realized nothing looked very appealing to wear over her flat breast (Anna Bonny, n.d.: online).

The brand currently features only one product, a breast patch meant to cover mastectomy scars (according to the design, the other breast should remain uncovered). The patch however has different declinations: undergarment, monokini (swimwear) and design limited editions. It has recently created a collection in collaboration with Chanel Metier d'arts and Maison Lemaire (Anna Bonny, n.d.: Instagram).

Surprisingly, Anna Bonny's breast patch is the closest to what could be considered a fashion product. It is made from silk and fine cotton and, most of all, it is created not as a 'solution' but as lingerie, designed for a certain physicality and not merely for its limitations. In its way, it is elegant, sexy and daring. Arguably, these kinds of results are only given by either first-hand experience or by an in-depth, empathic research which considers not only the physical needs but also the mental ones.

Marketing and communication strategies

In terms of marketing and communication, there's a variety of possibilities for companies wishing to target people with disabilities. Some choose to directly involve the potential customers, either as brand ambassadors or as consultants during the production process, following the prosumer logic (Toffler, 1984), others prefer to stick to more classic inclusion-focused forms of storytelling; some adopt an emotional communicative style encouraging empathy (or compassion), others favor a neutral tone of voice.

Whether or not a certain strategy is right, depends on a series of variables concerning, among others, the brand (i.e. its history, its heritage, its image), the product (style, material, colors, etc.) and the target.

The approach of a brand that *also* has an adaptive clothing line, like Tommy Hilfiger, will be different from that of a 'native' adaptive clothing one like Anna Bonny or IZ Adaptive. For example, the campaign developed by Tommy Hilfiger for its adaptive line is aimed first of all at legitimizing its entrance in this market segment; it seems to say: "Although we're known for our jeans, we now enter the world of adaptive clothing with the consent and support of those who ultimately wear them". It emphasizes the involvement of people with disabilities in both the design phase and the communication. Consistent with the brand's DNA, the mood is positive and optimistic: the video on their website shows the models happy and smiling, seemingly immune to the hardships of disability (Tommy Hilfiger, n.d.: online). This style of communication is somewhat ambiguous: it rejects the (sym)pathetic tone often used when talking disability, but it is also likely to mystify reality by removing from the picture the problems that people with disability face every day, as if they had been magically solved by snap buttons and one-hand zippers. At first glance, the empowering approach chosen by the American brand might appear similar to the one used to promote the Paralympics, in particular the 2016 video advertise, with its meaningful title "Yes I can" (Paralympics, 2016: online), and the 2022 one, titled "Super.Human" (Paralympics, 2022: online). Both videos focus on the exceptional capabilities of athletes with disability, however, they do not in any way conceal or dismiss the physical, emotional and psychological difficulties that Paralympic athletes face. Unlike Tommy Hilfiger did, they narrate – with irony or with emotions – what it really means to live with a disability, and how much struggle is required to overcome its limits.

This is also the narrative style of Anna Bonny: starting from the name – Anne Bonny being an infamous buccaneer from the golden age of piracy – the Spanish brand depicts without embellishments the reality of those who have lost a breast to cancer. Noelia Morales, founder of the brand, compares her own appearance to that of a pirate. On her own website, she writes:

> I was left with the dilemma of how to feel good with only one breast, a question every bit as hard as it sounds, and yet the solution was, in the end, a simple one. I became a pirate when I slashed a beautiful bra in half and slung the remains across my scar like an eye patch. It was a startling moment, I realized that I felt liberated, I knew I had uncovered a new world or perhaps more accurately recovered a lost one.
>
> (Anna Bonny, n.d.: online)

In the video 'Singular', she shows in a crudely intimate manner, the everyday life of a woman after breast surgery (Wallace, 2017: online), and she keeps the same style on the brand's Instagram feeds and for public speeches such as TedX Speech (TedXBarcelonaWomen, 2016: online).

An intermediary approach between the one of Tommy Hilfiger and the one of Anna Bonny is the one of Canadian IZ Adaptive. With a claim stating 'designed for sitting', the brand's communication is based on pure realism: it does not hide the complications of using a wheelchair, nor does it claim to solve them through clothing. Its strategy appears to be more 'honest' compared to Tommy Hilfiger's, though less intimate than the one of Anna Bonny. But, like the American brand, it privileges smiling faces and a positive attitude, both on their website and on their Instagram, as well as a body language shaped on assertiveness and empowerment.

Last, but not least since not communicating is also a form of communication, the fourth and final brand among the ones that this paper examines, Kiabi, has at present no specific communication for its 'Easy To Put On' collection.

Retail and omnichannel paradigm

The aesthetic connotation of the word 'fashion' also incorporates its distribution. Due to the rise of social media and online sales, fashion brands, today, adopt editorial and commercial directions that bring design, communication and product achievement, synergistically together towards a homogeneous integration of physical and digital stores in what we call *the new omnichannel paradigm.* However, phygital synergies in regards to adaptive fashion appear rather non-existent because, just like some old-school brands focus only on the brick-and-mortar experience, adaptive clothes exist almost exclusively in the realm of online retail; there doesn't seem to be any stores in which people with a disability can browse through a choice of items displayed within a fashion context. Offline sales of adaptive products are mostly relegated to specialized shops and presented in a way that is decidedly more medical than fashionable, with obvious consequences in terms of aesthetics and in terms of the narrative.

But just as sportswear is no longer sold solely in sportswear stores today, why can't it be the same also for adaptive clothing? Why can't it be simply sold as fashion?

Further investigations lead to questioning the consideration that fashion brands, even those who do offer adaptive clothing, have for this kind of product. For example, the same Tommy Hilfiger that pioneered in this market segment does not sell its adaptive clothing line in its stores. Indeed, shop attendants working in the Milan flagship store do not even know about its existence. As for the brand's e-commerce, accessing the adaptive clothing section requires a Google search as the collection is highlighted neither on the home page nor in the product catalogue. However, once one manages to reach the appropriate section, the wide range of products and the way in which they are presented and narrated, do in fact recreate a seemingly fashionable, albeit virtual, scenario.

On a similar note, despite the huge creative and commercial potential of adaptive clothes for children, Kiabi's 'Easy To Put On' collection is perhaps even less accessible than Tommy Hilfiger's adaptive one: the French brand sells its adaptive garments both online and in store, but the products are just scattered among the others without any particular highlight or explanation regarding their use and adaptive features (Kiabi, n.d.: online).

'Native adaptive' brands such as IZ adaptive and Anna Bonny, showcase their products and their values in a way that is both functional and consistent, despite being only available online. On its platform, the Canadian brand provides useful information on standing or seated sizing as well as a series of videos regarding its patent technology. However, the visual interface doesn't contribute to making the product desirable, displaying it in a context which is altogether unimaginative (IZ Adaptive, n.d.: online).

This is not the case for Anna Bonny, whose website is extremely sleek and refined, just like its Instagram feed, which works as an omnichannel bridge to e-commerce. This mood also shows in the brand's 'non-reconstruction manifesto', which celebrates a conceptual approach to self-acceptance. The website also features DIY tutorials for making your own breast-patch.

In terms of retail and omnichannel representation, another important issue arises from the lack of accessibility, in all senses. Not only are the products hard to come by and can almost only exclusively be found online, but physical stores are often not accessible to people in wheelchairs or with general motoric issues, while e-commerce platforms are often difficult to navigate for people with cognitive limitations or by the visually impaired. In general, the customer experience is all but frictionless: the person who might be a customer might either not be able to access the store, or not be able to see, hear or understand what the product is. How can fashion be adaptive, if it does not adapt fully to people's needs and limitations?

Education

What would happen, if the schools placed designing for diversity at the very center of the curriculum? What kind of students would emerge from this kind of education? The way in which the future industry players are taught leaves a big imprint on their work. Today, fashion schools worldwide mostly teach their students to design in a way that will suit the current market, which basically means designing with the industry as opposed to the people in mind. But this could change. The fact that conventional fashion education is becoming obsolete (while students themselves are becoming a more and more diverse crowd) is slowly but surely beginning to materialize in the graduate collections. Some of the students are already challenging the status quo by creating designs for diverse people and bodies, often drawing inspiration from their own personal experience.

In 2021, Ben Barry, a well-known disability fashion activist, became Dean and Visiting Associate Professor of Equity and Inclusion at Parsons' School of Fashion. This was quite significant, considering Parsons' influence in fashion education. Barry's teaching and research centers the intersectional fashion experiences of disabled, fat, trans and queer people and engages them in the design of clothing, fashion media and fashion system. Since he became Dean at Parsons' he has been working hard to shift the school towards an acceptable level of diversity and inclusion, developing design pedagogies that de-center whiteness and that center fat and disabled bodies. Because of Parsons' global impact, the international discourse around fashion education has certainly changed.

However, before diversity became the industry's latest keyword, in 2011, the Edinburgh College of Art launched a Diversity Network, led by Mal Burkinshaw – Program Director of the Fashion Department, connecting academics across the UK, facilitating knowledge exchange and sharing of best practice on the theme of diversity and engagement with users' needs and feelings. The purpose is also to educate students in the importance of developing a more responsible, diverse and emotionally considerate response to fashion design and communication. As a result, all fashion design projects at ECA now require the students to consider how their work will address and celebrate the needs of a very wide customer base. "As a child, you see fashion in magazines and you think that that is what you have to do", Burkinshaw explains:

> When I started teaching, I was also just perpetuating the existing system. It was around 2010 that I decided that I wanted to do things in a more genuine way. I connected with Caryn Franklin, one of the founders of All Walks Beyond the Catwalk – an initiative working to challenge the fashion industry's dependence on unachievable and limited body ideals – and they were looking to collaborate with someone in education. I started a dialogue with our students, explaining that the impact of design is bigger than they think, inviting them to become more responsible, more considerate. By 2014, we adopted the term *emotionally considerate design*. The students embraced it immediately, I guess it was also liberating for them. I created a course that asks students to work directly with a person, communicating with that person, taking notes and building a relationship. In a certain way, this replicates the idea of designers having a muse, but ultimately it teaches students about the problems that people have with fashion, how the clothes feel on their bodies, how they make them feel emotionally. Something they could never learn from a headless mannequin. The course was described as innovative, groundbreaking, revolutionary:

> in fact, I think it's just sensible. Incidentally, when we changed the curriculum, our students started to gain more and more recognition. At the beginning I was just like, wow, this is happening, but when I saw them winning awards at Graduate Fashion Week every year and move on to work for Gucci or Balenciaga, I also acknowledged the fact that there must be a connection between the way in which they are now being taught and the quality of their work. Often diversity and inclusion end up just being about who you put on the catwalk; I don't care about the catwalk, what I want is for the students to take their emotionally considerate approach in the industry in a natural way. Responsibility should be a prerequisite for fashion design: If you want to be a designer and all you care about is one body type, one that also hardly exists in the real world, how can you be a good designer?
> (Burkinshaw)

The Diversity Network has existed for more than ten years now and Mal Burkinshaw is in touch with fellow academics around the world. Once again, we ask: What would happen, if all fashion design schools integrated designing for diversity into the curriculum? And how would this ultimately influence the industry?

Conclusions

Considering both the specific case studies and a more general analysis of the market, it is time to address the elephant in the room: while there may be adaptive clothing, there is no such thing as adaptive fashion, and if there is, it is so niche that we failed to find it (whereas disability is all but a niche matter.) Brands that create adaptive clothes are seemingly entirely focused on offering 'solutions' as opposed to 'fashion'; these solutions can be functional, practical, well designed, but it is safe to say that hardly any, if any at all, are conceived of as fashionable garments.

In terms of style, the choice offered by adaptive clothes today is extremely limited: what most brands feature is usually a declination of the unisex sport suits and a few classic basics. Garments are often made in stretchy, technical fabrics, supposedly offering more freedom of movement and more durable items, while clean silhouettes in neutral tints ideally mock elegance and/or formality. The aesthetic result is often questionable, and besides sport-inspired attire and arguable formality, there doesn't seem to be room for anything else: no bright colors, no bold prints, no luxury fabrics or classy details, nothing playful, nothing cool and nothing sexy. Needless to say, none of the well-known high-end fashion brands has an adaptive clothing line, not even those who indulge in the drama of using a disabled model for a campaign or a runway show; the sole exception is Tommy Hilfiger, which however sits somewhere between ready-to-wear and sportswear.

More broadly, if we exclude Anna Bonny's revolutionary breast patch, most of the adaptive clothing that can be found today in the market, is just a replica of classic, conventional garments with the addition of some facilitating features. While they were most likely conceived for disabilities, one wonders if they were designed with actual people in mind or simply with the limitations caused by their conditions. Why replicate? Why not design something entirely new that will enhance, flatter, or, if desired, properly conceal the disabled body? Why not create an entirely new aesthetic code?

Incidentally, the so-called 'postapocalyptic' aesthetic, which draws inspiration from transhumanist philosophy and has been embraced by brands such as Ottolinger, Marine Serre, KNWLS and Balenciaga, is already redefining fashion by transcending conventional body features. This new trend could ideally incorporate adaptive clothing. However, it would appear that while having the occasional 'bionic model' walk the catwalk is 'fashionable', placing anything too fashionable within the context of disability, is not.

A brand making efforts in this direction – designing cool garments that can be worn "by everyone, even by those without a disability" (Indiegogo, n.d.: online) is the Italian D-Different, supported by the crowdfunding platform Indiegogo.

In terms of communication, while it is safe to say that the attempts are generally well-intended, what emerges is a kind of communication that is seemingly directed more at non-disabled people than at people with disabilities, despite these being the actual customers. Products are communicated in a merely functional manner, no effort is made to place them within the context of fashion or to make them appear desirable, with the sole exception of discreet, somewhat aspirational communication on social media. Brand communication, especially the brands that make adaptive clothing as a side-line, either depicts an edulcorated scenario, or falls into the so-called 'Inspiration Porn', a term first used by comedian and activist Stella Young to define all inspirational content featuring people with disabilities *doing things* (running, painting, etc.) which are supposedly meant to motivate non-disabled people (because if a disabled person can do it so should you.)

Regarding retail, adaptive clothing lines are almost exclusively relegated to online platforms with questionable aesthetics that don't always facilitate the purchase. Customers are deprived of the IRL shopping experience and of representation in the brick-and-mortar shops, which is possibly the reason why so many of them are not accessible.

In conclusion:

1 Brands making exclusively adaptive clothing have a long way to go in order to achieve an aesthetic coherence between product, communication and omnichannel paradigm.
2 Brands trying to target people with disability as a cluster of potential consumers by making adaptive clothing, often display a lack of consistency.

The product is poorly (or not) communicated, it is hard to access, not present in stores, and often regarded as a B-series product.

3 Although some of the contemporary BOL'S (big of luxury) have included diverse models in their communication, affordable or aspirational luxury companies have completely excluded this segment. The gap between fashion and adaptive fashion is enormous.
4 Fashion schools teach students to design in a way that suits the current market, despite the growing demand for adaptive clothing, its economic potential and the students' own possible inclinations. This precludes any shift in the industry.

How could fashion integrate disability and improve the offer of adaptive clothing?

Despite this, we can hardly expect an established *maison* to dismantle the establishment that has allowed her to flourish, the radical change will have to come from the new generation, which is why fashion schools play such an important role. Also, in the face of a huge market void, small practices (which have the privilege of being more flexible), artisanal manufacturers and companies working on fabric experimentations, could easily include adaptivity in their production, catering to consumers looking not for solutions but for fashion. On a similar note, retail also represents a business potential, considering the lack of fashionable options both online and offline. A small, accessible boutique (or online platform) offering a curated and well-displayed selection of adaptive garments, perhaps integrated with fashion accessories, could be the first step towards retail inclusion.

In general, in the world of adaptive clothing, where functionality plays a pivotal role, creativity is often put aside, so it is those who can think freely and creatively, without the constraints of industrial rules, that could best represent millions of people who are still excluded from the fashion realm.

Going back to our journey in Central Asia, and the possibilities that the fashion industry represents for its economy as countries such as Uzbekistan and Kazakhstan open up to a global market while still being significantly poorer than their Western counterparts (thus an easy target for exploitation), considering that the demand for adaptive clothing represents an economic potential of eight trillion dollars, increasing by 14% yearly, and considering also the (injustifiable) reluctance of the Western world to tap into this specific market segment, perhaps countries which still have a strong tradition of creating custom-made garments with high-quality textiles which defy Western aesthetic while at the same time being undeniably fashionable, might potentially be more capable of offering an adequate response than countries which are by now fully dominated by fast fashion. And perhaps, who knows, a booming adaptive clothing industry could also break down the barriers and help disabled people to really become a part of society, finally truly enjoying the unique beauty of life along the ancient Silk Road, whether in Tashkent or Almaty, or in one of the many rural villages of the steps.

References

Akipress.com. (2022, January 31). Officially reported number of persons with disabilities in Uzbekistan likely underestimated at 2.1%, World Bank finds. https://akipress.com/news:667500:Officially_reported_number_of_persons_with_disabilities_in_Uzbekistan_likely_underestimated_at_2_1_,_World_Bank_finds/

Anna Bonny Official Instagram account. (n.d.). [Instagram profile]. Retrieved January 21, 2023, from https://www.instagram.com/p/CbfF1JOjMa1/

Anna Bonny Official Website. (n.d.). About. Retrieved January 16, 2023, from https://www.annabonny.com/about/

Indiegogo Official Website. (n.d.). Retrieved January 20, 2023, from https://www.indiegogo.com/projects/d-different-la-nuova-moda-adattiva-made-in-italy#/

I-Z Adaptive Official Website. (n.d.). Retrieved January 18, 2023, from https://izadaptive.com/

Kiabi Official Website. (n.d.). Retrieved January 29, 2023, from https://www.kiabi.com

Paralympics. (2016). Yes I can, I just born today, Yes I can do anything [Video]. YouTube. Retrieved January 16, 2023, from https://www.youtube.com/watch?v=-cPakutgQZY

Paralympics. (2022). Super.Human [Video]. YouTube. Retrieved January 16, 2023, from https://www.youtube.com/watch?v=3dCpnjIDir8

Seitenova, A. S., & Becker, C. (2008). Disability in Kazakhstan: An evaluation of official data. World Bank. https://documents1.worldbank.org/curated/en/445781468039262888/pdf/424700Disabili1iscussion0Paper00802.pdf

Stewart, P. H., & Rittman, M. (2019). Interview: Children with disabilities in Kazakhstan are missing out. Human Rights Watch. https://www.hrw.org/news/2019/03/14/interview-children-disabilities-kazakhstan-are-missing-out

TedXBarcelonaWomen. (2016). Pitch: Piratas de un solo pecho [Video]. YouTube. Retrieved January 16, 2023, from https://www.youtube.com/watch?v=u-WA9WKW5O8

Toffler, A. (1984). *The third wave: The classic study of tomorrow*. New York: Bantam.

Tommy Hilfiger Official Website. (n.d.). Tommy Adaptive. Retrieved January 15, 2023, from https://it.tommy.com/tommy-adaptive

Wallace, C. (2017). Singular – Anna Bonny. Retrieved January 16, 2023, from https://vimeo.com/190698377

White, J., et al. (2022). Uzbekistan inclusive education diagnostic study. Prepared by the University of Notre Dame's Pulte Institute for Global Development and Notre Dame's Institute for Educational Initiatives' Global Center for the Development of the Whole Child, for review by the United States Agency for International Development Mission in Uzbekistan. https://curate.nd.edu/downloads/v692t43957m

Index

Note: – *Italicized* page references refer to figures, **bold** references refer to tables, and page references with "n" refer to endnotes.

Kolibri 360 GmbH
Ferdinand-Jühlke-Straße 7
99095 Erfurt, Deutschland
produktsicherheit@kolibri360.de